THE EAGLE AND THE CROWN

THE EAGLE AND THE CROWN

AMERICANS AND THE BRITISH MONARCHY

FRANK PROCHASKA

YALE UNIVERSITY PRESS
NEW HAVEN AND LONDON

Published with assistance from the Annie Burr Lewis Fund

For information about this and other Yale University Press publications, please contact:
U.S. Office: sales.press@yale.edu   www.yalebooks.com
Europe Office: sales @yaleup.co.uk   www.yaleup.co.uk

Set in Minion by IDSUK (DataConnection) Ltd.
Printed in Great Britain by TJ International Ltd, Padstow, Cornwall.

Library of Congress Cataloging-in-Publication Data

Prochaska, F. K.
    The eagle and the crown : Americans and the British monarchy / Frank
Prochaska.
      p. cm.
    Includes bibliographical references and index.
    ISBN 978-0-300-14195-5 (cl. : alk. paper)
    1. United States–Relations–Great Britain. 2. Great Britain–Relations–United States.
    3. Great Britain–Kings and rulers–Public opinion. 4. Monarchy–Great Britain–Public
    opinion. 5. Public opinion–United States–History. 6. Great Britain–Foreign public
    opinion, American. I. Title.
    E183.8.G7P76 2008
    327.73041–dc22
                                                                                2008027982
A catalogue record for this book is available from the British Library.
10 9 8 7 6 5 4 3 2 1

To Robert Baldock

There is a natural inclination in mankind to Kingly Government.
Benjamin Franklin, 1787

CONTENTS

ILLUSTRATIONS

Plates

10. Queen Elizabeth, President Ford and Cary Grant at the White House, 1976. Courtesy of the Gerald R. Ford Library
11. Princess Diana dancing with John Travolta at the White House, 9 November 1985. Reagan Library
12. Princess Diana and Clint Eastwood at the London film premiere of *The Fugitive*, 3 September 1993. Rex Features
13. Princess Diana at the Red Cross Day, Washington D.C., 17 June 1997. Tim Graham/Getty Images
14. The Queen visits Jamestown, 4 May 2007. Getty Images

FOREWORD

The legacy of the colonial period was protean in politics and enduring in culture. In the nearly two and a half centuries between the accession of George III and the death of Diana, Princess of Wales, the love–hate relationship with the British monarchy has been part of America's conversation about itself. This is an account of that conversation, of a nation that overthrew British rule only to become captivated by the magnetic attraction of royal renown. A fascination with the monarchy has been a continuous theme in American opinion from its colonial beginnings, and it persisted despite the demonization of George III during the Revolution. For all their egalitarian principles, many Americans have been highly susceptible to the transcendent glamour of hereditary kingship – what has been called 'a family on the throne' – and find little contradiction in saluting the stars and stripes one moment and bowing to the British sovereign the next.

Republics resemble monarchies in many ways, and from its early days the newly-formed American nation, which derived its political and cultural heritage from Britain, looked across the Atlantic for time-honoured traditions, family ties and possessions that would give a sense of inheritance to a people otherwise defined by their novelty. Expansion and rapid social change unsettled United States citizens, leaving them uneasy about class but preoccupied with status. Titles, honours and distinctions of rank alleviate the monotony of democracy. And with exquisite paradox, Americans fell under the spell of royal tradition from the lofty heights of republican virtue. This book, which constitutes a tour of monarchy and public opinion in America, seeks to illuminate that paradox but also the greater paradox to which it is joined – America's simultaneous belief in the future and reverence for the past.

The book begins with the high politics of the Founding Fathers and George III, but shifts to cultural issues and American attitudes to royalty as the British monarchy lost its political significance in the young, independent nation. For a century or more after the Revolution the dominant culture in the United States, as expressed in the press, literature, and public events, remained under the sway of the mother country. Was it not remarkable that the usage 'Victorian' became a commonplace in the United States? It was a tribute to the power of British civilization in the nineteenth century, an era in which America saw itself linked to the mother country by the bonds of language, law, and liberty. It was also a tribute to the British monarchy itself, which effectively cultivated America for diplomatic and commercial reasons.

The decline of British power and the rise of the United States, together with the vast increase in migration to the United States from non-English speaking parts of Europe, gradually changed American attitudes towards the Crown. In the twentieth century, it was largely royal ceremonial and visits to the United States by members of the royal family that kept the monarchy in the headlines and in the American imagination. Kings and queens, princes and princesses provided the personages that propelled the monarchy's popularity in the United States. America's curiosity towards the public and private life of the royal family is a fascinating subject in itself, and the character of this curiosity, often romantic, sometimes prurient, is as revealing of United States culture and Anglo-American relations as the Jay Treaty or Queen Victoria's role in the Civil War.

Historically, monarchy may be seen as the fount of celebrity. From the Prince of Wales, later Edward VII, to Princess Diana, members of the royal family have been major players in the emergence of America's obsession with fame, offering an exclusive and classy contrast to the instant creations of the media. Hereditary kingship also propels British ceremonial, which has dazzled the citizens of a young nation comparatively lacking in hallowed settings and traditions. American expressions of joy and sorrow at royal marriages and funerals, coronations and jubilees have been extraordinary, given the rejection of the monarchy during the Revolution. Are they simply ephemeral reactions to what have become media events, or do they represent some deeper human response to pomp, class, and the hereditary principle?

The evolution of the relationship between the American people and the British monarchy is an absorbing story, which should tell us a good deal about America and perhaps something new about monarchy itself. But this book is not simply about the royal presence in America. The Founding Fathers were more monarchical in their assumptions than is widely believed. They created a veiled monarchy in the United States, giving presidents quasi-regal status and the trappings of royalty. Theodore Roosevelt, not one to minimize the powers of his office, once described the President as an 'elective King'. Attributing kingly powers to America's highest office, a recurring theme in United States history, has recently revived in political discussion. Thus the British monarchy, a largely benign presence in the United States after the reign of George III, continues to provide a point of reference in the nation's conversation about itself.

*   *   *

This book springs from a longstanding interest in the history of the British monarchy. This particular topic originated out of a discussion following a talk on early American material culture by my colleague Kariann Yokota at Yale. I wondered aloud whether Americans celebrated the Jubilee of George III in 1809. No one present knew the answer so I had a look at the American newspapers of the day and found that many of them mentioned the festivities in Britain and several looked favourably on the King. This finding led me to examine the views of the Founding Fathers on the monarchy, which in turn led to the issues of diplomacy, political and social custom, the media, and the American temper. The study broadened further with a visit to the Royal Archives to explore the Crown's attitude towards the United States. Thus an innocent inquiry about George III's Jubilee became a survey of the relationship between the American people and monarchy over the past 250 years, an inexhaustible subject that has received surprisingly little attention from historians on either side of the Atlantic.

It is a pleasure to thank the institutions and individuals who have assisted in the writing of this book. As ever I am deeply indebted to archivists and librarians, but owe special thanks for their advice and support to Judith Schiff, Susan Roberts, and Kevin Pacelli at Yale's Sterling Memorial Library. Ellen Cohn and her staff at the Franklin Papers project, housed in the Sterling Library, provided expert guidance on the Founding Fathers. A book on the monarchy and America would be a poor thing without access to royal sources. By permission of Her Majesty Queen Elizabeth II, I have been able to use material from the Royal Archives at Windsor, for which I am very grateful. Other institutions that have aided my research include the Library of Congress, the Houghton Library at Harvard, and the National Archives at College Park, Maryland.

My warmest thanks go to Robert Lacey, John Sainty, Stuart Semmel and Yale's expert readers for their perceptive remarks on the manuscript. Donald Lamm, Edward Purcell, Stuart Proffitt, and Joseph Roach contributed in various ways, from advice on publishing to comment on constitutional issues and celebrity culture. I am grateful to Letha Sandweiss and the Yale University

Women's Organization for the opportunity to test some of my ideas in a series of lectures. *History Today* published a shortened version of the first chapter in August 2007 under the title 'The American Monarchy'. As a former author with Yale University Press, I am delighted to be back in the fold, and would like to thank the staff in both London and New Haven for their care and proficiency. Finally, I am ever grateful to my wife Alice and our children Elizabeth and William for their comment and encouragement. They support me in dedicating the book to a dear family friend and guide, who nursed this book along from its inception.

CHAPTER 1

THE FOUNDING FATHERS

We were educated in royalism; no wonder, if some of us retain that idolatry still.

Thomas Jefferson, 1789

In September 1761, the colonial Englishman Benjamin Franklin, on tour in the Low Countries, eagerly anticipated a return to his home in London to attend the Coronation of King George III. His time, as he said, 'was so taken up with seeking for places at the Coronation' that he had little leisure.[1] With his invitation secured, he reached London in time for the festivities, but a storm delayed his arrival and he had to content himself with watching the pageant from a distance. His son William was part of the procession that walked into Westminster Abbey.[2] From his vantage point, the elder Franklin would not have known that the ceremony itself was a shambles. Among other mishaps, the authorities had forgotten the canopy, the sword of state and chairs for the King and Queen; and the Dean of Westminster, it was said by an eye witness, 'would have drop'd the Crown, if it had not been pin'd to the Cushion'.[3]

Franklin, fascinated by royalty, would have forgiven the King had he sat on the crown. He wrote to a friend that George III's virtue and sincerity would dissipate faction 'like the morning Fog before the rising sun' and predicted that His Majesty's reign would 'be happy and truly glorious'.[4] Franklin's admiration for his monarch knew few bounds in the years following the Coronation. After a dinner at Versailles hosted by Louis XV in 1767, he reported that 'no Frenchman shall go beyond me in thinking my own king and queen the very best in the World and most amiable'.[5] As a frequent guest at court, he attended George III's birthday festivities in 1771, and the following year wrote to his son of the King's 'great regard' for him.[6]

As Franklin's devotion to royalty illustrates, it was no easy matter to break with so universal a system of government as monarchy, especially for colonial subjects who thought of themselves as patriotic Englishmen and their King as a guardian of the Protestant faith and 'the Father of his People'. George III was no less revered for being so remote. Distance made him a more difficult target and enhanced the monarch as symbol. With an ocean between them, few colonists ever set eyes upon a member of the royal family, but they demonstrated their allegiance through ritual celebrations of coronations and royal birthdays.[7] When the Philadelphia physician Benjamin Rush visited the House of Lords in 1768, he gazed at the throne with 'indescribable' emotions:

> I asked our guide if it was common for strangers to set down upon it. He told me no, but upon my importuning him a good deal I prevailed upon him to allow me the liberty. . . . When I first got into it, I was seized with a kind of horror which for some time interrupted my ordinary train of thinking. . . . I endeavored to arrange my thoughts into some order, but such a crowd of ideas poured in upon my mind that I can scarcely recollect one of them.[8]

Colonial subjects like Rush would come to decry George III, but royal authority was slow to weaken in a land of English-speaking emigrants on the fringes of the known world, whose leaders looked to the King for political legitimacy. As the colonists believed the monarchy to be the guarantor of their rights, even the disaffected were hesitant to blame the King for their discontents. As the tensions mounted, popular indignation centred on the ministry and not the monarch, who was typically described in resolutions as 'the best of sovereigns'.[9] Oliver Wolcott, a signer of the Declaration of Independence, wrote that the reservoir of respect for George III had been so deep on the eve of the Revolution that 'the abilities of a Child might have governed' the colonists.[10] Rufus King, a Senator from New York and American Minister to Britain in the 1790s, recalled in later life that Americans of his generation 'were born the subjects of a King, and were accustomed to subscribe ourselves "His Majesty's most faithful subjects" '.[11]

As such remarks suggest, the colonial tradition of looking to the Crown for redress was very powerful. While Americans often acknowledged the authority of Parliament, they found reasons for refusing to accept it in specific cases, as, for example, over taxation. Dismissing the monarch was more difficult given the deep roots of royalism in the colonies.[12] Franklin said he could understand the sovereignty of the Crown but not the authority of Parliament.[13] Subject to party politics, Parliament had little symbolic importance in American political rituals, whereas the King was 'the empire's living embodiment'.[14] As John Brooke observed in his distinguished biography of George III: 'the fathers of the American republic were the heirs of the Tory tradition in British politics'. And he added: 'perhaps the only true Tories in the world today are to be found in the United States. Which may account for the otherwise surprising fact that we sometimes meet Americans, especially from the east coast states formerly under British rule, who are far more monarchical than the average Briton'.[15]

Although the colonists' regard for George III was slow to wane, events on the ground increasingly strained their patience. In the 1770s, the tightening of political authority and the behaviour of the British Army towards colonial civilians heightened fears that the American arcadia was being sacrificed to satisfy European dynastic interests. As the crisis deepened, it became increasingly common for the colonists to depict the King as the head of a tyrannical government. But in the years before the outbreak of hostilities, no one tried more valiantly than Franklin to reconcile the conflicting claims of the colonists and their King. It was not until March 1775, after eighteen years in Europe, his hopes dashed for a settlement of differences, that the reluctant revolutionary sailed home to serve the American cause.

Pamphleteers fuelled the growing anxieties as the crisis turned violent at Lexington and Bunker Hill. The King, intent on defending his authority, played into their hands by his determination to bring the colonists to heel. The result was a breakdown of the paternalism that marked relations between the King and the colonists, whom he described as his 'rebellious children' at the beginning of the conflict.[16] In *Common Sense* (1776), that great salvo against the British Crown, Thomas Paine accused King George of despotic warmongering and argued that 'monarchy and succession have laid . . . the world in blood and ashes'. In another striking phrase, which would have endeared him to rebellious American Protestants, he called monarchy 'the Popery of government'. As relations with the mother country deteriorated, Paine found a receptive audience willing to support his call for a manifesto declaring independence because of 'the cruel disposition of the British court'.[17]

The defiant colonists needed a scapegoat and the zealous denunciation of George III in the Declaration of Independence was an astute propaganda device. The Loyalist Thomas Hutchinson argued that its passages were 'most wickedly perverted to cast reproach upon the King'.[18] But Thomas Jefferson understood the value of personalizing the enemy. Having discredited Parliament, the revolutionaries needed to discredit the monarchy in order to define their cause and rally the troops. Thus Jefferson turned his aim on the King. Describing him as 'a Prince, whose character is thus marked by every act which may define a Tyrant' was meat and drink to pure republicans like Paine. So too was the Declaration's litany of more than a score of royal 'injuries and usurpations' the King heaped on the colonists. Nothing did more to shape the unhappy reputation of George III in America than what Samuel Adams called this 'catalogue of crimes'.[19]

By the time of the Declaration of Independence, Franklin's disillusionment with the King was palpable. Burning towns and Indian atrocities provoked by the British were much on his mind by the end of 1775, leading him to see the King as demonstrably hostile to the colonists and dissolving all ties of allegiance. Some years later, with the country at war for its survival, he compared George III unfavourably with Nero.[20] Like a lover scorned, he found it difficult to forgive his former sovereign and those Americans who remained loyal to the Crown. This was evident in details great and small. In the privacy of his study, Franklin crossed out the words 'God preserve him [the King]' in his personal copy of his book *Experiments and Observations on Electricity made at Philadelphia in America.*[21] More poignantly, he erased from his life his only son William, who remained loyal to the King and spent his final years in England.[22]

* * *

George III loomed large in America's foundation myth, and thus became a fixture in United States history, an antitype of the Founding Father. The animosity whipped up against the King had profound effects on American perceptions of monarchy, or what it perceived to be monarchy. But it did not spill over into a repudiation of the heritage of the mother country, for the colonists saw themselves as 'a projection of English Civilization'.[23] 'Throughout the war and after', the historian Edmund Morgan observes, 'Americans maintained that they were preserving the true tradition of English history, a tradition that had been upset by forces of darkness and corruption in England itself.'[24] During the conflict, large numbers of colonists remained sympathetic to the Crown. John Adams estimated that they constituted as much as a third of the population at the time of the Revolution.[25] These Loyalists, or American Tories, represented a cross-section of the colonial population, from Anglicans and the members of the commercial and governing classes to artisans, farmers, seamen and thousands of slaves.[26]

During the hostilities, fewer Loyalists left the country than was once thought. As one authority argues, 'only a fraction' of them 'were ever able or perhaps willing to emigrate'.[27] Others returned, which augured well for cultural continuity between the new nation and the mother country. There was much bitterness and many instances of persecution during the Revolution, including the tarring and feathering of Tories. But it was a remarkable feature of the republic that most remaining Loyalists were eventually reintegrated into local and national life. This was made easier because the American Revolution was a civil war without carnage at the political centre. Unlike the revolutionaries in the English Civil War and the French and Russian revolutions, the Americans did not kill the King, which eased the process of reconciliation both at home and abroad.[28] Had the revolutionaries executed George III – as opposed to burning his effigy and destroying his images – one can only imagine the enduring tensions between the British and American people.

The hostility to Loyalists and to George III has tended to obscure the cultural and constitutional affinities between the two nations. It has also obscured the limits imposed on royal authority in Britain by the late eighteenth century. Though memorable and politically dynamic, the denunciations of the King as a tyrant had little foundation in reality. John Adams, for one, disapproved of the description of the King as a tyrant in the Declaration of Independence, but was unable to change it.[29] As suggested, a belief in the despotism of George III

1. Pulling down the statue of King George III, 6 July 1776, New York City.

was invaluable in shaping the vision of the United States as a nation founded in patriotic struggle. In turn, the rejection of European dynastic and political interests contributed to the conviction that America is a nation uniquely blessed, which has characterized American self-perception since the Revolution. But the belief in American 'exceptionalism', like the belief in the 'free-born Englishman' that nourished it, has always been better propaganda than history. The Puritan John Winthrop fashioned his 'City upon a Hill' in the hills of Suffolk, England, not the hills of Massachusetts.[30]

*   *   *

George III survived the American Revolution, but the break up of the first British Empire left him scarred. The loss of the colonies was an affront, but it also threatened to relegate Britain, in his words, to 'a very low class among the European states'.[31] But while the King retained an aversion to what he saw as an unwarranted rebellion, he was not oblivious to shifting realities. In the aftermath of the Revolution, improved relations were, if anything, more agreeable to Britain than to America. Beneath the bitterness and recrimination, the foundations of cooperation still existed between the two countries. In December 1782, the King said to the House of Lords that 'Religion, language, interests and affection may, and I hope will, yet prove a bond of permanent union between the two countries.'[32]

A memorandum in the King's hand now in the Royal Archives expressed a measure of royal reconciliation with the former colonists. Though undated, the internal evidence suggests that the King composed the document 'America is Lost' during the peace negotiations in early 1783. Written under the influence of the free trade doctrine of the First Lord of the Treasury, the Earl of Shelburne, the memorandum provides a snapshot of the King's shifting views as his Empire unravelled. It was a unique royal document, written at a momentous time in American history, but it was also a statement of policy that would bear fruit in the years to come:

America is lost! Must we fall beneath the blow? Or have we resources that may repair the mischief? What are those resources? Should they be sought in distant Regions held by precarious Tenure, or shall we seek them at home in the exertions of a new policy? The situation of the Kingdom is novel, the policy that is to govern it must be novel likewise, or neither adapted to the real evils of the present moment, or the dreaded ones of the future. . . .

This comparative view of our former colonies in America is not stated with any idea of lessening the consequence of a future friendship and connection with them; on the contrary it is to be hoped we shall reap more advantages from their trade as friends than ever we could derive from them as Colonies;

for there is reason to suppose we actually gained more by them while in actual rebellion, and the common open connection cut off, than when they were in obedience to the Crown.[33]

The King's prescription made a virtue of necessity, but it did not mark a permanent change of mind. After the peace agreement he was hesitant to welcome a diplomat representing the United States.[34] Nonetheless, he received John Adams, the first American Minister to the Court of St James, with all due

2. John Adams presenting his credentials to George III.

propriety in June 1785. On the day, Adams, visibly nervous, reciprocated the formal welcome with all the courtesies that attended a private audience with a British monarch. 'I shall esteem myself the happiest of men', Adams said in his prepared remarks,

> if I can be instrumental in recommending my country more and more to your Majesty's royal benevolence, and of restoring an entire esteem, confidence, and affection, or, in better words, the old good nature and the old good humor between people who, though separated by an ocean and under different governments, have the same language, a similar religion, and kindred blood.[35]

Adams recorded the King's reply, the first words ever spoken by a British monarch to a United States Minister of State:

> I not only receive with pleasure the assurance of the friendly dispositions of the United States, but that I am very glad that the choice has fallen upon you to be their minister. I wish you, sir, to believe, and that it be understood in America, that I have done nothing in the late contest but what I thought myself indispensably bound to do by the duty which I owed to my people. I will be very frank with you, I was the last to consent to separation; but the separation having been made, and having become inevitable, I have always said, as I say now, that I would be the first to meet the friendship of the United States as an independent power.[36]

As their historic exchange suggests, the King and Adams recognized that despite the recent animosities powerful cultural and commercial interests encouraged friendly relations between Britain and America. Other cultures existed in the young republic, including those from the Netherlands and France, but by far the most predominant culture was British, albeit with variations within it, from New England Puritans to Virginian slave owners. About three quarters of the American population of 3,250,000 in 1790, excluding slaves, traced their ancestry back to England, Scotland, or Wales.[37] Moreover, its white population was 98 per cent Protestant, fortified with a set of values that would have a lasting impact on the United States.[38] The nature of the rebellion itself, which was fought between people of the same culture and language, promoted an eventual settlement of political differences, including reconciliation with George III and his descendants.

Travellers to the fledgling republic from abroad often remarked on the homogeneity and 'essential Englishness' of American culture. The agricultural reformer William Strickland wrote to a friend in 1794 that the attachment of the northern states, especially those of New England, 'to the *Old Country*, as they call England, is truly remarkable'.[39] A French visitor to the United States in the same decade observed that the manners of former colonial subjects 'must necessarily resemble, in a great degree, those of England. To the American manners particularly, those relative to living are the same as in the provinces of England'.[40] But it was not simply American manners, language, religion, and folkways that resembled the traditions of the mother country.

* * *

Americans, as Franklin's grandson Benjamin Franklin Bache put it, created a constitution before they 'had sufficiently *un-monarchized* their ideas and habits' (his italics).[41] Republics, such as Venice, and 'elective' monarchies, such as Poland and the Papacy, were familiar to the Founding Fathers. But hereditary monarchy was the principal constitutional model on which Americans had to draw before the French Revolution.[42] When the Founding Fathers devised a substitute for the Crown what they knew about government was the example of kingship.[43] Though few Americans said it openly after 1776, many of them believed that some form of limited monarchy was the most practical system of government on offer. In a world in which mankind was thought to be fallen, his reason frail, a mixed government with its separation of powers and emphasis on the rule of law was thought well suited to man's imperfect nature.

As Adams wrote to Benjamin Rush in 1790: 'No nation under Heaven ever was, now is, nor ever will be qualified for a Republican Government, unless you mean ... resulting from a Balance of three powers, the Monarchical, Aristocratical, and Democratical. . . . Americans are particularly unfit for any Republic but the Aristo-Democratical Monarchy'.[44] Such phrases as 'Aristo-Democratical Monarchy' suggest just how arbitrary definitions of republican – and monarchical – government were in the late eighteenth century.[45] The Latin *res publica*, the 'public thing', was a shapeless idea, which had been defined variously in the past as the state, the commonwealth, mixed government, limited monarchy, a polity, or simply the public domain.

It was widely recognized that England's balanced constitution of King, Lords and Commons constituted a republic.[46] Both Alexander Hamilton and James Madison observed that the British government, with a powerful hereditary king, was often described as a republic.[47] Even Paine recognized that kingship was not inconsistent with republican government. As he put it, 'what is called a *republic*, is not any *particular form* of government'.[48] Adams admired the phrase 'monarchical republic', by which he meant a form of government in which kingship did not descend into despotism. But as the author of a classic work on constitutions, he concluded that the word 'republic' was unintelligible.[49]

The following is an idealized description of Britain's constitutional monarchy from the mid-eighteenth century, which may be read as a classical republican text:

> The pride, the glory of Britain, and the direct end of its constitution is political liberty. . . . Thus have we created the noblest constitution the human mind is capable of framing, where the executive power is in the prince, the legislative in the nobility and the representatives of the people, and the judicial in the people and in some cases the nobility, to whom there lies a final appeal from all other courts of judicature, where every man's life, liberty and possessions are secure, where one part of the legislative body checks the other by the privilege of rejecting, both checked by the executive, as that is again by the legislative; all parts moving, and however they may follow the particular interest of their body, yet all uniting the last for the public good.[50]

George III wrote these lines as a youth under the guidance of Lord Bute.

In keeping with his political education, King George's conception of the royal prerogative bore little resemblance to the assumptions of Charles I and James II, or Paine and Jefferson. As a Prince, he had written that the Revolution of 1688 had rescued Britain 'from the iron rod of arbitrary power' and even had a good word for Oliver Cromwell as 'a friend of justice and liberty'.[51] As King, he wished to recover as much control of the executive as possible within the vague parameters of the Constitution, but he never sought to repeal the legislation that comprised the Revolutionary Settlement of 1688.[52] He was a political manager who fully understood and endorsed the classical republican framework of King, Lords and Commons, with its restrictions on royal authority. As the twists and turns in his relations with ministers suggest, he operated in an ideological context in which kingship was in flux, though generally working to reduce the monarch's authority. Checks and balances were so much a part of the political language of the eighteenth century that they were the constitutional currency of British monarchists and American republicans alike.

When Americans declared that 'Our President is not a King' they either did not consider the limits of George III's powers or had another king in mind.[53] Though King George publicly approved of a harsh policy towards the colonists, he did not declare war on America nor lead the nation into battle. While he often stands accused of wilfully prolonging the conflict, none of the measures that ignited it was of his own making.[54] He planned, advised and reprimanded, but deferred to his Cabinet on strategy. In theory, the Prime Minister served at the King's pleasure, but during the American Revolution George III generally followed the lead of his ministers. 'It was not the Crown but Parliament that was encroaching on the liberties of America', remarked his biographer, Brooke.[55] Parliament carried every measure against the colonies by large majorities. As George III himself wrote in September 1775, 'I am fighting the battle of the legislature.'[56]

The American denigration of the King as a despot served to justify the Revolution; but *pace* Jefferson and Paine, it is debatable whether George III was the 'executive' in British politics in the late eighteenth century, given the constraints on his prerogatives and the emergent power of the office of Prime Minister.[57] By the Act of Settlement the King could not even leave the country without the consent of Parliament. Ironically, posterity accused the King of wishing to serve as his own Prime Minister and of trying to direct the war when in fact he did not attempt these roles.[58] Clearly, George III felt the limitations of his authority, which had increased with the incremental reform of royal finance and the growing weight of public business – he did

3. *The Whitehall Pump*, 1774. Lord North pumping water from a fountain topped with the head of George III, on to the prostrate bodies of Britannia and America.

not have a private secretary until afflicted by blindness in 1805. Nor, unlike President Washington, did the King invoke that telling instrument of executive power – the veto – which had fallen into disuse in Britain after the reign of Queen Anne.[59]

As the English journalist and editor of the *Economist* Walter Bagehot noted in the *English Constitution* (1867): 'Living across the Atlantic, and misled by accepted doctrines, the acute framers of the Federal Constitution, even after the keenest attention, did not perceive the Prime Minister to be the principal executive of the British Constitution, and the sovereign a cog in the mechanism.'[60] The Founding Fathers had experience of the British Constitution, but their recollection of it was out of touch with its shifting reality, which often led them to overstate the monarchy's power. Under the influence of the English jurist William Blackstone's *Commentaries* (1765–1769) they had convinced themselves that the British King had the sole prerogative of making war and peace.[61] James Bryce, the British historian and statesman, believed that had the Founding Fathers spent more time studying the actual practice of monarchy, rather than Blackstone's dated ideas of kingship, they might have seen things differently.[62]

The Founding Fathers paid little heed to the conflict between King George and his ministers in the late eighteenth century, which ended with the modern conception of a constitutional sovereign. A crucial moment came after the defeat at Yorktown in 1781 when George III had no choice but to accept the resignation of Lord North and reluctantly swallowed the indignity of accepting American independence.[63] The King threatened to abdicate, but gave way. That the monarch had to accept advice even when it was unwanted was largely lost on the rebellious former colonists, for the effective American propaganda campaign had skewed perceptions of the King's power. But it should not be assumed that George III, as a constitutional monarch, had the authority of 'Commander in Chief', which has been interpreted at different times to give the President virtually unlimited authority. It is one of the great ironies of the United States Constitution that the Founding Fathers invested more power in the Presidency than George III was able to exercise as King.

*   *   *

The confusion over what constituted a republic – or a monarchy – helps to explain the uproar over the shadowy schemes to re-introduce a king in America. According to a historian who investigated the issue nearly a century ago, 'several plans of monarchical character received serious consideration in the United States between 1776 and 1787'.[64] During and after the Revolution, there was a steady drip of gossip accusing Federalists of having royalist sympathies. On his return to America from France in 1789, Jefferson, who detected a royalist under every Federalist bed, said he was 'astonished to find the general prevalence of monarchical sentiments'.[65] In the tense and heady atmosphere rumours spread of European princes, including Prince Henry of Prussia, being offered the throne.[66] Just how much support such schemes received will probably never be known, for secrecy and caution marked the behaviour of those favourably disposed to monarchy.

In revolutionary America, discretion was the better part of valour for those with royalist sympathies. Take the case of the Army officers, who in May 1782, angered by their hardships and the inefficiency of Congress, sought to enlist Washington as an American monarch. (Jefferson later accused various officials from the Northeast, including Rufus King, then a Massachusetts lawyer, of being in league with the scheme.)[67] On behalf of his Army colleagues, Colonel Lewis Nicola, an Irishman who had once served in the British Army, wrote a guarded letter to General Washington, in which he remarked that republics were inherently weak; and he suggested that 'strong arguments might be produced for admitting the title of king, which I conceive would be attended with some material advantage'.[68]

Washington wrote a withering reply. He was at a loss to understand what he had done to encourage such a letter: 'If I am not deceived in the knowledge of myself, you could not have found a person to whom your schemes are more disagreeable. . . . If you have any regard for your Country, concern for yourself or posterity, or respect for me, banish these thoughts from your Mind.'[69] As Nicola and his chastened comrades discovered, Washington, who was always sensitive to accusations of monarchical sympathies, had an extraordinary capacity for self-denial. (Perhaps he would have been more susceptible to their entreaties had he had a son of his own.) Yet while he repudiated monarchy, Washington accepted that honourable men thought it might rescue the nation from anarchy. By early 1787, he admitted that 'the utility; – nay the necessity' of monarchy might become evident, though he hoped the creation of a stable government would prevent it from coming into being.[70]

*   *   *

Contrary to opinion widespread in America today, the Founding Fathers were not averse to kingship, at least of the undespotic, limited variety. (During the French Revolution Thomas Paine saw Louis XVI as an agent of progress, a 'republican monarch'.)[71] The political thinking of the Founding Fathers had been shaped by the British Constitution, which most of them, including Jefferson, believed to be the finest in the world. This was in keeping with the views of leading political philosophers in Europe, who had reason to abhor the traditions of absolutism on the continent.

As George Bancroft acknowledged in his classic *History of the United States* (1864–1875), loyalty to the House of Hanover had been synonymous with the love of civil and religious liberty for much of the eighteenth century:

> Neither Franklin, nor Washington, nor John Adams, nor Jefferson, nor Jay had ever expressed a preference for a republic. The voices that rose for independence, spoke also for alliances with kings. The Sovereignty of George the Third was renounced, not because he was a king, but because he was deemed a tyrant.[72]

Various American thinkers, most notably John Adams and Alexander Hamilton, leaned towards incorporating monarchical elements in the American Constitution. As an officer at Valley Forge in 1778, Hamilton had signed an oath in which he repudiated any allegiance to George III.[73] But his admiration for England led to a good deal of ridicule from his enemies, who retailed stories that he was in league with British paymasters.[74] Jefferson had Hamilton in mind when he wrote to Lafayette: 'It is from the eastward that these champions for a king, lords, and commons, come. They get some important associates from New York, and are puffed up by a tribe of Agioteurs which have been hatched in a bed of corruption made up after the model of their beloved England.'[75]

Jefferson had a point when he accused Hamilton of monarchical sympathies. Hamilton wrote in his notes in 1787 that republics suffered from corruption and intrigue, while monarchical power provided vigorous execution of the laws and acted as a check on the other branches of government. 'The monarch must have proportional strength. He ought to be hereditary, and to have so much power, that it will not be his interest to risk much to acquire more'.[76] In his subsequent remarks on constitutional questions, Hamilton dropped all references to the virtue of 'hereditary' monarchy. In the *Federalist* essays he mocked those who equated the authority of the American presidency with that of a hereditary British king. In a purposeful sleight of mind, he inflated the monarchy's powers so as to make the powers of the Presidency, which he wished to be extensive, seem relatively modest.[77] In *Federalist* number 70, he agreed with the writer who said that ' "the executive power is more easily confined when it is one"; that it is far more safe there should be a single object for the jealousy and watchfulness of the people'.[78]

Like other Americans with royalist leanings, Hamilton judiciously covered his tracks and retreated from any notion of replicating in the republic a hereditary institution that had been complicit in so much turmoil. For years, he sympathized with the idea of what he called an 'elective monarch', who could serve for life on 'good behavior'.[79] Indeed, he put forward this proposition in a long speech to the Constitutional Convention in 1787. The delegates rejected the idea, yet in the end the Constitution did not preclude the emergence of an elective monarch for life, at least in theory, for it permitted a president to be re-elected for successive four-year terms. As the Founding Fathers were aware, monarchy did not necessitate the hereditary principle or life tenure. Elective monarchy had a long history, with examples from Anglo-Saxon England, the Holy Roman Empire, Poland and the Vatican. As Hamilton noted, '*monarch* is an indefinite term. It marks not either the degree or duration of power'.[80] As Dr Johnson's *English Dictionary* defined it, monarchy simply meant government by a single person.

Hamilton paid a price for his monarchical tendencies, and he ruefully observed that 'the mad democrat will have nothing republican which does not accord with his own mad theory'.[81] Ardent democrats, with unsullied purity, were on the lookout for royalist sympathizers and exploited the popular aversion to monarchy for electoral purposes. Jefferson, unlike Adams, could never reconcile himself to George III. Despite sharing the King's interests in science and architecture he came away from an audience at St James's Palace in 1786 feeling that he had been 'ungraciously' snubbed.[82] Jefferson's table talk was rich in whispered innuendo about royalist intrigues and contributed to the political atmosphere of suspicion. Once, over dinner, he heard Hamilton 'avowing his preference for monarchy over every other government'.[83] In the raucous politics of the republic loose talk about the advantages of monarchical rule was enough to place a person under suspicion. William Maclay, the severe republican senator from Pennsylvania, was always on the lookout for high-toned manners and love of ceremony, which he saw as evidence of a 'Court Party' intent on the creation of an American monarchy.[84]

The distinction between absolute monarchy and limited monarchy was often lost on American politicians, particularly anti-Federalists with a political axe to grind. 'No man . . .', Hamilton wrote in 1792, 'contemplated the introducing into this country a monarchy', by which he meant absolute monarchy. But he added that a constitution like that of Great Britain had an appeal.[85] As he recognized, in devising a mixed government that sought to create checks and balances, America drew on those malleable classical republican traditions that were consistent with the evolution of Britain's limited monarchy. The diffusion of power between the various elements or classes of society was thought to ensure that the state did not degenerate into tyranny, oligarchy, or mob rule.

In creating a viable constitution, the Founding Fathers turned naturally to Britain, for it was the principal exemplar of mixed government, providing a working model on which to experiment.[86] But having savaged George III as a tyrant they had difficulty using him as a prototype. Still, the figure they had before them was not an abstract, generalized monarch but King George.[87] Despite the widespread animosity towards him, a mixed government of King, Lords and Commons retained a compelling logic to the many Americans who desired security and a just measure of liberty. It was 'an arrangement of power that appeared to the colonists as it did to most of Europe as "a system of consummate wisdom and policy"'.[88] A 'pure democracy' had little charm, for it was widely seen as at best impractical and at worst anarchical. As Edward Rutledge of South Carolina wrote to John Jay in 1776, 'a pure democracy may possibly do, when patriotism is the ruling passion, but when the State abounds with rascals . . . you must suppress a little of that popular spirit'.[89]

Americans sought to widen the definition of republic to embrace more fully the affairs of the public at large; but while they strained to reconcile egalitarianism with mixed government, their colonial experience eased the translation of King, Lords and Commons into President, Senate and the House of Representatives.[90] Adams wrote to Jefferson in December 1787 on the new Constitution, observing that 'you are apprehensive of Monarchy; I, of Aristocracy. I would therefore have given more Power to the President and less to the Senate.'[91] The Founding Fathers gave the classical republican model an American twist that turned the House of Lords into a Senate of notables, though without an aristocracy it was not always clear who they were.[92] The constitutional system adopted in the United States, with its ideal of checks and balances, was a creative modification of classical republican ideas suited to American social realities. But when those checks and balances do not operate effectively – as has happened from time to time in American history – the powers of the Presidency are arguably more akin to those of Charles I than to those of a limited monarch like George III.

*   *   *

Benjamin Franklin Bache observed that Americans 'dismissed the name of king, but they retained a prejudice for his authority. Instead of keeping as little, they kept as much of it as possible for their president.'[93] For all their revolutionary rhetoric, Americans treated 'His Excellency' George Washington as a republican version of 'His Majesty' King George. Some Americans, sensitive to the symbolism of power, believed Washington required a title and pored over the titles of the European princes to find one that had not been appropriated. Thomas McKean, Chief Justice of Pennsylvania, thought 'Most Serene Highness' desirable. Washington himself was said to have preferred the style of 'High Mightiness' used by the Stadtholder of the Netherlands.[94] The reigning Stadtholder, William V, was among the Europeans who saw George Washington as an uncrowned monarch. As he said to Adams: 'Sir, you have given yourselves a king under the title of president.'[95]

In the Senate, the titles issue was contentious. A titles committee suggested 'His Highness the President of the United States of America and Protector of the Rights of the Same'. Adams, who believed that social distinctions and love of ceremonial were innate human characteristics, took the lead on the titles issue; but the Senate rejected his suggestions for the Presidency, which were 'His Elective Majesty' or 'His Mightiness'. In the end, the Senate, like the House of Representatives, voted that Washington should be called simply 'The President of the United States'.[96] But the issue of how presidents were to be addressed did not end there. Article 2 of the Constitution gave them what was arguably the more significant and problematic title – 'Commander in Chief'. The title 'president', as David McCullough notes, had associations with cricket clubs and fire companies.[97] But 'Commander in Chief' had longstanding royal associations, having first been used by the absolutist Charles I.

Whatever his title, the President was not short on authority and prestige. Given American uneasiness with unmerited privilege, the Founding Fathers rejected the hereditary principle. But as Bagehot observed, the President was 'an unhereditary substitute' for a king, an elective monarch serving for a fixed term.[98] Though the source of Washington's authority was not biological, as President he was given 'semi-royal status' that suited his august demeanour and vital role in the revolutionary struggle.[99] The African-born Phillis Wheatley paid poetic tribute, which suggested just how common it was at the time to think of the Presidency as a variant of kingship: 'A crown, a mansion, and a throne that shine / With gold unfading, Washington! Be thine.'[100] Adams, too, took comfort from the admixture of kingship in the Presidency: 'Limited monarchy is founded in Nature. No Nation can adore more than one Man at a time. It is a happy Circumstance that the object of our Devotion [Washington] is so well deserving of it.'[101] Others were less positive. Bache, from his pulpit as editor of the radical newspaper the *Aurora*, called Washington 'the *George* of America' and described his powers as approaching 'terrestrial omnipotence'.[102]

During the framing of the Constitution, the highly-contested office of the President came under attack as an instrument of monarchy. Some, like George Mason in the Virginia Convention, worried lest an 'elective monarchy' prevail. (The disorderly nature of Poland's elective monarchy lurked in the background.) So did his colleagues James Monroe and William Grayson, who feared that foreign intermediaries might intervene.[103] Governor Edmund Randolph of Virginia, who attended the Constitutional Convention, regarded a unitary executive as 'the foetus of monarchy'.[104] Patrick Henry, another Virginian, famously denounced the Constitution's 'deformities' and saw the Presidency 'squinting' towards monarchy:

> If your American chief be a man of ambition and abilities, how easy is it for him to render himself absolute. The army is in his hands, and if he be a man of address, it will be attached to him. . . . Away with your president! We shall have a king: the army will salute him monarch.[105]

Various commentators worried about insufficient checks on presidential pretension, given the extraordinary powers invested in the Commander in Chief under Article 2 of the Constitution, which in practice gave the President a free hand in foreign affairs. With the power to make treaties, grant pardons, fill vacancies, appoint supreme court judges, ambassadors, consuls, and 'all other officers of the United States', it was not surprising that critics saw American kingship in the making, for these powers resembled – indeed exceeded – the powers exercised by the British Crown, which were in the process of being eroded. Rawlins Lowndes, in the South Carolina Convention, declared the proposed presidential office 'the best preparatory plan for a monarchical government he had read'. It 'came so near' to the British form that, 'as to our changing from a republic to a monarchy, it was what everybody must expect'.[106]

American commentators, having demonized the King, had little inclination to understand the development of constitutional monarchy in the reign of George III. So when they said that America would lapse into monarchy, they meant something more absolute than the limited monarchy in Britain. Alarmed by the moral temper in the early republic, Benjamin Rush wrote that 'a hundred years hence, absolute monarchy will probably be rendered necessary in our country by the corruption of the people'.[107] In 1787, Franklin, with philosophical detachment, observed in the Constitutional Convention:

> It will be said that we do not propose to establish kings. I know it. But there is a natural inclination in mankind to Kingly Government. It sometimes relieves them from Aristocratic domination. They had rather have one tyrant than five hundred. It gives more of the appearance of equality among Citizens, and that they like.[108]

Though Congress rejected princely titles it happily acquiesced in presidential ceremonial that bore the hallmarks of royal tradition. Hamilton, among others, ruminated over 'courtly forms to inspire reverence for the law'.[109] The dignity of the nation's head of state required recognizable customs, if only to appear on a level with European heads of state who were monarchs, at least until the French Revolution reduced their number. But more important than form was a concession to kingship that has been little appreciated in America. It was of no small significance that the Founding Fathers made the President both the executive *and* the ceremonial head of state. When presidents in their inaugural addresses say they wish to represent 'all the people', they are taking on a monarchical role, ensuring that the nation's highest office will have royal overtones, with some of the attendant, uncritical awe associated with kingship. Later European republics, those of France, Germany, and Italy for example, separated these roles as a safeguard against the abuse of power.

*   *   *

The Founding Fathers turned naturally to British precedent to answer constitutional questions but also to answer questions of political etiquette. They cast off British rule, but retained a liking for British ceremonial practices and customs, albeit on a scale befitting a former colony with modest resources. Adams and Hamilton urged Washington to follow the forms of 'European courts' and indulge in a show of 'Splendor and Majesty'.[110] A look at Washington's Presidency illustrates that a 'Republican Court' emerged, complete with artillery salutes, parades, odes set to the music of 'God Save the King', bewigged footmen, levées, lavish dinners, speeches redolent of those from the throne, a presidential barge manned by thirteen river pilots in formal dress (the British royal barge at the time had 21), and travels through the states that were reminiscent of royal 'progresses'.[111] When Washington moved about the country he did so, as an English witness noted, 'in a very kingly style'.[112] The courtly formality enraged radicals and anti-Federalists, who thought it recreated the divisive rituals of monarchy.

Inaugurations mimic coronations. The first inaugural in 1789, which set the tone for future administrations, had many of the trappings of a crowning. Dignity and grandeur, thought essential to the union and the nation's highest office, were the order of the day. In a pale imitation of George III's golden state coach pulled by eight cream Hanoverian stallions, 'Washington rode to Federal Hall in a canary-yellow carriage pulled by six white horses and followed by a long column of New York militia in full dress.'[113] Armed soldiers lined the route to St Paul's Church, where the bishop gave his blessing. Back at the Senate, the President called his address 'His Most gracious Speech', which raised a few eyebrows, for it was noted that those words were the same as those placed before the speech of the King at the annual opening of Parliament. When a critic protested that the usage represented 'the first Step of the Ladder in the Ascent to royalty', the President greeted the complaint with surprise, saying that it was 'taken from the Practice of that Government under which we had lived so long and so happily formerly'.[114]

Washington, dubbed the 'Monarch of Mount Vernon' by the polemical journalist James Thompson Callender, saw domestic and foreign advantage in the political use of courtly language and ceremony.[115] As he was well aware, the monarchy's dazzling pageantry and resounding titles had helped to sustain Britain's hold over the colonists. At the first session of Congress it was suggested that a throne be set up in the Senate chamber for Washington's use, but the idea did not get sufficient support and was dropped.[116] In his public addresses, the President's tone was such as his former sovereign might use. In a republican nod to monarchical usage, Washington came to be called 'the Father of his Country', a variant of 'the Father of his People', a phrase often applied to the paternalistic George III. In the many portraits by Gilbert Stuart and other artists, Washington was typically portrayed in regal pose. America's iconography, from presidential portraiture to civic pageants, drew heavily on monarchical traditions.[117]

As the President of a new and vulnerable nation, Washington was acutely sensitive to the need for *politesse* in his dealings with Britain, which remained the most powerful country on earth despite the loss of the colonies. In 1789, on hearing that George III had been struck down by insanity, he expressed sympathy for the King. On the King's recovery he held a fête, which was a portent of better relations with the British Crown. Though the American newspapers made little of it, reports of the celebration reached London, where it was seen as a compliment to his Majesty. The *Whitehall Evening-Post* noted the event, but could not resist a hostile aside about Washington's powers. Assuming that he would always be re-elected, it called the President 'dictator of America for life'.[118]

In 1797, George III spoke to Rufus King, the American Minister, of the 'wisdom' of the United States government, adding that Washington was the greatest of living men.[119] This may have been simply polite conversation, for on the President's death two years later, the King and his courtiers uttered not a word of condolence, which the American Minister saw as a 'want of magnanimity'.[120] Though lacking sympathy for Washington, the English court could not fail to notice that republican America mimicked British political traditions. This was so in matters great and small, from the Senate borrowing its procedures from Parliament to the State of the Union Address, authorized by Article II of the Constitution, which had its origins in the address from the throne. Jefferson, who recoiled from such royal usages, thought Washington's address to Congress in 1790 too kingly and declined to appear before the legislative branches.[121]

George III would have been amused to discover that the former colonists celebrated President Washington's birthday rather as his British subjects celebrated his own, with the sound of cannon, bells, and drums. It was followed by a levée, a formal reception long associated with royalty.[122] The levée, though frowned upon by radicals, became a fixture of the nineteenth-century American court. Even Jefferson, who had discontinued the practice on becoming President, held one in 1805, to the dismay of some of his admirers.[123] In a striking union of republican content and monarchical form, James Madison celebrated the Fourth of July with a levée.[124] Such practices fed the popular criticism of the nation's monarchical tendencies and the penchant of presidents for pomposity and splendour, for stately nods and seclusion from the people.[125]

Regal customs were not restricted to the office of the President, but also featured in governors' mansions and mayoral offices, where the incumbents revelled in the stately pageantry. For decades, the Governors of Massachusetts held regular levées at the State House, from whence a procession moved to the Old South Meeting House, where an oration was delivered before returning to the State House for a sumptuous banquet concluded with patriotic toasts.[126] In 1791, the citizens of Pennsylvania celebrated the birthday of their governor 'with the discharge of cannon, and other military parade; and more than this, the humble imitation of European courts, in levée congratulations on the occasion!!!'[127] Such provincial republican expressions of royal ceremonial did not go uncriticized. As one newspaper observed: 'The dignity of our officers of government is not increased by their dangling a sword at a *levee* in imitation of Gothic custom'.[128] Had there been no Revolution in France, said a correspondent in the *Pennsylvania Gazette*, 'the "well born" among us would, before this Period, have endeavoured to establish Orders of nobility'.[129]

Although there were no American orders of nobility, George Washington set a regal tone for the nation. Though uneasy about his ceremonial role, he played the republican king to weekly audiences at his formal levées. The scripted bows and curtsies would not have looked amiss at the court of his former monarch.[130] In New York and in Philadelphia, where the capital relocated in 1790, the President received his guests on Tuesday afternoons. In imitation of Queen Charlotte, Mrs Washington, attended by her husband, opened her drawing room on Friday evenings 'to exact those courtesies to which she knew she was entitled'. None were admitted to these 'select' and 'courtly' receptions but those who had an official station or 'who were entitled to the privilege by established merit and character'. The courtiers and 'would-be Lords' who attended these rituals applauded Washington for his 'heroic and patriotic virtues' in the cause of '*American* liberty'.[131] With full dress required, the democratic rabble, with their frock coats and patched knees, need not apply.[132] Ironically, procedures in the republic did not permit petitions to be presented to the President, unlike levées held by British monarchs.

Levées in Philadelphia were held in the presidential dining room, with the table and chairs removed. Typically surrounded by his Cabinet, the President wore a black velvet coat and breeches, a cocked hat in his hand and a long sword by his side, his hair powdered like an English lord. 'On these occasions', as one witness reported,

> he never shook hands, even with his most intimate friends. The name of everyone was announced. . . . The visitor was received with a dignified bow, and passed on to another part of the room. . . . The gentlemen present moved into a circle, and he proceeded, beginning at his right hand, to exchange a few words with each. When the circuit was completed he resumed his first position, and the visitors approached him in succession, bowed, and retired.[133]

In this courtly republican dance, spontaneity was rarely evident, though on one memorable occasion the statuesque Washington bent over to kiss the cheek of the widow of his former lieutenant Nathanael Greene.[134]

After witnessing one of Washington's receptions a colonel from Virginia despaired for the safety of the nation. As he observed, the President's 'bows were more distant and stiff' than any he had witnessed at St James's.[135] Attacks on these formalities, the 'mock pageantry of monarchy', were a recurring theme in the young republic. In 1793, the *Carlisle Gazette* decried the government's royal associations and took particular umbrage at the presidential levée: 'It certainly springs from the uniform habits of Royalty, it is degrading to the excellent understanding of the President; and can only be necessary in a Monarchy where the Royal Puppet is publicly danced by the Minister.'[136] Maclay, a tenacious critic of inherited ceremony and titles, saw levées as the thin end of a royal wedge. But even Maclay succumbed to court dress, and, as he put it, 'did the needful. It is an idle thing but What is the life of Man but folly.'[137]

George III, always attentive to etiquette and ritual, approved of the royal overtones of the American court. With delicious irony – and a wink – he remarked to Rufus King that he noticed that President Adams wore formal attire in Congress and used the word 'Gentlemen' and not those of 'fellow citizens' in his speeches as Washington had done.[138] At home, John Adams, dubbed 'His Rotundity' and the 'Duke of Braintree', was often criticized for his princely style. His love of decorum led his enemies to conclude 'that he sought a hereditary monarch, with himself as king and son John Quincy groomed as his dauphin'. Even Washington mocked him for his 'ostentatious imitation [and] mimicry of royalty'.[139] Adams's critics complained that elaborate dress, birthday odes, and drawing rooms created a ceremonial distance between the officers of state and the people. They were evidence that republicanism had failed to strike the evil at its source. 'It is dangerous in the extreme', wrote 'A

Farmer' in 1793, 'to set up any man as an idol . . . witness Cromwell's grip in the name of republicanism.'[140]

*   *   *

The Founding Fathers had endowed the nation's highest office with quasi-regal status. But for all the airs and graces, America's 'first family' proved less potent than a royal family in the creation of national identity. Lacking the historic continuity of a hereditary family in the White House, presidential government, with its succession of lacklustre incumbents in the nineteenth century, proved less intelligible and captivating than Britain's monarchical system. The adoption of courtly ceremonial only partly compensated for the failure of the republican form of government to create emotional ties with the citizenry. Constitutional monarchy had the capacity to create instinctive personal loyalty for impersonal parliamentary government. As Bagehot would argue in the 1860s, this was a distinctive advantage that monarchies had over republics:

> Royalty is a government in which the attention of the nation is concentrated on one person doing interesting actions. A Republic is a government in which that attention is divided between many, who are all doing uninteresting actions. Accordingly, so long as the human heart is strong and the human reason weak, Royalty will be strong because it appeals to diffused feeling, and Republics weak because they appeal to understanding.[141]

America's adaptation of 'elective' monarchy and the borrowing of British procedures and ceremonial suggests just how deeply indebted the new nation was to its colonial past. Perhaps not surprisingly, later British commentators saw this indebtedness more clearly than Americans, who have been prone to see the United States as a unique constitutional experiment. In *The American Commonwealth* (1888), Bryce, who was to become a popular ambassador to the United States, argued that the Founding Fathers created 'a reduced and improved copy of the English king. He is George III . . . diminished by his holding office for four years, instead of for life'.[142] In his book *Popular Government* (1885), the English jurist Sir Henry Maine was likewise forthright about just how much the Presidency owed to the British monarchy: 'On the face of the Constitution of the United States, the resemblance of the President to the European King, and especially to the King of Great Britain, is too obvious to mistake.'[143]

In Britain, as Bagehot and a host of nineteenth-century constitutional writers agreed, a republic had 'insinuated itself beneath the folds of a Monarchy'.[144] In America, a monarchy had insinuated itself beneath the folds of a republic. The phrase 'monarcho-republicanism' was sometimes used to describe the British Crown. It had a variant in the American Presidency, which many a participant in the Revolution recognized and several endorsed, though rarely with frankness. Adams had classified America as a 'monarchical republic', by which he meant that it was, like England, a monarchy in that the executive power was in the hands of an individual, and it was a republic in so far as the Constitution provided for the representation of the people.[145] Jefferson, the scourge of American royalists, felt that the spirit, if not the letter of monarchy, had persisted in the republic. He feared an eventual tyranny of executive power in Washington, believing this to be a feature of Federalist politics.[146] As he wrote to James Madison in 1789: 'We were educated in royalism; no wonder, if some of us retain that idolatry still.'[147]

The Founding Fathers rejected hereditary kingship, but a penchant for 'the rule of one' had a recurring echo in the republic, which the Constitution did little to silence. Many Americans assume that democratic principles are incompatible with monarchy, which they have been brought up to associate with tyranny, forgetting that monarchies are today among the most advanced democracies.[148] The suggestion that their President is an elective king and the United States a monarcho-republic makes them uncomfortable. American historians, well aware of the monarchical elements in the Constitution, have typically pulled their punches, often on the grounds that a president, however regal, serves for a limited term, forgetting that monarchy does not require the hereditary principle or life tenure. In *The Imperial Presidency* (1973), Arthur Schlesinger conceded that United States presidents had 'monarchical moments', especially in the post-war years, but he avoids the 'K' word, preferring to see the Presidency as 'imperial'.[149] But is not an emperor a king writ large?

Allusions to the imperial Presidency and the unitary executive have become commonplace in contemporary America. But as we shall see, references to United States presidents as kings have been a feature of the nation's conversation about its political leadership throughout American history. Such references have increased dramatically of late, as a glance at many a newspaper and website will attest.[150] In 2004, an article in the *Atlanta Inquirer* put it squarely: 'What we have is an elective monarch who, if we are to believe the current wearer of the crown, rules by divine right.'[151] A survey of presidents from Theodore Roosevelt to George W. Bush sees them as a new breed of monarchs surrounded by courtiers, with vastly expanded executive authority and 'unmistakable signs of having assumed the trappings traditionally bestowed on European heads of state'.[152] If only Americans knew, some of their presidents would give monarchy a bad name.

*   *   *

The similarities between the British and United States political systems, the former a disguised republic, the latter a disguised monarchy, encouraged reconciliation between the two previous combatants and prepared generations of Americans for a love affair with the British royal family.[153] In a nation without a hereditary king, the constitutional and ceremonial continuities between the two nations also prepared America for treating their presidents as republican substitutes for royalty. Brought up on monarchical idols, Americans continued to succumb to the idolatry. The want of a royal family encouraged the emergence of political dynasties in America, from the Adamses to the Bushes. But the Presidency, for all its powers, proved a prosaic replacement for the poetry of royalty. Without a hereditary family on the throne at home, the American people remained captivated by the genuine article abroad, which helps to explain the emergence of what was to become, as one nineteenth-century witness put it, 'our absurd national mania for everything that assumes a title'.[154]

CHAPTER 2

ROYAL RECONCILIATION

One scarcely encounters an American who does not want to owe something of his birth to the first founders of the colonies, and as for offshoots of the great families of England, America seemed to me to be entirely covered with them.

Alexis de Tocqueville, *Democracy in America*, 1840

In the early republic King George went through a transformation in the American mind, from perfidious tyrant to harmless personage. For several years after the peace of 1783, Anglo-American relations were fraught, and the belief that George III was a despot remained widespread in the population at large. The outbreak of the French Revolution in 1789 marked something of a turning point. In the revolutionary context of toppled dynasties and European tumult, Americans began to see the once reviled George III as an embattled, if rather pathetic, Christian gentleman, an upholder of family values against French savagery and irreligion. The executions of Louis XVI and Marie Antoinette in 1793, which the American press covered with more than a little sympathy for the French King and Queen, rejuvenated United States interest in the British royal family. For most Americans, despite their nation's revolutionary origins, the English language and Christian culture trumped Jacobin principles. Such tendencies were in keeping with the political and religious establishment in Britain, where the conservative values of that devoted monarchist Edmund Burke prevailed.

Many Americans initially saw the tensions between Britain and France as a contest between tyranny and democracy, but once revolutionary France declared war on Britain in 1793 and descended into the Terror, a United States

policy of favouring France over Britain was seen to reverse the natural order
of things. Where did the nation's loyalties lie? The Jeffersonians preferred
France, the Federalists Britain. But which country was more likely to be the
firmer ally and more lucrative trading partner? France had been an ally in the
Revolution but now threatened the independent nations of Europe. Britain
had battled America but was the source of its intellectual claims to freedom.
With foreign relations in a critical condition and a European war in full swing,
the issues of peace and trade needed urgently to be addressed by both the
United States and Britain. Early in 1794, Washington appointed John Jay as
special envoy to normalize trade relations and resolve issues left over from the
American Revolution.

Jay was of Huguenot ancestry but indistinguishable from the English in his
manners and habits of mind. Part of his mission was to assess British prosperity,
gauge public unrest, and take the measure of the King. Somewhat to his surprise
he found the monarchy esteemed in Britain. He described George III, who
received him cordially, as an affable and affectionate family man, who patron-
ized the arts, sciences, and agriculture: 'He is industrious, sober and temperate,
and has acquired much various knowledge and information. . . . That he is a
great and wise king, I have not heard asserted. . . . I have heard him described as
being a great man in little things, and as being generally well-intentioned, perti-
nacious and persevering.'[1]

Jay's mission, as he put it rather grandiloquently, was 'a solemn question of
peace or war between two peoples, in whose veins flowed the blood of a
common ancestry, and on whose continued good understanding might
perhaps depend the future freedom and happiness of the human race'.[2] He
found the King conciliatory and Lord Grenville, his counterpart in negotiations, amiable and high-minded. The eventual Treaty, signed in November
1794 and ratified by the Senate in 1795, was about as much as the United
States could hope for. Among other things, Jay obtained commercial privileges
in the British East and West Indies, though America had to recognize its
obligation to pay the pre-war debts owed to British merchants. Enemies of the
administration greeted the Treaty with scorn. Angry mobs burned Jay's effigy
and radical editors denounced President Washington for his treachery and
monarchical tendencies.

Despite the public outcry, the Treaty's political and commercial advantages
soon became apparent. Eventually hailed as a triumph of diplomacy, its first
Article 'of Amity, Commerce and Navigation' promised 'a firm inviolable and
universal Peace, and a true and sincere Friendship' between the two nations.[3]
George III, who followed the negotiations closely, praised the Treaty as having
removed 'all grounds of jealousy and misunderstanding'.[4] A decade earlier he

had declared America 'lost', but his wish that something might be salvaged from friendly trading relations with the former colonies was now about to be realized. The Treaty was a belated victory for pro-British, Loyalist traditions in the republic, which were on the rise against the background of the French Revolution.

Independence had freed Americans from British rule but not from material and cultural dependency on the mother country. Arguably, the Revolutionary War was little more than a hiatus in trading relations, with Britain resuming domination with the return of peace.[5] America's exports depended on the British Empire, while the United States was among Britain's best customers. Commercial rapprochement stemmed from 'habit, ready credit, existing obligations and wartime conditions'.[6] In the years immediately after the Jay Treaty, about a sixth of America's exports found their way to Britain, while a third of America's imports came from Britain, most of them in the form of manufactured goods. These figures were to increase significantly in the years after the end of the Napoleonic Wars in 1815.[7]

Despite the residual misunderstandings left by the American Revolution and the sometimes off-hand treatment of United States citizens by officials in England, improved commercial relations encouraged the reassertion of the familial relationship between the two peoples. In turn, improved relations contributed to the revival of United States interest in the royal family, which was re-emerging from the tumult of the 1770s and 1780s. Feelings of pride and confidence in the young republic were widespread, but partisan presidents subject to highly-contested elections could not easily fill the social and psychological vacuum left by the loss of a hereditary royal family. With the passing years, Americans began to make a distinction between monarchy, which they typically deplored, and kings and queens, who were increasingly seen as an inoffensive, historic part of 'the sentiment and poetry of England'.[8]

*   *   *

Across Britain and the Empire George III's subjects celebrated his Golden Jubilee in October 1809. In America, an unknown number of citizens celebrated, but rather more discreetly. Most would have been former Loyalists, who looked with respect, if not veneration, to the King across the water. Reports of the Jubilee appeared in a host of American newspapers, which gave details of the festivities in Britain, typically months after the event because news travelled so slowly in the age of sail.[9] Various papers noted with approval that the King released debtors from British jails, while a few complained that he failed to release captive Americans on board British ships.[10] More humorously, the *Salem Gazette* was among the many papers that retailed the different proposals on how to celebrate the event, from candlemakers recommending a general illumination to old maids recommending compulsory marriage for all single men.[11] Several papers in the Northeast printed a Jubilee poem by Norman Nicholson, a shepherd from the Grampian Mountains in Scotland, whose sentiments would have incited a riot in 1776:

> The flock o'Great-Britain ye've lang weel attended,
> The flock o'Great-Britain demanded your care. . . .
> But ah! Royal GEORGE, and ah! Humble
> NORMAN
> Life to us haith drawn to a close; . . .
> An' may the heist Jub'lee among angels meet us,
> To hail the auld Shepherd, and worthy auld
> King![12]

By the time Americans saw Nicholson's verse, George III, long blind, had begun his descent into senile gloom. Thomas Jefferson, writing to Governor Langdon of New Hampshire in 1810, uncharitably described the King as a 'cypher' in 'a strait waistcoat'.[13] But the King's decline and consequent absence from political life served his reputation in the United States, for he could no longer be dubbed a tyrant or blamed for reverses in relations. Paine's parody of the King as a German despot laying waste his kingdom was hard to square with the view that he was an inconsequential madman. In the early nineteenth century, most American commentators depicted George III as unwell and unwise, but many would have agreed with Jay's assessment that he was affable and well intentioned. Some would have seen him through the eyes of John Wesley, who rallied to his sovereign as a God-fearing family man.[14] With the years, the King's virtues as a Christian gentleman became more apparent on both sides of the Atlantic.

A tolerance for kingship was built in to Christianity. Indeed, some commentators, like the Catholic writer Hilaire Belloc, have argued that the root of monarchy lay in religion, in 'man's instinct for worship'.[15] Colonial Americans, like their British counterparts, had imbibed the biblical message that God was a king, the 'King of Kings', who had other kings under him. Just as it had been difficult for the Founding Fathers to break with so universal a system of government as monarchy, American Christians, not least the Anglicans among them, found it difficult to disengage from a religious world steeped in kingship, in which, as the popular ballad intoned,

> Kings are by God appointed,
> And Damn'd are those who dare resist,
> Or touch the Lord's Anointed.[16]

While the French Revolution linked republics with atheism, it highlighted the British monarch as the defender of the faith, the resplendent centre of religious sentiment subject to the workings of providence.[17]

The American reaction to the death of George III in January 1820 was respectful, with little recrimination. The King continued to rally the patriots and frighten the children on the Fourth of July, but given his long absence from public view he had become an historical figure during his lifetime. The United States press covered his death belatedly. The news only reached the *Arkansas Gazette*, for example, four months after the event.[18] A spate of widely-circulated stories appeared that characterized the King as a dignified and kindly, if rather eccentric, Christian gentleman. One first-hand account from an American traveller retailed a story of the King speaking warmly about Washington and Franklin.[19] The *Ladies' Literary Cabinet* pointed to his undisputed piety, temperance and personal courage.[20] The *Salem Gazette* published an article from the *Christian Observer* that praised the King's domestic virtues, the purity of his court and his steadfastness in the face of French tyranny.[21] Gradually, a distinction was being made, as the *Carolina Centinel* put it, between 'the vices of the government of George III' during the American Revolution and 'the virtues of his private life', which as 'the head of his family, rendered him so worthy of national esteem'.[22]

A notable article published in several New England papers reassessed the King's political talents and the effects of the American Revolution on British fortunes. It was evidence that Loyalist echoes could still be heard in the republic. The King's reign, observed the article, was distinguished by a host of critical events that demanded great abilities in a monarch:

> In all these he was eminently successful, if we except the American revolution on which he undoubtedly set his whole heart: But the conquest of America was beyond the power of any monarch of his time. Although the late reign is remarkable for great vicissitudes of fortune, it may truly be observed of it, that, on the whole, the march of British power and importance was steady and progressive – the British lamented the loss of America, without considering, that, as to all physical support, the Americans were useless to the mother country. The event has shewn, that to all useful purposes, America is still the vassal.[23]

*   *   *

George IV, George III's successor, could hardly be called a Christian family man, a fact widely recognized by Britons and Americans alike, who were by now prone to see British royalty through a moral lens. Whether the king was the 'selfish, unfeeling dog' of the diarist Charles Greville's imagination, or simply a misguided profligate redeemed by charm and taste is a matter of opinion.[24] Like monarchs elsewhere, he put on fancy dress and full regalia and had the painters in to convince himself that he was part of a great tradition. But the political and military ground had been cut from under his feet. His personal failings and political vagaries weakened the reputation of the Crown, but promoted the growth of cabinet government. As the American public was coming to recognize, the reign thus marked another step in the development of constitutional monarchy.

Despite the Crown's diminished authority, the American press followed the policies and personal conduct of George IV with considerable interest. It was said that he was favourably disposed to the American cause during his father's reign, but this was wishful thinking since the Prince had no interest in revolutionary principles.[25] As Prince Regent (1810–1820), he sought accord with the former colonies. When relations deteriorated in 1811 and America broke off diplomatic ties, he replied to the departing Minister William Pinkney with the 'utmost amity' towards the United States.[26] During the War of 1812 he followed the lead of his ministers and took a desultory interest in the campaigns. When the British captured Washington and set fire to the White House he applauded, for it was 'well calculated to humble the presumption of the American government'.[27]

In histories of the War of 1812, the Prince Regent is rarely mentioned. At the time the American press criticized him for his part in it, though he was not demonized the way his father had been during the Revolution.[28] Despite the great strain in Anglo-American relations, the war did not notably affect America's fascination with the royal family even while it was underway. Perhaps this was because most Americans did not suffer unduly during the war – only about 1,500 United States soldiers died – and they had little reason to fear much change in their daily routine from British arms.[29] Given the apparent limitations of royal authority, they were less likely to blame the monarchy for the policies of the British government than they had been during the Revolution. During his time as Minister in London at the end of the war, John Quincy Adams dismissed the Prince Regent for his frivolity: 'He is Falstaff without the wit, and a Prince Henry without the compunctions. His only talent is of mimicry, which he exercises without regard to dignity or decorum. . . . His supreme delight is to expose persons dependent upon him to ridicule, and to enjoy their mortification.'[30]

Unlike his father, George IV neglected his duties in favour of his pleasures. His enemies criticized him for laziness, profligacy and waste rather than for any abuse of power. After the War of 1812 and the revival of trade, he gave Americans little to oppose, apart from his wayward morals. Given the distractions of his private life, he rarely took notice of the United States, which in any case remained a delicate issue for a son of George III. To American diplomats he could be cold and reserved, though to Richard Rush, who was appointed Minister to Britain in 1818, he was perfectly charming.[31] Adams reported that he seemed ignorant of the American political system, not able to comprehend how a government could be managed where the members of the executive did not sit as members of the legislature.[32] With the improvement in relations after the War of 1812, most Americans who thought about it took his policy towards the United States to be about as friendly as could be expected from a king of England.[33]

Meanwhile, the royal family continued to excite American interest. In 1817, the American papers covered the death of Princess Charlotte, George IV's only child and presumptive heir to the throne, as if it were a death in the family. A thousand or so newspaper articles, drawing heavily on English sources, touched on her tragic death in childbirth and its implications for the succession. A change in British policy was not widely expected. As the *New-York Columbian* put it: 'The line of Kings may be altered; but her policy will be the same. The King is but a phantom – the miserable dupe and tool of the ministry.'[34] The more romantic reflected on the power and grandeur of the British throne. From Philadelphia, the Scottish-born American Helen Currie paid tribute in a poem titled 'In memory of the amiable and illustrious Princess Charlotte of England':

We long'd to see a female reign,
   We long'd to see thy worth reveal'd,
Elizabeth's reviv'd again,
   But now thy destiny's seal'd.[35]

The death of Princess Charlotte made the American headlines, but the King's treatment of his wife soon overshadowed the event. In Britain, the Queen Caroline affair was the cause célèbre of the era, comparable to the acrimonious marital break-up of the Prince and Princess of Wales in the 1990s. The Queen's trial in 1820 provoked the most extensive radical campaign of the post-war years in Britain and prompted a theatrical display of emotion that bordered on the saturnalian. Verse satires, caricatures, and vast quantities of inflammatory material belittled the King, though it did not in the end pose a threat to the monarchy. Still, the respectable classes on both sides of the Atlantic had to draw on a deep well of forgiveness in the case of George IV. For Americans, the Queen Caroline case was an irresistible opportunity for royal gazing coupled with a dash of moral superiority. From their republican eyrie, censoriousness was a predictable reaction to what was widely portrayed as royal injustice.

When foreign intelligence reached the United States of the impending royal divorce, American news hounds were quickly on the distant scent. It was an early example of the use of royal scandal to increase newspaper sales in America. The idea was simple enough: to give readers the impression that they were getting reports of momentous political and social consequence, even if the news was stale back in Britain. As a New England columnist declared in December 1820: 'since the commencement of the Queen's trial, the people of this country, as well as England, have suffered the subject to engross their chief attention'.[36] (The Divorce Bill had been dropped a month before he reported its importance.) The events surrounding the Queen were of such importance, observed the *Connecticut Courant*, 'that we have thought a detail of every circumstance attending them which could be comprised within the limits of a weekly paper, would be expected by our readers'.[37]

In America, as in Britain, the King's errant behaviour galvanized the literate public. Even admirers of the monarchy in the United States tended to fault the King and side with the Queen:

> In our own country much interest has been felt for the fate of this unfortu-
> nate woman, who, alone and unprotected, has stood as yet unmoved and
> unsullied amid the tempest of filth and calumny with which she has been
> assailed by the royal debauchee, her husband, and his sycophantic allies, the
> ministry.[38]

The newspapers took no small pleasure in retailing the royal embarrassment, the ensuing political unrest, and the costs of the Queen's trial. 'If the Queen of England's guilt should be proved, that circumstance, so far from rendering a divorce proper, would be a strong reason why the King and Queen should still continue husband and wife, as they would then be fit companions for each other.'[39] When the Queen suddenly died within a year of her trial, the press paid their respects and moved on to other royal issues.

A rapid expansion of the American press – there were under 200 American newspapers in 1800 and over 3,000 by 1850 – was taking place in the reign of George IV. In keeping with the growing demand for society news and stories of human interest, editors turned naturally to the British court. From George IV's accession in 1820 to his death a decade later, newspapers and magazines produced a steady flow of information on the line of succession, royal levées, royal fashions, royal travels, royal expenditure, and royal misdemeanour. Often such information came directly from the London papers, but whatever its origin it was starting to take up more and more space in the American prints, especially those in New England and the cities of the Eastern seaboard, where cultural, familial, and trade links with Britain remained particularly strong.

During the reign of George IV, ambivalence characterized American attitudes towards the royal family. Much comment was unflattering, though good humoured. As a spectator at the Coronation in 1821, the writer Washington Irving thought the procession 'magnificent' and the King 'amazingly grand' but 'not so great a king as Louis the 18th by at least a hundred weight'.[40] Meanwhile, the American press, which had attacked the King for mistreating his wife, now looked for a replacement among the princesses of Europe. It regaled readers with the splendour of the Coronation but mocked it as extravagant folly.[41] It gawped at the King's jewels but despised them as 'trappings of a monarchy that would support a republic'.[42] It dismissed the King as a profligate but sang his praises, as in the *Providence Gazette*: 'And may this long be Briton's song, God save great George our King'.[43]

Sadly for the royalists of Rhode Island, even God could not save the dissolute King. When news of his decline reached the United States in the summer of 1830, bulletins of his condition were soon followed by details of his demise. At his death the King received notices on both sides of the Atlantic that would have killed a production in the West End. The moralizing obituaries in America dwelled on the King's decadence and brutality towards Queen Caroline, which his taste and refinement could not offset. The *New York Evangelist* applauded the religious reforms of the reign, especially the removal of disabilities on Catholics and Protestant dissenters, but thought that the King's 'profligate character' encouraged 'gross sensuality' among the English nobility.[44] The *Casket* compared George IV's disposition to Charles II: 'the same reckless levity, the same fondness for illicit pleasures' and castigated him for his 'mortifying neglect' of his wife.[45]

On hearing the news of the King's death, President Jackson drafted a letter of condolence. It was a model of the tact that typified relations between the American and British courts:

> I have received with deep regret the doleful intelligence of the decease of your august Sovereign George the 4th and offer you my sincere condolence at an event so well calculated to remind nations of their dependence upon the author of all good. But whilst I thus mingle my sorrows with yours, permit me to congratulate you and your majesty's subjects generally, that this dispensation of providence has been so mercifully ordered as not to be without a solace which may well excite their gratitude. In the succession of

his brother William the 4th I feel confident that the people of England will find all the blessings of the succeeding reign; and that Foreign powers will see in it the same guarantees for a just and liberal intercourse preserved and strengthened. The long experience of his majesty's first minister confirms this pleasing anticipation, and would authorise us to look for a policy calculated to avert forever if it were possible, the horrors and miseries of war.[46]

As a mark of respect for George IV, ships in the New York harbour hoisted their colours to half-mast.[47] An American in London wrote home that 'all classes of the people express for him the highest regard and warmest kindness, and deprecate his death with fervor and apparent sincerity'.[48] He had apparently not read the obituaries in the British press, which were, if anything, more critical of the King than those in the United States. An article in *The Times* of London, which captured the mood, described the King as unloved by his subjects who had to pick up the bill for his extravagance: 'Nothing more remains to be said about George IV but to pay, as pay we must, for his profusion.'[49] Years later, the novelist William Thackeray, lecturing in the United States, summed up George IV as 'a great simulacrum', a view nicely judged for an American audience.[50]

*   *   *

By the end of George IV's reign, many Americans felt threatened by Jacksonian democracy with its radical, egalitarian ideals and appeal to a mass electorate. It was the era in which Alexis de Tocqueville travelled to America and noted the dangers inherent in a republic that had many ambitious men but few lofty ambitions, and the prospect of political power concentrated in their hands. For more cosmopolitan Americans, who feared the tyranny of the majority, the United States lacked the tradition and charm of the old world. It also lacked an aristocracy, which in Britain made the transition to democracy less abrupt and disorienting. The Burkean conservative Charles Francis Adams, the grandson of John Adams, spoke for many privileged Americans when he wrote in his diary that the spirit of change was 'too active' in America. An Anglophile, he worried about the growth of democracy in Britain and hoped that the British 'will beware in time of the danger to be incurred in adopting our principles'.[51]

Having spent their moral capital in the Revolution, Americans turned to commercial expansion in the early republic. In the mid-nineteenth century Americans were not so inclined to proclaim the United States as the model system of government for the nations of the world. For all the lofty sentiments of the Declaration of Independence, political corruption and self-aggrandizement were as common in the United States as elsewhere. In the 1830s the Minister in London was still defending slavery – nearly half of the presidents before the Civil War were slave owners – and his successor was explaining away the repudiation of American state bonds.[52] The Presidency itself was looking increasingly tarnished, realizing some of the misgivings of the Founding Fathers about the role of the executive. Meanwhile, Britain remained the world's foremost power and it boasted a hereditary monarch as its head of state. And despite their residual anti-British sentiment, which came to the fore on meeting patronizing English visitors to the United States, Americans still looked to Britain for material progress and cultural guidance.

Such cultural dependency was hard to avoid, even among non-English-speaking emigrants on the frontier where the United States was forging its character. It left many Americans in the grip of the mother country so that, as has been said, 'colonial society was a copy of English society of the same period, a little caricatured'.[53] Before the Revolution, British culture had penetrated the unruly settlements beyond the Atlantic seaboard, spearheaded by learned teachers and preachers from New England, Virginia and cities like Philadelphia. In the early republic the distinctive regional customs derived from the colonial experience persisted.[54] The force of the past remained so powerful that it would have been surprising had the migrants teeming into Ohio and Kentucky and the lands beyond, though increasingly polyglot, rejected the law, literature, manners and mores of the mother country. The very crudities of the frontier encouraged the citizenry to look back to a land that for generations had been the fount of America's cultivated style and civilized values.[55]

To many Americans the cultural dependency of the United States on Britain was historical and for that reason readily understandable.[56] Whether they liked it or not they could not easily escape their inheritance. In so far as they saw themselves bound to the mother country by ethnicity it undermined the perceived need to forge a separate American identity.[57] A French visitor described the people of New England in the 1830s as not merely English but 'double-distilled English'.[58] The historian Henry Adams, writing of his New England childhood in the mid-nineteenth century, observed: 'The tone of Boston society was colonial. The true Bostonian always knelt in self-abasement before the majesty of English standards; far from concealing it as a weakness, he was proud of it as his strength.'[59] As Ralph Waldo Emerson remarked: 'Every book we read, every biography, play, or romance, in whatever form, is still English history and manners.'[60]

The capacity of English civilization to absorb other traditions was remarkable, and it was not simply to do with its literature, settled institutions, and material culture but also something less tangible. To Gerald Johnson, the

American author of *Our English Heritage* (1949) it had to do with a compelling narrative, 'a story, partly history, partly legend, largely poetry and drama'.[61] For all the anti-British rhetoric of Fourth of July celebrations, Americans remained intellectually indebted to Britain. In newspapers and magazines, in book prefaces and memoirs 'the longing for English praise, the submission to English literary judgment, the fear of English censure, and the base humility with which it was received, was dwelt on incessantly'.[62] Such subservience had a further influence, for it underpinned American deference to British royalty, who were central to the historical narrative.

Whether from literary Boston or the raw backwoods, Americans were highly sensitive to British opinion because they cared so much about it. During his extensive travels in North America in 1827 to 1828, Captain Basil Hall of the Royal Navy noted the American insecurities, the longing for praise and recognition, 'all the while praising everything so highly themselves'.[63] While Americans often criticized Britain as decadent and class-ridden, British visitors to the United States tended to see their cousins across the Atlantic as provincial bumpkins, lacking the refinement provided by culture and ancient institutions like the monarchy. The novelist Frances Trollope, who lived in the United States for some years, took this patrician attitude in her best-selling travel book *Domestic Manners of the Americans* (1832). In her opinion, Americans were Englishmen abroad, but that was little compensation for their defects: 'I do not like their principles, I do not like their manners, I do not like their opinions.'[64]

During his tour of the United States from 1831 to 1832, the aristocratic Tocqueville rather liked Americans and their principles. But he also saw Americans as displaced Englishmen and noted that an egalitarian culture required diversions to offset the blandness and monotony of daily life. By the time of his visit, the American Revolution was a distant memory; and reports of British royalty, with their titles, vast wealth, and aristocratic manners filled a social vacuum, not least on the frontier. Royalty dazzled and provided an enthralling, if remote, dimension to life in a country with more space than tradition. Americans were uneasy with the hierarchical social order personified by royalty, but social fluidity brought insecurity in its wake, leaving United States citizens unsure of their place in society. Tocqueville observed that Americans, lacking an established class system, developed a fixation with status, which was to blame for the restlessness that often afflicted democratic citizens: 'One scarcely encounters an American who does not want to owe something of his birth to the first founders of the colonies, and as for offshoots of the great families of England, America seemed to me to be entirely covered with them'.[65]

As Tocqueville travelled across the United States, Calvin Colton, a Yale graduate and former missionary, was penning his impressions of English society as a journalist for the *New York Observer*. It was of no small consequence, he wrote, that 'Americans have no king, no court, no aristocracy'. A royal house, in his estimation, provided 'majesty' and 'splendour', while Britain's titled aristocracy provided 'a social and moral influence, diffusing itself downward and over the entire mass of the community, above which they tower and move in such exalted, dazzling, and inapproachable eminence'. He dissented from those English commentators who said that without a royal court Americans must be destitute of the most refined taste and culture, but he observed that the advanced civilization of the mother country could not be expected in 'an infant Republic, that has struggled into existence and been raised to its importance by dint of toil'.[66]

Colton was not one of those Americans who traced their ancestry to the noble houses of England – he came from worthy Massachusetts stock – but he was susceptible to the royal spell. The want of a royal family was not to Colton a 'grave charge'; yet in his opinion Americans had cause to revere Great Britain and its monarchy in the reign of William IV. For him, British institutions were:

> a bulwark of the liberties of mankind. And we have as much affection – yes, we will say, affection for William IV, as could reasonably be demanded by anyone of his Majesty's subjects from a republican of the United States. We are not conscious of any thing, but the kindest feelings and the best wishes for his Majesty's person and family.[67]

Arguably, such opinions betrayed the very lack of sophistication Colton detected in the American character. But they would have diverted William IV, who once condescended to receive Colton at a Buckingham Palace levée.

* * *

'Look at that idiot', George IV once said about his brother, the Duke of Clarence, 'they will remember me if ever he is in my place.'[68] Compared to George IV, his successor William IV was a model of dullness, prone to falling asleep after dinner while the dutiful Queen Adelaide embroidered. Americans duly noted the King's 'discreditable *liaisons*', but they found his Coronation relatively economical and his opinions mild and expected his policy towards the United States to be, like his predecessor's, generally friendly.[69] Many Americans would have read Sir Walter Scott's poem 'A Vision of the Coronation', a paean of praise to 'a patriot King' in their daily papers.[70] Few of them would have remembered that as Duke of Clarence he had spent some months in New York during the American Revolution as a young midshipman – he was not impressed by the city's amenities – and that General Washington hatched a plan, which had to be aborted, for his capture.[71] Those older citizens who did know the King from his days in New York now recalled him not so much as an enemy of the Revolution but as a 'frolicksome boy' often seen ice skating while in port.[72]

Affable but boorish, William IV was widely popular in Britain, except in ultra-radical circles, which treated him as just another royal nuisance. While he could hold forth on the Poor Law, he was more at home cultivating his turnips. As a constitutional monarch, he was a conservative and a conciliator but without subtlety or vision. Wellington said of him that he did not even have any serious interests or opinions.[73] Colton observed what should have been obvious about the monarchy for decades: 'The King of Great Britain has not . . . so much power as the President of the United States.'[74] William IV's intention was to ensure the stability of the kingdom, which to him meant keeping the royal show on the road. If that included being nice to Americans, so be it. With little inclination to interfere in politics, he reluctantly presided over the passage of the 1832 Reform Bill, which widened the franchise and ended the monarchy's political influence through traditional forms of patronage and honours. In the new context, influence compensated for the loss of royal authority. Increasingly, the monarchy's purpose was to display what Burke called 'the decent drapery of life'.

For William IV and the other children of George III, America was something of an embarrassment, a subject to be avoided lest unhappy memories intruded. In the early decades of the nineteenth century contact between Americans and the royal family was limited. Diplomats presented their credentials to the monarch and were invited to levées and drawing rooms, but most American visitors to Britain rarely saw the King or Queen, though they might get a sight of royalty at the opera or the races at Ascot. During a trip to England William Henry Seward, a state senator from New York and later Secretary of State under Lincoln, had to bribe a guard at Windsor to catch a glimpse of William IV.[75]

Over the years, the King's attitudes towards the United States had softened, driven by his easy nature, the needs of diplomacy, and cordial relations with Andrew Jackson, whose Presidency was coterminous with his reign. Washington Irving, who had become Secretary to the legation in London by the beginning of the new reign, noted that 'our diplomatic situation at this Court is favourable and gratifying as we could desire, being treated with marked respect and friendliness by the Royal family'.[76] It was a sign of improved relations that Irving, who was responsible for distributing Coronation tickets to 'Persons from the Court of the President of the United States', had to turn many away, including the Consul-General.[77]

Irving was the most English of American authors, and he left a pleasing picture of the court of William IV, whose traditions he obviously admired. 'The King keeps all London agog; nothing but sights and parades and reviews. He is determined that it shall be merry old England once more.' At a grand dress ball at the Duke of Wellington's house, the King spoke in an affable manner to everybody, including the Americans present. Irving noted William IV's easy manner and 'old middy' (midshipman) habit of wiping his nose with the back of his forefinger: 'Upon the whole, however, he seems in a most happy mood, and disposed to make everyone happy about him, and if he keeps on as he is going, without getting too far out of his depth, he will make the most popular King that ever sat on the English throne.'[78]

The King warmly welcomed the United States legation and treated American visitors to England without superciliousness. When some courtiers bated an American woman with the question whether she came from a nation that 'calculated', the King answered that she came from a nation that 'fascinated'.[79] When he received the American Minister Martin Van Buren in 1831, he took pains to make a favourable impression, saying that the common origin and kindred relations between the two countries 'should stimulate both nations to practise forbearance towards each other'.[80] The King also spoke handsomely of President Jackson, observing 'that all good men were traduced'.[81] After the assassination attempt on the President's life in early 1835, he sent a message of sympathy, which elicited from Jackson the comment that the King's character was 'lofty and benevolent' and that he was 'amongst the greatest of his country's benefactors'.[82]

Though the monarchy's increasingly benign image tempered views about William IV, he nonetheless came in for occasional ridicule from American travellers who often felt obliged to express reservations about royalty. The future author and Dean of the Harvard Medical School Oliver Wendell Holmes saw the royal family at the opera in 1834. As an upright republican he was not one to exclude the monarchy from tart observation. He wrote home that the King looked 'like a retired butcher' and the Queen a milkman's wife. He added that 'the King blew his nose twice, and wiped the royal perspiration repeatedly from a face which is probably the largest uncivilized spot in England'. He was kinder to Princess Victoria – 'a nice, fresh-looking girl, blonde, and rather pretty'.[83] (In later years Holmes warmed to the royal family, and in 1886 spent Derby Day in the 'jolly' company of the Prince of Wales, later Edward VII.)[84]

A peek at royalty from the opera pit did not compare with meeting royalty at the palace, and Americans presented at court tended to shed their critical faculties. After leaving a royal reception at Buckingham Palace during his time as Minister, Richard Rush said that the spectacle, 'like old English buildings, and Shakespeare, . . . carried the feelings with it, triumphing over criticism'.[85] The naval officer Charles Stewart, who published a memoir of his British travels, wrote a detailed description of the levée that he attended at St James's Palace in 1832. He described the King as 'a plain-hearted and generous-spirited sailor', and found, somewhat to his surprise, that the assembled company was very much like the American elite in manners and taste, though a little more ostentatious in their display of jewellery. The next day he attended Queen Adelaide's last drawing room of the season, which he portrayed as a scene of such brilliance and splendour that it satisfied everything his imagination had desired.[86]

Colton also left vivid descriptions of both a levée and a drawing room that he had the honour of attending with the United States diplomat Aaron Vail in the mid 1830s. Though he did not get beyond an exchange of bows with the King, the reception impressed him as a transient display of royal magnificence that bore similarities to the more modest presidential events in Washington. But Colton, like Stewart, preferred his outing to the Queen's drawing room, which he described as the ultimate in regal splendour, 'the most brilliant scene

4. *President's Levée,* aquatint by Robert Cruikshank.

I had ever witnessed . . . a dazzling pageant'.[87] When the door opened to the royal presence, the 'moving diorama' inside left the impressionable American breathless. And when, in the manner of royal small talk, Queen Adelaide asked him how long he had been in England, he answered and parted in a swoon, to join the growing number of United States citizens seduced by the royal magic.

Compare Colton's experience at Buckingham Palace with the corresponding experience of Charles Dickens at the White House a few years later. On an initial visit to meet President Tyler, the White House and its denizens failed to impress the worldly writer, whose views, published in *American Notes* in 1842, chagrined many of his readers in the United States. He compared the home of the President to an English clubhouse with grounds that had 'that uncomfortable air of having been made yesterday', while the other guests he met in a dreary waiting room spat on the carpets.[88] On returning to the 'republican court' for a party one evening, he was surprised to find it called a levée. For all the democratic rhetoric of the day, levées remained a fixture of White House ceremonial. In Jackson's administration there had been complaints about the disgraceful conduct of the crowd, which resulted in police officers having to be stationed at the gates of the executive mansion.[89]

Dickens seemed to expect the levée he attended to turn into a mêlée. On his report, there was little in the way of presidential magic; but the lack of stately grandeur witnessed by Colton at Buckingham Palace was not without compensations for an English man of letters, who arrived with his wife amidst the dense crowd of carriages. He noted the mass of undistinguished citizens who crowded the drawing room and was relieved to find that a measure of propriety prevailed. For all the lack of refinement and 'the madness of American politics', he was most taken by the affection shown to Washington Irving, who had been recently appointed Minister at the Court of Spain. 'I have seldom respected a public assembly more, than I did this eager throng, when I saw them turning with one mind from noisy orators and officers of state, and flocking with a generous and honest impulse round the man of quiet pursuits.'[90]

CHAPTER 3

VICTORIA FEVER

Stubborn Yankee pen wont write,
  Your Gracious Majesty.
And yet thy throne I've ever deemed a nucleus of light;
  All earthly grandeur to me seemed
Around thee clustering bright.

Factory girl, Lowell Massachusetts, 1842

Many Americans would have agreed with the proposition that Queen Victoria succeeded 'an imbecile . . . a profligate . . . and a buffoon'.[1] But having reconciled themselves to the 'imbecile' and the 'profligate', they had warmed to the 'buffoon'. For all their faults, the 'wicked uncles' had no quarrel with the United States. They left the monarchy's power eroded, which reduced the scope for American criticism, while enhancing its social influence, which increased the scope for amity between the two countries. In the reign of Victoria, the friendship between America and the royal family was to reach unprecedented heights. The Queen's genius was to enhance the monarch as a symbol of constitutional rectitude, while associating royalty with the prevailing middle-class sentiments of the age. Her religious upbringing accommodated the pieties of her day, and she identified with the practical morality that was such a feature of the mid-nineteenth century in both Britain and America.

Manners and morals aside, the onset of the Queen's reign coincided with the vast expansion underway in the British manufacturing industry. In the second quarter of the nineteenth century about 40 per cent of United States imports came from Britain.[2] Though friendship does not always follow trade,

Americans viewed Queen Victoria against the backdrop of advancing technology, the greater availability of manufactured goods, and widening prosperity on both sides of the Atlantic. The array of British articles in American shops buttressed the outpouring of favourable royal publicity in the United States. That the usage 'Victorian' became ubiquitous in the republic was an extraordinary tribute to the influence of the mother country. It was shaped not only by the English 'colonization' of the American mind but also by the belief in the Queen's moral sovereignty in an age of material improvement and by the clarion calls in mid-century America to Anglo-Saxon patriotism.[3]

The arrival of the young Queen dispelled much of the suspicion that marked United States attitudes towards the royal family in the early decades of the nineteenth century. The American press had been fascinated by Victoria as the heiress presumptive, an interest heightened by the novelty of a female sovereign. Her accession prompted memories of Queen Elizabeth, who still loomed large in nineteenth-century American education. To romantic royalists Victoria was not a constitutional ornament; nor did they wish her to be one. Nor did she see herself as a figurehead, for as a personality she was obstinate, kindly and impetuous by turns, inclined to assert her independence. 'The King of England's dead', wrote the young New York attorney George Templeton Strong in his diary:

and so long live Queen Victoria! Who will do quite as well, I dare say. She'll be a fool if she marries; let her think of Elizabeth. A mere nominal queenship – and actual cyphership – is a state she'll keep clear of, if she has the independent spirit of a cockroach.[4]

In 1837, the *New Yorker* newspaper reported on the 'true dignity and winning modesty' with which the 'fair' Victoria passed through the trials of her accession to the throne. It was more like a novel of Disraeli than a chapter of history that she 'should be called, without a whisper of dissent, to sway the destinies of . . . the richest, most powerful and most enlightened nation on the face of the earth'.[5] Americans rejoiced in their own system of government, but its relative lack of pomp and ceremony made monarchical pageantry all the more alluring. The sight of the most powerful men on earth bending their knees to a mere child in an act of loyalty, however absurd it might seem, had a romantic grandeur that fired the imagination. It also had a strange logic. As the *New Yorker* observed: 'The sovereign is but a ceremony – the embodied personification of the majesty of the laws and the inviolability of public order. The individual is nothing; – the rallying-point of loyalty, the focus of a people's affection for their country, her institutions, interests, and honor, are everything.'[6]

Given the theatricality of a monarchy with such a colourful and illustrious history, it was not surprising that the Queen attracted enormous attention in America. One of the most attentive onlookers was Andrew Jackson, who was more deeply interested in monarchy than generally supposed. During his Presidency, the old soldier received many personal messages from European royalty. In 1833, the Duchess of Kent, Princess Victoria's mother, conveyed her best wishes to him and to the United States through the American chargé d'affaires in London. Jackson, who was eager to become more intimate with foreign rulers, reciprocated her regard through his envoi. No European royalty held such an attraction for him as Princess Victoria. They exchanged portraits and when she ascended the throne Jackson saw himself in the role of her American protector, a seemingly unlikely role for the self-made popular tribune.[7]

In his retirement, Jackson followed the preparations for the Coronation of his 'little good friend' in 1838 with great interest.[8] As he recognized, the individual might be everything in America, but no single individual, not even the President, served as the focus of such loyalty and national pride as a hereditary monarch who was seen to be above politics. With youth, the weight of history, and the appeal of royal ceremonial behind her, Queen Victoria, heir to an ancient throne, touched parts of the human psyche that presidents could not reach, especially lacklustre ones such as Jackson's successor Martin Van Buren.

At the time of the Coronation a rumour spread in the United States that President Van Buren wished to offer his hand in marriage to the Queen and that his son John was sailing to England with the formal proposal. It was an opportunity for some revelry at the President's expense: 'He has shown himself . . . totally unqualified to be the President of a Republic, but we dare say he would answer quite well for a pageant of royalty. – The husband of a queen regent, by the laws of England, is just nobody, – a part which Mr Van Buren will be able to play to perfection.'[9] John Van Buren attended the Coronation and later dined with the Queen, but he did not pull a proposal of marriage out of his pocket from his father. Instead, like an American Podsnap, he told her how big the rivers and prairies were in the United States.[10]

The Coronation, though muddled and inadequately rehearsed, left most Americans in London in awe. One lady said that its novelty explained the attraction, but it was far more than that to most American witnesses.[11] The correspondent for the *New York Observer* declared that the coronation of the Pope was 'mere tinsel in comparison'.[12] 'Be assured as a pageant it was unsurpassed in all history,' wrote another witness: 'I plead guilty to that weakness though I hold myself as good a republican as walks the earth; and I will confess to you, (between ourselves) that the whole roomful of Americans, who surrounded

5. Coronation of Queen Victoria, 1838.

me, were as foolish as myself. I cannot help it; and what is more, I will not: – so set that down to my account.'[13]

Not all Americans were as impressed. Amidst all the detailed coverage of the Coronation, there was the occasional soul-searching in the United States press, which portrayed the pomp and pageantry of the ceremony as 'exceedingly brilliant and imposing' but 'repulsive to republican taste and simplicity'.[14] Among those who wanted to have it both ways, the *Richmond Enquirer* praised the splendour then declared it 'ridiculous'.[15] The editor and divine, Richard Cary Morse, who attended the Coronation with a group of American friends, wrote to his wife that while everyone around him was thrilled by the spectacle, his own reaction was one of repugnance. 'I wondered that such a delicate race as the aristocracy should be fond of such shows of their weakness. Is it possible that the English are such children as to be duped by these gewgaws?'[16]

The Coronation was an opportunity for the American legation in London to make a show of republican simplicity. This was not just a matter of principle, but of necessity, for the legation was sorely short of funds. So much so that at the time of the death of William IV, the Minister, Andrew Stevenson of Virginia, had to pay for the mourning clothes of his officials out of his own pocket.[17] The United States delegation invited to Westminster Abbey for the Coronation consisted of Stevenson and his guests, who travelled in two 'plain but chaste and elegant carriages'. Mrs Stevenson wrote that the 'ambassadors were all blazing with diamonds' but that she and her husband were, 'like our equipage, handsome and genteel, without being fine'.[18] Whether the British saw the unadorned coaches as vehicles of democracy or simply assumed that the United States could not afford to pay for more becoming transport is unclear, but to the puritans in the American legation they were seen as a sign of a progressive nation.[19]

There was a tendency of American visitors to Britain to go native. This was especially true of the diplomats resident in London, who felt at home in the larger sense when they landed on their ancestral soil.[20] More and more Americans were coming to England.[21] The Coronation turned more than a few of them into royalist sympathizers, and they extended the royal mythology and prestige as they passed along their experiences. Among them was the bachelor Richard Vaux, Secretary to Minister Stevenson, who had the distinction of dancing with the Queen at a Coronation ball. He was the first, and probably the last, American to be so privileged; and while he went on to have a brilliant career, he dined out on the story for the rest of his life. On hearing of the event, his Quaker mother, who distrusted dancing and titles, wrote to her son: 'I am told thee has been dancing with the queen. I do hope, my son, thee will not marry out of meeting.'[22]

One could compile a book of Coronation verse from maudlin poets in New York and Boston, Baltimore and Poughkeepsie, Richmond and Charleston.[23] Most were written by Americans who had never seen a member of the royal family in person, but a growing number of Americans did experience the grandeur surrounding the throne in the reign of Queen Victoria. What would the Founding Fathers have made of the presentation of American debutantes at Buckingham Palace? Such presentations might never have happened if the State Department had adopted Jefferson's suggestion that a resident Minister in London was unnecessary. The Queen's nodding approval of American debutantes not only disseminated Victorian values among wealthy Americans, but also could open doors closed in New York or Washington to girls of doubtful reputation or background.[24] Years later, the historian Beckles Willson asked Whitelaw Reid, the Ambassador to London in the reign of Edward VII, about American participation in court presentations. They agreed that 'the practical tribute to feudal institutions involved had acted as a valuable social safety-valve, furnishing a vent for the natural aspirations of a restless and wealthy young democracy'.[25]

Social climbing on a feudal scale could be a daunting – and expensive – as this playful description of an American girl's presentation at court from a New Hampshire paper in 1839 suggests:

> The fatal day arrives, and it rains, as usual. Miss Letty, jaded, fatigued, hurried, nervous, excited, and fretful, is at last 'rigged out,' metaphorically speaking, and the coach arrives, and she sets out for St James'. . . . At length the gentlemen ushers of the gold and silver sticks introduce her to the saloon of the Throne, where her Majesty stands in regal state. 'Miss Tinicum, of Communipaw', the curtsey is made, the Queen nods, and Miss Letty is walked off into another room, and here ends the whole ceremony – the sensitive labors of a whole month, night and day, and the loss of a small fortune, thrown away on a single nod from Miss Victoria Rex, who probably did not condescend to look earnestly at the lady thus introduced to her.[26]

Presentations at court, the Coronation, the Queen's appearance, and palace arrangements generally fascinated Americans. On the spot was Stevenson, who kindled interest in the royal family by posting dispatches and letters to the press from his ministerial office. While he could not describe the Queen as beautiful, wise, or divine, he was much taken by her expressiveness, unaffected manner and capacity for business, features that endeared her to Americans: 'No one can approach the present Queen without being struck, not only with her easy and charming deportment, and that peculiar softness of disposition and temper, for which she is remarkable, but with the entire self command and repose of manner.'[27] These were the qualities captured by the English-born American painter Thomas Sully in his portrait of the Queen, commissioned by the 'Society of the Sons of St George' of Philadelphia, which was on show in that city in 1839.[28]

'Victoria Fever' and 'Queen Mania' raised occasional hackles in the American press. The newspaper coverage across the country suggests that royal watching was not restricted to the Northeast, though to Jeffersonians it was seen as a reflection of urban, as opposed to country, taste and fashion. To critics of the inequalities in Anglo-American relations, ogling royalty was symptomatic of a deeper malaise. One British traveller remarked that the United States was 'as much subject to the *English System* as the Colonies once were to the English

King'. Taking up this cue, the *United States Magazine* lamented that 'our paper money, banking, credit, and stock operations, are dependent, even to their minutest ramifications, on the temper of the Bank of England and the change-jobbers of London'.[29] On this account George III's wish that Britain might reap greater benefits from Americans as friends than as colonists had come true.

What would Jefferson or Franklin have made of the humorous letter from the mystified American visitor to Philadelphia, or what he called 'Victoria-delphia,' in 1839?

> When I landed at Dock street wharf I fancied I was in some city in the English dominions. The moment I landed on terra firma I espied a large placard posted on a wall at the corner of a street; it ran as follows: 'The splendid painting of Her Majesty Queen Victoria [Sully's portrait] still continues open at the Masonic Hall'. I walked a little further on, when I stopped opposite a fashionable barber's shop; at the window, among other articles, was a variety of hair brushes, with portraits of 'Her Most Gracious Majesty' on them . . . I entered the exchange – the first thing I saw was a bust of Her Majesty standing on the mantelpiece. I walked out, and doubted in my own mind whether the days of old had not returned, and we were yet bowing beneath the sceptre of England. I strolled up Chestnut Street – saw at an auction store some Yankee clocks for sale, with a Victoria portrait for an ornament. I stopped at a perfumer's to purchase something in his line – saw some 'Queen Victoria soap, composed expressly for the coronation'. . . . I stopped to look into a music store. There was the 'Victoria grand march,' the Victoria quadrilles,' etc. . . . I could bear this no longer; I went down into an oyster cellar, got something to eat, and walked as fast as I could to the wharf; there was no boat to go until the next day, so I had to go to the 'Victoria,' formerly 'Baltimore House,' where I went to bed. . . . At daylight I got up and went down to the wharf, and got on board the steamboat as well as I could. Saw a fine brig with the English ensign flying. 'What is her name?' said I; 'Oh,' said a little boy, 'that's the Victoria.'[30]

*   *   *

Any unmarried woman may be in want of a fortune, but an unmarried Queen has dynastic interests to consider as well. This was not lost on American commentators, who after the Coronation turned their attention to Victoria's matrimonial prospects. 'Venus is decidedly in the ascendant', enjoined the *New York Mirror* early in 1840, 'and the desire to follow her majesty's example will be almost universal.'[31] The *Boston Weekly Magazine* noted her intention to comply with the wishes of her country in marrying but applauded her desire to avoid giving her hand to any suitor who was not 'in possession of her heart'.[32] Having dismissed President Van Buren as dynastically impaired, Americans warmed to rumours of Prince Albert of Saxe Coburg. It pleased American Protestants that the Queen could not marry a Catholic and 'if it's a love match,' pronounced the *New York Commercial Advertiser*, 'and the husband worth the having, long life to them and a worthy line of kings.'[33]

There was no shortage of material to indulge American readers about the impending nuptials, much of it recycled in the women's magazines. It gave credence to Bagehot's dictum that 'women – half the human race – care fifty times more for a marriage than a ministry'.[34] The Queen's so-called 'Declaration of Love', which was read in Parliament and widely quoted in the United States, struck a chord with the moral majority:

> Deeply impressed with the solemnity of the engagement which I am about to contract, I have not come to this decision without mature consideration, nor without feeling a strong assurance, that with the blessing of Almighty God, it will at once secure my domestic felicity, and serve the interests of my country.[35]

George Templeton Strong noted in his diary that the papers were overflowing with stuff about the royal nuptials, 'which is doubtless very interesting and important to her Majesty's loyal subjects, but which to us republicans is, or ought to be, rather dull and profitless'.[36]

For all their republican airs, however, most Americans found nothing 'dull' or 'profitless' in the royal marriage. Sarah Stevenson, the Minister's wife, who attended the wedding in the chapel of St James's Palace, described the Queen as 'if not an angel, at least such stuff as angels are made of'.[37] She sent a piece of the royal wedding cake to a friend in New York. London Yankees attended the many parties in honour of the wedding, and Minister Stevenson had an audience at Buckingham Palace, where he presented a congratulatory letter to the Queen from President Van Buren. Meanwhile, across the Atlantic, enthralled Americans observed the wedding with verse:

> Lady! God send thee, in thy new condition,
>   Healthy, happiness, and all prosperity;
> May'st reap of thine each a rich fruition!
>   True, I am not thy subject – nor to thee
> In home bow – yet this my warm petition,
>   Make I to Heaven for your Majesty:
> Fair Queen, thus over broad Atlantic's waters
> I wish thee health, and many sons and daughters![38]

Americans took an abiding interest in the Prince Consort and generally liked what they saw. They took him to be liberal in his views and benevolent in his feelings, a model marital partner who would promote the Queen's happiness and domestic peace. The American diplomat Edward Everett, who sat next to him at dinner at Windsor, found him to be 'an exceedingly modest, intelligent, well educated person, greatly above the average . . . of those of his rank in Europe'.[39] But some Americans, true to their origins, thought the Queen should have married an Englishman. At least one, Arthur Cleveland Coxe, the Rector of Grace Church in Baltimore, took Prince Albert to task for his German blood. Besotted by royal ceremonial, Coxe was deeply sympathetic to monarchy: 'I defy any one to look at the Throne of England without veneration', he declared after a visit to the House of Lords. The Prince Consort, however, disappointed him, for 'he is an alien to true British feeling, and an enemy to the Anglican Church. He would Germanize the nation if possible.'[40]

Most American commentators forgave the Prince Consort his German origin – he was a Protestant, at least. As with so much commentary on royalty, there was a particular interest in physical appearances, which was a reflection of the monarchy's greater visibility by the 1840s. 'A very decent looking lad', observed a reporter.[41] 'A well looking lad . . . with foxy mustachios' wrote another.[42] A former editor of the *Trenton Emporium*, Stacy Potts, who was travelling in England in 1841, published a first-hand description of the Prince for American consumption that set the tone: 'Prince Albert is decidedly a handsome young man; and though he wears the abominable mustachios which almost brutalize the faces of three-fourths of the fashionable here, he appears to be a modest, unassuming, quiet, family kind of personage.'[43] A potato named after him soon became a favourite with Midwestern farmers for its high yield.[44]

The birth of nine offspring to the royal couple consolidated the Queen's reputation for domesticity and sweetness of disposition. Articles on the royal christenings and the royal nursery filled many a column of print in the United States. In an era when the young were becoming more prominent in Anglo-American families, anything to do with the privileged world of the Queen's children, who 'shone as a race apart, denizens of a red and gold Valhalla', was sought after.[45] It was a social market fed by the Queen and the Prince Consort, who were highly sensitive to their reputation beyond the Palace gates. Emily Faithfull, the English editor and promoter of women's employment, wrote in an American magazine: 'Royalty did a daring thing when it commenced to have its portraits taken with babies climbing over its shoulder, and pipes in its hand.'[46]

In the Americanization of the Queen, the devout considered her religion to be of crucial importance, for she could be exalted as a model of righteousness and good conduct, a royal *mater familias*. Bagehot, who recognized the importance of faith in popularizing royalty, observed: 'The English monarchy strengthens our government with the strength of religion.'[47] Clearly, American Christians, whose religious traditions drew heavily on Britain, saw the monarchy as attuned to their own faith. Christianity was widely thought to give particular scope to women as wives and mothers and, by extension, enormous benefits to society. That the greatest monarch on earth was a Protestant and a woman was no small matter in the United States. And though head of the Church of England, she did not alienate American sectarians. Her faith was not worn on the royal sleeve but was moral and down to earth. An American religious periodical remarked that Victoria was largely an object of interest in the United States because of her reputation for domestic virtue at the summit of society.[48] With the strength of religion behind her, she served as the epitome of decency on both sides of the Atlantic.

But Queen Victoria's popularity in America was driven not simply by her reputation for religion and rectitude. It was also driven by the course of United States politics. In the 1830s, not a few Americans had become increasingly sensitive to the growth of executive power in Washington. It was a trend that had been encouraged by Andrew Jackson, who was well known for expanding presidential privileges, not least the use of the veto, once the prerogative of English kings. In a cartoon of 1833, titled 'King Andrew the First', he was shown in royal garb with a veto in his hand. The orator Henry Clay, the leader of the Whig Party and failed presidential candidate, accused the Democrats of eroding the Constitution and the nation's liberties by their extension of presidential authority. In 1833, he observed that if vetoes and other political abuses continued at the current rate, the United States government 'will have been transformed into an elective monarchy'.[49] Six years later his fears for the nation had not abated: 'by the vast accumulation of executive power, actual and meditated, our system is rapidly tending towards an elective monarchy'.[50]

The fear of an impending American monarchy was much in the news in the 1840s.[51] It even reached into the White House. In his inaugural address in 1841, President William Henry Harrison, who died of pneumonia soon after assuming office, reminded his audience that many of the Founding Fathers regretted the extensive powers granted to the executive branch, and he lamented that American politics had for some years been moving towards a 'virtual monarchy'. He thought it 'a great error of the framers of the Constitution not to have made the officer at the head of the Treasury entirely

6. *King Andrew the First*, a Whig handbill.

independent of the Executive'. Nothing, he observed, was wanting 'to the powers of our Chief Magistrate to stamp a monarchical character on our Government but the control of public finances'.[52] (A dispute between Parliament and the Crown over the control of public money, it may be remembered, contributed to the downfall of Charles I.) The Whigs went so far as to accuse Jackson of fulfilling Patrick Henry's definition of a tyrant by wielding both the purse and the sword.[53]

The disparity in the reputation of Queen Victoria, who was not under attack for any abuse of power, and United States presidents, who often were, occasionally discomfited patriotic Americans. Many of them felt obliged to defend their elected presidents, however much they disapproved of them, because they were the ceremonial heads of the nation. In 1842, New York dignitaries gave a grand dinner to honour Lord Ashburton, a British Commissioner in Washington. It created quite a stir in the press for the guests, both Whigs and Democrats, greeted a toast to President Tyler in silence, but stood to applaud a toast to the Queen.[54] When New York notables honoured the Queen and Bostonians saluted her birthdays with cannon fire in the harbour, it reminded Americans of the ceremonial grandeur associated with an ancient monarchy, which was lacking in the republic with its succession of divisive heads of state who struggled to represent the nation entire. Ironically, Queen Victoria was becoming a viable substitute for the President in connecting Americans to a wider historic culture.

The very ordinariness of life in the republic – and the growing emphasis on simplicity in its political manners – magnified the Queen's magical effect on America. As the sovereign of the world's foremost power she was also a potent symbol, especially to traditionalists who longed for stability in an era of undistinguished leaders and unresolved tensions between the northern and southern states. Tocqueville had noted in the 1830s that 'American statesmen of our day seem very inferior to those who appeared at the head of affairs fifty years ago'.[55] Presidents Martin Van Buren, William Henry Harrison, and John Tyler made the Founding Fathers look all the more impressive. Their successors were no more illustrious. During his tour of the United States in 1861, Anthony Trollope remarked: 'who has heard of Polk, of Pierce, of Buchanan? What American is proud of them?'[56] Was there a cavity in the United States Constitution that no president could fill?

But the failure of American presidents and the nation's political institutions only partly explains the reason for the Queen's popularity in the United States. Quite naturally, nations want their head of state to take the lead in representing their manners and aspirations, but the fact that American presidents, even popular ones, have a limited term and political opposition undermines their capacity to play the part of a national idol. Politics is 'the systematic organization of hatreds' as Henry Adams put it, and the more divided the nation politically the more difficult it becomes for a President to reconcile the dual positions of the executive and the head of state. In times of political crisis the party chief tends to eclipse the chief of state.[57]

The Founding Fathers had created a Constitution before the emergence of political parties, and they failed to anticipate the potential danger in combining the executive and ceremonial offices. Compared to the American Presidency, a British constitutional monarch, with tenure for life and independent of political faction, has a significant advantage in representing the nation at large. Unlike Polk, Pierce, or Buchanan, Queen Victoria could do no wrong. What she lacked in power she made up in dignity and the splendour of her court. As Bryce put it in his classic study *The American Commonwealth*, 'the President enjoys more authority, if less dignity, than a European king'. And he added that the eight presidents between Andrew Jackson and Abraham Lincoln were 'intellectual pigmies' by comparison with the leading men of their day.[58] At the beginning of the Civil War, Bagehot thought that the quality of American leaders had not only 'degenerated frightfully' but that the Constitution itself had fallen prey to mob rule.[59]

*　*　*

In many ways, America's response to the royal family was a transatlantic version of what was happening in Britain. More specifically, it was a response similar to that which was to be found in provincial Britain, where the public also witnessed royal events at a distance from polite court culture. As the virtues of Queen Victoria and her family became ever more widely celebrated, Americans, like their British cousins, looked increasingly to the Crown for moral leadership and a focus of identity. Meanwhile, the royal family culti-vated expectations of its moral leadership for its own purposes in an era when royal political power was in decline. Prince Albert was particularly sensitive to the need for better royal public relations and felt that the monarchy would be made safe by taking the moral high ground. By shedding party political asso-ciations the Crown would have the independence to see Britain's problems in the round and to act as 'a balance wheel on the movement of the social body'.[60]

The historian of Victorian England G. M. Young observed that as the monarchy's 'power pursued its inevitable downward curve, its influence rose in equipoise'.[61] Against this background, the monarch's position as 'head of society' came increasingly to the fore, which ceremonial display reinforced. The Queen provided diplomatic cover for her ministers, smoothing relations with the United States through formal gestures. Meanwhile, members of the royal family, precluded from politics, commerce and the professions, collapsed into respectability, becoming creatures of Society with a capital 'S'. As it exchanged authority for influence, the monarchy became allied not only with ascendant middle England, but also with ascendant middle America, whose religion, manners and morals still mirrored those of the mother country. Between them the Queen and the Prince Consort were remaking the monarchy in a new image – a matriarchal family of symbolic power that satis-fied the traditionalist needs of a transatlantic Anglo-Saxon culture.[62]

The royal family buttressed its growing reputation for morality with an atten-tion to ceremonial etiquette that both captivated and unsettled Americans, whose susceptibility to courtly rituals fit uneasily with their democratic princi-ples. When egalitarianism came up against royal decorum, difficulties arose for United States officials. American ministers abroad had typically worn the simple clothing recommended by their department, but they had leeway if the customs of the country they were in required more formal dress. But in 1853, William

L. Marcy, the Secretary of State in President Pierce's administration, issued a circular requiring that United States diplomats abroad wear the plain dress of an American citizen. Marcy, whose experience of royalty was negligible, took the singular view that special dress had no ritual significance and undermined the dignity of a democracy.[63]

Marcy's dress code put James Buchanan, the American Minister in London, on the defensive, for Palace officials took a dim view of sartorial laxity. Sir Edward Cust, the Master of Ceremonies of the Court, explained that to appear before her Majesty in street clothes would be disrespectful. Though Buchanan ridiculed the ribbons and lace, he feared that refusing to follow the traditional dress code would curtail his social life and cut off his sources of information.[64] The British press was decidedly unsympathetic to what it saw as impertinent republican swagger. The *Morning Chronicle* put it sharply:

> There is not the least reason why her Majesty . . . should be troubled to receive the gentleman in the black coat from Yankee-land. He can say his say at the Foreign Office, dine at a chop house in King Street, sleep at the old hummums, and be off as he came, per liner, when his business is done.[65]

The Crimean War put 'this tempest in the wardrobe' into perspective. At his presentation at the Palace in August 1853, Buchanan wore plain dress embellished with a black-handled sword, which at least set him apart from the servants. 'As I approached the Queen, an arch but benevolent smile lit up her countenance – as much as to say, you are the first man who ever appeared before me at Court in such a dress. I must confess that I never felt more proud of being an American.'[66] This was not the end of the muddle surrounding diplomatic etiquette between Britain and the United States during Buchanan's mission that touched on national honour. He was more than a little embarrassed when the Secretary of the American legation in London, Daniel Sickles of New York, remained seated during a toast to the Queen at a public dinner because Victoria, rather than Washington, came first on the list. The controversy reached such a pitch in the press on both sides of the Atlantic that Buchanan sent Sickles back to Washington on a diplomatic pretext.[67]

Americans did not usually cultivate controversy in their encounters with royalty, but their mix of earnestness and provincialism could lead to embarrassment. The British court was well aware of American touchiness, and in her audiences, dinners and drawing rooms, the Queen, who served the diplomatic purposes of her ministers, sought to ease relations between the two countries. In a world in which she had to offer her hand to some pretty unsavoury foreigners, cultivating thin-skinned Americans was not the most onerous of her concessions to duty. She had not inherited a dislike of the United States from her parents, rather the reverse; and the evidence suggests that the Queen rather liked many of her American visitors, who were usually on their best behaviour in her company.

In 1855, the Foreign Office proposed that Her Majesty give an audience to former President Fillmore, who was on a visit to England. The Foreign Minister Lord Clarendon wrote to the Queen:

> At this moment our relations with the United States are of the utmost importance & the Americans are always *on the watch* for the manner in wh. their most distinguished citizens are received in this country . . . An honor done to Mr Fillmore by Your Majesty wd have a good political result.[68]

The Queen accordingly did her diplomatic turn. There is no first-hand report of what was said between them, but various writers have remarked that she found him 'the most courtly and elegant of any American ever presented to her'.[69] The audience must have gone well enough, for she invited Fillmore to a dinner, which was also attended by Buchanan and his niece Miss Harriet Lane, a popular presence at court, who would soon become her uncle's First Lady at the White House.

George Mifflin Dallas, the truculent former Vice-President in the Polk administration, was Buchanan's successor as American Minister. Like so many United States diplomats, he was by turns beguiled and repelled by the Victorian court. He followed Buchanan's lead when presented to the Queen by wearing a plain black coat, bought in his native Philadelphia, which he said represented 'common sense' over 'traditional fooleries'.[70] Like Buchanan, Dallas enjoyed being at the diplomatic heart of the world. But as the representative of an independent democratic nation he eschewed what he called the 'balderdash about mother country, kindred, and so forth' in his public pronouncements. In a letter to a friend he predicted the downfall of the very court culture that gave him pleasure:

> All this magnificence of ceremonial and pretension is fast being undermined, even among the proudest peers, by our republican principles accompanied by our wonderful prosperity; and before any one of your children reaches fifty, it will have vanished, like the hues of a rainbow, for ever. Let them see it before it fades away.[71]

Dallas did not live to see the ceremonial splendour of Edward VII's court, much less the wedding of Prince Charles. When his letters from London were published in 1869, a review in the *Spectator* remarked on the insecurities of a diplomat unsure of his acceptance by those with whom he had officially to mix, a man who feared that Anglomania was getting the better of him and so railed against the barbarity of class. In his letters home, Dallas confessed to a 'democratic pride' and excessive touchiness when in the company of aristocrats whose principles and conduct differed from his own.[72] 'The condemnation of the thing sought after and prediction of its downfall do not deceive,' observed the *Spectator*. . . . 'It is not difficult to sympathize with him, but equally impossible to avoid more than a suspicion that political society is really more advanced in old Europe than in America.'[73] Misunderstandings between the two political cultures, concluded the English reviewer, were inevitable until the United States had a more worldly political class, by which he meant that America's lack of an aristocracy with a tradition of public service sometimes showed.

Such issues took on a greater significance because the legation in London was the most important foreign posting in the state department, though it was not upgraded to embassy status until 1893. In the first century of the republic American ministers to Britain were a prominent lot. Five of them became presidents: John Adams, James Monroe, John Quincy Adams, Martin Van Buren, and James Buchanan. Among those who served in the reign of Victoria, apart from those already mentioned, were the historians George Bancroft and John Lothrop Motley; the men of letters Charles Francis Adams and James Russell Lowell; the son of President Lincoln Robert Todd Lincoln, and the statesmen Thomas Bayard and John Hay. Such able men worked steadily at the job of improving relations and served the banner of Anglo-American Victorianism as they served the United States.

United States diplomats typically felt at home in Britain, but they were highly sensitive to the undercurrent of anti-Americanism, which, while on the wane in the reign of Victoria, still surfaced from time to time, particularly among the aristocracy, who found advocates of the American demos a little rough around the edges. Americans generally found it vexing to be treated like backward Englishmen by English visitors to the United States. The British actress Fanny Kemble, who lived in America in the mid-nineteenth century, found 'the whole country like some remote part of England that I had never seen, the people like English provincial or colonial folk; in short, they were like *queer* English people'.[74] It was no less galling for Americans visiting Britain to discover 'that the ultimate reward for social success was to be taken for an Englishman or woman, rather than a representative of the breed of civilized Americans'.[75]

Tocqueville noted that an American, 'transported to Europe, suddenly becomes meticulous and difficult company'.[76] The sometimes chilling correctness of their hosts unnerved even seasoned American diplomats on the grand stage of British politics and culture. When in the presence of royalty or statesmen as renowned as William Gladstone or Benjamin Disraeli, they could look a little unsophisticated. In such circumstances it was perhaps not surprising that they fell back on egalitarian principles, which manifested themselves in matters like the dress code. But United States emissaries must have known that their British hosts, who had a sharp eye for signs of innocent American behaviour, were often laughing at them behind their backs for their republican moralizing. James Russell Lowell, who was highly sensitive to British of the United States, wrote an essay 'On a Certain Condescension in Foreigners' in 1871: 'Could the eyes of what is called Good Society ... look upon a nation of democrats with any chance of receiving an undistorted image? ... It will take England a great while to get over her airs of patronage toward us, or even passably to conceal them.'[77]

* * *

For all the anti-American undercurrents in Britain and the ambivalence of United States diplomats, the response of the American public to Queen Victoria and her court remained enthusiastic. It bore testimony to continuing Englishness of American culture and the contention that hereditary monarchy exerted a powerful hold on the imagination. This was not simply because kingship was traditional and theatrical, but because it was comprehensible: 'The mass of mankind understand it [monarchy]', remarked Bagehot, 'and they hardly anywhere in the world understand any other.' Uncrowned republics, by contrast, were in his estimation relatively unfathomable.

> The nature of a constitution, the action of an assembly, the play of parties, the unseen formation of a guiding opinion, are complex facts, difficult to know and easy to mistake. But the action of a single will, the fiat of a single mind, are easy ideas; anybody can make them out, and no one can ever forget them.[78]

From its earliest years as an independent nation, the complexities of their government could be confusing to Americans. The sovereignty of an abstract, written Constitution was harder to fathom than the sovereignty of a living monarch, who disguised the complexities of the British Constitution. As Bagehot put it: 'A family on the throne ... brings down the pride of sovereignty to the level of petty life.'[79] An American constitutional writer noted that the English political system, with its hereditary sovereign above all parties, was not only more comprehensible than the American system but also more elastic. The British Constitution, though 'absurd in theory' was 'very efficient in operation', for it sensibly allowed shifts of opinion to change prime ministers without waiting for a fixed election. America, he suggested, was the reverse – inefficient because 'inelastic' in operation.[80] Such opinions would have found favour with Bagehot, who was not enamoured of the American Constitution. No Englishman, he argued, would be much impressed with arguments that assume 'that the limited clauses of an old state-paper can provide for all coming cases, and for ever regulate the future'.[81]

* * *

The American reaction to Queen Victoria's Coronation, marriage and the christening of her children bears out Bagehot's insight that 'a royal family sweetens politics by the seasonable addition of nice and pretty events. It introduces irrelevant facts into the business of government, but they are facts which speak to "men's bosoms" and employ their thoughts.'[82] As an 'American Lady abroad' wrote home to her children: 'republican as I am in feeling and in principle, I could never see her [Victoria's] fresh English face, nor witness the joyous demonstrations attending her appearances, without feeling a soft moisture gathering in my eyes.'[83] Ceremonial heightened royal prestige, while suggesting that the monarchy was politically harmless. Its capacity to satisfy people's longing for splendour and serenity dazzled successive generations of Americans, whose rituals at home were a pale imitation of Britain's. Increasingly, the public treated royalty with that mix of ambivalence and wonder typical of young republics in their dealings with hereditary monarchies.

'The heart of Kings is unknowable', says *Proverbs*. To many Americans the monarchy in the reign of Victoria came to serve as a *tabula rasa* on which the public imprinted its own desires and fantasies. No doubt many United States citizens, particularly those on the frontier without English ancestry, had little or no interest in royal news. But the advent of cheap print and a growing middle-class readership in an era of material progress heightened the monarchy's celebrity well beyond New England and the cities of the Eastern seaboard. Meanwhile, royal values continued to metamorphose into a utilitarian philosophy of goodness, which was in tune with a commercial, voluntary society – and republican values. In the United States the Loyalism of the colonial years was transforming into a reverence for Anglo-Saxon culture, which the Queen embodied as the most dignified, illustrious, and symbolic part of the historic relationship between the two kindred peoples.

American diplomats might dismiss the 'balderdash' about the mother country and predict the collapse of the Victorian court, but the royalist din drowned out their voices. A sense of social hierarchy was seemingly inconsistent with American values, yet United States newspapers and magazines produced a wealth of stories to supply the expanding market for royal news. Increasingly, American editors commissioned royal stories from Britain, which further blurred the distinctions between British and American Victorianism.[84] Whenever there was a royal occasion, reporters, writers and churchmen on both sides of the Atlantic reached for their pens and pulpits, and eventually their cameras and microphones. Paradoxically, the more they said and wrote, the more magical royalty appeared. The wave of media attention would make members of the royal family mysterious yet seemingly accessible, turning them into servants of the emerging American cult of celebrity.

CHAPTER 4

THE PRINCE IN THE PROMISED LAND

No community worships hereditary rank and station like a democracy.
George Templeton Strong, *Diary*, 1860

No episode better illustrates the magical effect of royalty on America than the visit of the Queen's eldest son, the eighteen-year-old Albert Edward, the Prince of Wales (later Edward VII) to the United States in the autumn of 1860.[1] It was love at first sight when the citizens of America's disguised monarchy met the heir to the throne of the crowned republic from which they derived their traditions. Other members of the royal family had visited North America in military or naval capacities – the Prince's grandfather, the Duke of Kent, had stopped in Boston on his way to the West Indies in 1794. But no heir apparent had ever done so. With a demanding schedule, the Prince travelled 5,134 miles in the United States, arriving in Detroit from Ontario on 20 September and departing from Portland Maine a month later, with stops in various towns and cities along the way.[2] To millions of Americans in disparate places, the trip provided a memorable glimpse of British royalty, prompted a reassessment of transatlantic relations, and offered an insight into the ambivalence of being American.

The Prince's visit came at the close of a tour of Canada, where he had been invited to lay the foundation stone of the Federal Parliament in Ottawa and to open a railway bridge in Montreal. From the monarchy's point of view, the visit was an opportunity to test royal popularity abroad, which in an era of advancing democracy could not be taken for granted. The underlying purpose of the Canadian trip was to cement imperial relations, to rally disparate Canadians around the British banner, and to further trade and industry. The visit, remarked

The Times of London, 'will illustrate not only the loyalty of these prosperous Provinces, but the immense extent of British dominion and the deep-laid foundations of British power'.[3] And so it did, as most Canadians rallied to the son of their sovereign with enthusiasm, pleasure and pride.

When President Buchanan, who was well known to the royal family from his time as Minister in London, heard of the Canadian visit he wrote to Queen Victoria with an invitation to extend the Prince's tour to the United States, with the promise that the American people would give him a warm welcome. 'In this they will manifest their deep sense of your domestic virtues, as well as their convictions of your merits as a wise patriot and constitutional sovereign.' The Queen, who thought it prudent that the Prince become acquainted with America, accepted the invitation on her son's behalf and relayed the royal family's feelings of respect 'for the Chief Magistrate of a great and friendly State and kindred nation'.[4] She proposed that on leaving her dominions the Prince would travel under the name of Lord Renfrew, as he did when travelling in Europe. Lord Renfrew, as the American public were told, was only one of the Prince's eleven titles.[5]

As the Queen's letter suggested, there was no official business to get in the way of the entertainments and sightseeing in the United States. The Prince Consort, who worried about his son's lack of seriousness, took the trouble to give him notes on the cities he was to visit and speeches he was to deliver.[6] But unlike the Canadian part of the tour, the excursion to the south was to extend goodwill, not imperial purpose. This suited the good-natured, sociable Prince, who had developed a taste for diversions as an Oxford undergraduate. A Palace memo recommended that the Prince should avoid politics and 'endeavour to give his visit the character of a national compliment to the Americans'.[7] This appealed to his American hosts, who took it for granted that their uniquely blessed country was deserving of compliments. For them the royal tour was an opportunity to reflect on matters of national etiquette, and they turned it into a conversation about themselves.

Foreigners often commented on the distinctive mix of confidence and anxiety, swagger and hypersensitivity, in the American character, which was a social consequence of the breathtaking rate of change in the United States.[8] Mrs Frances Trollope, like her contemporary, travel writer Basil Hall, had decried the boastfulness she found in the United States, which she attributed to a lack of chivalry and refinement.[9] During his tour of 1842, Dickens had found the mass of Americans frank and hospitable but assertive and humourless.[10] The novelist Anthony Trollope, who visited the United States not long after the Prince's tour, described Americans as 'thin skinned' and 'self-idolaters', views similar to his mother's, 30 years earlier.[11] Not surprisingly, Americans had

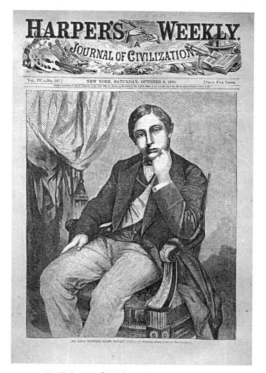

7. Prince of Wales, *Harper's Weekly.*

become highly sensitive to what they believed to be injustices heaped upon their country by visitors from the mother country, which they often took personally. One English tourist, who followed in the Prince's footsteps during the royal visit, remarked, for example, that Americans were 'bent on showing him that they are not the barbarians they are often supposed to be'.[12]

Little distracted by politics, the American press focused its attention on the crowds, the spontaneity of the reception, the dress and decorations, and the spectacle of it all. The Prince brought the monarchy to life, made it visible and theatrical, which had an irresistible appeal to a nation short on pomp and ceremony. The British court had developed formal procedures for managing reporters, who were becoming increasingly potent as a source of royal promotion in an era of press expansion.[13] But the Lord Chamberlain, who dealt with newspapers in Britain, had no sway in America where the tour became a free for all. That the Prince travelled incognito in the United States as Lord Renfrew was a fiction disregarded by everyone he met and treated with wry amusement in the papers: 'The *alias* of the son of Victoria in America is only comparable to Sheridan's quizzical stage direction of the "army" which "enters *incog*".'[14] *Vanity Fair* revelled in the Prince's many titles and noted that 'Abe

Lincoln has, from time to time, been recognized under such cognomens as the Rail Splitter, the Flat Boatman, and Honest old Abe.'[15]

The inexperienced Prince had a large diplomatic staff in support, headed by the Duke of Newcastle, Secretary of State for the Colonies, and Lord St Germans, Lord Steward of the Queen's Household. Good humour had characterized the tour in Canada, but, in the United States the raucous greetings and press sensationalisms, which amused the Prince if not his entourage, could be trying. Maintaining the dignity of the Prince vexed Lord Lyons, the British Ambassador in Washington, who feared Irish disturbances and despaired of the American crowd, which he described in a letter to the Prime Minister as 'curious and violent', without regard for any one else's convenience.[16] The turbulent eruptions of the crowds caused frequent alarm to the Prince's minders, who had to be nimble in protecting him from the crush of well-wishers. 'The United States are England without its upper classes', declared an English journalist, 'and hence there is nothing to moderate the enthusiasm of an American mob.'[17] The *New York Times* put it rather more delicately: 'We will give the Prince a hearty Republican welcome such as no prince or monarch has yet received from a Republican people.'[18]

From Ontario, the Prince had travelled with his staff on a steamer to Detroit, crossing into the United States on the evening of 20 September. A line of ships greeted the royal guest on his arrival. The torches of 600 firemen illuminated the shoreline packed with noisy and unruly onlookers, one of whom was pushed into the river. Another man crawled under a table to avoid the crush and became entangled under a woman's petticoat, only to be soundly kicked by her infuriated husband.[19] In the 'emancipated menagerie', the royal party resorted to the ruse of a decoy carriage, which enabled the Prince to reach the hotel unscathed. Such a turnout had never been seen 'since the days when Detroit acknowledged the rule of the great grandfather of the present Prince of Wales', observed Kinahan Cornwallis, a reporter for the *New York Herald*, who followed the royal party across Canada to the United States.[20] Whether out of admiration or mere curiosity, 30,000 wildly enthusiastic residents of Detroit had, as an English witness put it, a single wish: 'to see a Prince of Wales, and tell it for the rest of their lives'.[21]

Once in the United States, the government provided the royal party with special trains, which included a luxurious director's car for the Prince, charged at five cents per mile per person. The Midwestern part of the tour was a test for the royal party, as the monarchy was thought to be less popular there than in the east and the west. This was a mistaken assumption, judging from the coverage of the royal tour carried by steamboats and the Pony Express to New Orleans, Dallas, Houston, San Antonio, Salt Lake City and San Francisco. Any

8. *Another Feather!*, *Vanity Fair*, 20 October 1860.

worries that the reception would be less than ecstatic evaporated in Chicago, where an enormous crowd rushed down the station platform, broke through the ropes and followed the royal carriage to the hotel. After a day of visiting the city's sights, including a drive down Michigan Avenue amidst the cheering crowds, the party left for Dwight, Illinois, a small town 80 miles away, where the Prince spent a couple of days reducing the quail and plover populations of the surrounding grasslands.

From Dwight, the Prince travelled to St Louis, where he attended the agricultural fair; then to Cincinnati, Pittsburgh, and Baltimore, where vast crowds and sensational reports followed his every movement. On his way to a lavish ball in his honour at Pike's Opera House in Cincinnati some overzealous onlookers seized him by the leg and pulled him into the crowd. The soirées, the ovations, and the excesses of republican tribute were reminders of the relationship between the old world and the new. Though English commentators applauded the ties that bound the two nations together, they could not resist turning the enthusiasm for the great grandson of George III into expressions of American insecurity. Even American commentators could be embarrassed.

'How few European celebrities', remarked a reporter, 'are able to endure without loss this trying ordeal of American enthusiasm?'[22] Who would have imagined 60 years ago, said the *New York Times*, that a Prince of Wales would be such an object of adulation. 'No President could excite such a fervor.'[23]

President Buchanan, dubbed 'our present majesty King James' for the occasion, greeted the Prince upon his arrival in Washington on 3 October. Harriet Lane, the niece and First Lady of the bachelor President, dubbed the 'Democratic Queen', joined him. John Engleheart, Newcastle's Private Secretary, described her as 'the handsomest young lady we have seen in the States'.[24] The Prince's advisers had worried about amenities in the White House, which could not compare with those of many an English stately home. (Anthony Trollope noted that there were private houses in London 'considerably larger'.)[25] At dinner, the President told the waiters to hurry up with the courses, as he thought the Prince was about to fall asleep. The stiffly formal Buchanan prohibited dancing, but after dinner he relaxed his aversion to card playing, which had been banned in the White House. At the end of the evening, the President had to sleep on a sofa because the guests occupied all the White House beds. He had taken the precaution of removing the portrait of the vivacious Miss Lane from the Prince's bedroom.[26]

The following day the Prince toured the Capitol building and attended a levée held in his honour. It was yet another of those 'democratic' ceremonies that Henry Adams, the grandson and great grandson of presidents, would call the 'droll aping of monarchical forms' in his satirical novel *Democracy* (1880).[27] The White House, as Cornwallis put it, had never seen 'such a flutter of crinoline'.[28] The Prince was unaccustomed to ladies appearing at a levée, nor had he ever witnessed such unruliness at a Palace reception. The incessant hand-shaking and backslapping, which tactile Americans preferred to bowing, came as a further surprise. The Prince endured the cordiality with composure, though he must have been flummoxed to see the familiarity with which the guests addressed the President. The *New York Times* noted the 'mobbish' behaviour of the guests, including ladies who climbed onto the shoulders of the men to get a glimpse of the Prince: 'The royal party have certainly seen Democracy unshackled for once.'[29]

From Washington, on a fine October day, the Prince travelled down the Potomac with President Buchanan and Miss Lane to Mount Vernon where the party spent the afternoon inspecting the house, which was 'sadly dilapidated' according to Engleheart, who left a detailed record of the tour.[30] After some appreciative remarks at Washington's graveside, the Prince planted a chestnut tree in the grounds, a gesture of royal respect for the reputation of the President that was meant to send a signal that the British monarchy had warm

9. Prince of Wales at Tomb of Washington, wood engraving, *Harper's Weekly.*

regards for the United States and that any ill feeling between the two English-speaking nations was a thing of the past. It was a symbolic act of homage that touched a deep chord in the American public:

> Twas gracefully and nobly done,
>   A royal tribute to the free,
>   Who, Prince, will long remember thee,
> Before the grave of Washington.[31]

One American correspondent remarked that 'when princes visit the graves of rebel democrats', it represented a new order of things between nations. There was nothing like it in monarchical history: 'The man whose humble tomb the prince reverently visited was the chief instrument, in the hands of Providence, in wresting its most brilliant gem from the very crown he is to wear.'[32] 'If the Americans forgive George III in the person of the Prince of Wales,' recorded the *Saturday Review*, 'they will have forgiven every thing. . . . Nothing delights the bulk of our own countrymen like an opportunity for a burst of sentiment.'[33] To American commentators, forgiveness was a one-way street. Yet the royal visit to Mount Vernon impressed the British hardly less than the Americans. 'The Prince of Wales at the Tomb of Washington' was the subject set by Cambridge University for the poetry prize in 1861.[34]

In Philadelphia, the citizens received the Prince with somewhat greater restraint than elsewhere. He attended the races at Point Breeze and went to see *La Traviata* at the opera, where a deferential audience rose spontaneously to sing 'God Save the Queen'. On an outing to a model prison, which Dickens had mentioned in *American Notes*, he asked a convict if he wished to converse: 'Talk away, Prince', the prisoner replied. 'I'm here for twenty years.'[35] The Prince's rejoinder must have been succinct, for he was no sooner seen in Philadelphia than he was off again, 'like a salesman hurrying back to meet the Fall trade', remarked one wit. If the citizens of Philadelphia, unlike those of other cities, showed less zeal for their celebrated guest than elsewhere, it was a tribute to their sense of themselves as urbane and unhurried: 'We think it probable that the Prince thinks no worse of us, but a little better, that the great majority of our citizens and our municipal authorities did not go into spasms on his account.'[36]

The Prince's reception in New York was less sedate, befitting a commercial city of a million social climbers. Clearly the shopkeepers, who did a brisk business in fancy goods and jewellery, owed him a debt of gratitude.[37] Discerning Americans could purchase dolls of the Prince made locally and could eventually smoke tobacco named after him from North Carolina.[38] New York, which spent an estimated $750,000 on the royal visit, threw everywhere else on the tour into the shade.[39] This was the intention of the city fathers, who formed a committee of 400 leading citizens to make the elaborate preparations, which left more a few Gothamites discombobulated. An 'Air' written for the occasion by J. F. Bartholt, called on the city's 'Fifth Avenuelles' to replenish their wardrobes and prepare their houses:

> The Young man is coming, to visit this Nation,
>   And view the great wonders of Yankee Creation;
> Let's show him around, let the Wonders be seen,
>   Let the band's play no tune, but God Save the Queen.
>   Chorus. – Singing, etc.
> . . .
> But in seriousness earnest, should he pay us a Visit,
>   And into our affairs, be a little Inquisit;
> Don't make fools of yourselves, and kick up such a fuss
>   That when he gets back, he'll play 'Dickens' with us.
>   Chorus. – Singing, etc.[40]

Not every New Yorker was happy to greet the Prince with a rendition of 'God Save the Queen'. Many of the city's 200,000-strong Irish population felt the Prince represented a nation that had starved and oppressed their homeland. The Irish press took a dim view of the behaviour of the New York elite, whom they accused of shelving their republican principles in favour of toadying to foreign royalty. The *Irish American*, for example, saw 'the spirit of flunkeyism ... at the root of the whole affair'.[41] True Americans did not grovel, declared the *Freeman's Journal and Catholic Register*, but believed 'in the *new* world, that the honors, dignities and emoluments of the government are not fit things to be transmitted and inherited'.[42]

When the news broke that the State Militia was to participate in the grand welcoming ceremony for the Prince, the 69th Regiment, known as the Irish Brigade, refused to join the parade, which led to ill feeling and recrimination. Colonel Michael Corcoran, who led the revolt, became a hero of the Irish dissenters:

> The Stars and the Strips with the Green did unite,
>   He raised them upright in his Country's defence;
> And said to his men all to Washington we've called,
>   We'll defend it or fall but won't honour the Prince.[43]

Though the Irish refusal to join the parade did little to tarnish the spectacle of the Prince's visit to New York, it was the single most important gesture of opposition to the royal tour in the United States.[44]

'What a spectacle-loving people we are,' declared George Templeton Strong, who was among the party that welcomed the Prince. 'I fear we are a city of snobs.'[45] A *'nation'* of snobs, according to *Punch*, which revelled in former colonials truckling to a member of the royal family.[46] A parade of 6,000 troops from the New York State Militia – albeit without the Irish Brigade – received the Prince with full military honours upon his arrival in the City. A mass of humanity – some reports put the figure at 500,000 people – applauded the Prince as he drove through the city in a six-horse barouche heralded by a military column.[47] Spectators packed the streets and windows and climbed lampposts and trees, while platform tickets sold for five dollars a seat. At one point, someone threw a bouquet of flowers into the Prince's carriage, with the lines:

> Accept, dear Prince, this humble gift,
>   With every kind and loyal prayer;
> May Heaven your Highness ever lift
>   Above each sad and worldly care.[48]

Young and old hurrahed; pickpockets did a brisk business; ladies waved their handkerchiefs, and the most frenzied among them pinched the Prince during a walkabout.[49] But perhaps it was his double, a man whose name was kept secret lest he be mobbed as a celebrity. The Prince stopped at City Hall where he surveyed the passing regiments from a carpeted platform. By the time he reached the Fifth Avenue Hotel, the *Herald* reporter Cornwallis, who had followed every mile of the royal tour, could not restrain the hyperbole. It was couched in the language of race patriotism that was increasingly a feature of United States culture:

No grander ovation to the representative of the elder branch of the Anglo-Saxon race, was possible. Here the *entente cordiale* with England was proclaimed to the skies by hundreds of thousands of freemen, who hailed the coming and showered hearty blessings upon the head of the son of that peerless Queen, whose virtues shed a halo round the throne of England, and constitute the pride and joy of all where England's tongue is spoken and England's honor loved – of England our mother country.[50]

The *New York Times* saw the orderly crowd as a tribute to democratic institutions and compared it with the mobs in European cities that had to be scattered by bayonets. 'Even in London, where political liberty is as fully guaranteed as it is here, there would be an endless array of policemen to keep order and enforce the laws. Nothing of the kind is required in New York.'[51] Fortunately, the city's finest were on duty the next morning when a man dressed in sailor's uniform rushed towards the Prince as he left the hotel and cried: 'You never shall be King of England, if you live a hundred years.'[52] He was promptly arrested, questioned, reprimanded and released. It turned out that he was an English anti-monarchist named Edward Moncar, who was the second mate on a ship in the harbour. By the time the story reached Texas by Pony Express, it was reported that a lunatic had attempted to assassinate the Prince while on parade.[53]

The unruffled Prince proceeded to New York University, where the Chancellor presented an address, then on to the Astor Library and the Cooper Institute and the New York Free Academy. After a drive through Central Park, where he planted emblematic saplings of oak and elm, he lunched with the Mayor and a few select guests, including ex-President Fillmore and the financier Cyrus Field. Up next on the schedule was the Institute for the Deaf and Dumb, where the 'mutes' treated him to their compositions. What he and the Queen would have made of the recitation of a royalist poem in sign language can only be imagined.[54]

To cap the day's festivities, a grand ball was held at the Academy of Music attended by 3,000 of the city's elite. The United States may have been England without an upper class, as the journalist said, but this was not for want of a desire to create one. If a plethora of diamonds and dowagers were the test, then an aristocracy existed in New York that rivalled London or St Petersburg. Where else in the world, asked Cornwallis, could a display of dresses, diamonds, and 'chiselled beauty' be displayed to such effect?[55] (The *Saturday Evening Post* published a detailed description of the 'toilettes of the ball' worn by the leading ladies.)[56] Tickets were not for sale but were restricted to guests invited by the organizing committee, which suggested the limits of democracy among New York's moneyed class. The event, which cost the organizing committee over $40,000, was the closest thing America could offer to an aristocratic ball in Europe, brilliant but less restrained.[57]

Surveying the dazzling scene, the *New York Times* correspondent exclaimed: 'All that art could effect at the suggestion of luxury being supplied in the most lavish profusion.'[58] In the dress circle, a cornucupia of flowers was on display that would have done justice to a show at the Royal Horticultural Society. In the supper room, lined by a regiment of waiters, the Prince's crest 'blazed out in plumes of diamond-like light over the floating folds of a vast tent of pink and white drapery'.[59] The food, supplied by Delmonico's, was worthy of the Bourbons, but with a nod to the Saxe-Coburgs. The Prince, dressed in evening costume, appeared through a side door, whereupon several ladies lost their composure and stepped on the chairs to get a better look. In the reception line gentlemen debated whether shaking the hand of so august a personage was indecorous. But when the Prince proffered his hand, they decided it would be ungracious to decline the honour. 'I think of having my right-hand glove framed and glazed, with an appropriate inscription,' Strong wrote in his diary.[60]

Expectant daughters of the plutocracy jostled for their fairy-tale chance to dance with the fabled Prince. Then disaster struck. Just after the band played 'God Save the Queen' a cracking sound was heard and part of the floor collapsed under the weight of the crowd, toppling over flower vases and ladies in their finery.

The staging before him fell with a crash,
and Fifty young ladies, as quick as a flash,
Sank down in a kind of ethereal hash.[61]

Carpenters soon repaired the damage and the Prince danced the night away with the recovered debutantes, which increased speculation about his marital plans. The charms of Miss Fish, daughter of the former governor, and Miss Van Buren, granddaughter of President Van Buren, no doubt enchanted the Prince, but the rumour spread that at the end of the evening he slipped his minders and retired to one of the city's more luxurious brothels.[62] If so, it was not mentioned in the high-toned press.

Speculation about the marital prospects of heirs to the throne, which first appeared in 1860, was to become a staple of American interest in British royalty. *Punch* touched on this 'tender theme', wondering whether the 'transcendent charms' of American girls might drive the heir to the throne frantic:

> A German princess must he marry?
> And who can say he may not carry
> One of Columbia's fascinating daughters
> O'er the Atlantic?
> Hopes that to her the kerchief may be flung,
> To the ultimate exaltation of a young
> American lady to the British throne.[63]

The *Saturday Evening Post* assumed that an object of the Prince's visit was to look over the girls. 'We take it for granted because it is the most sensible thing that the heir to the British Crown can do, to marry an American wife.' There were a million American girls ready to wed the Prince, even 'if they knew they would have their sweet heads cut off, like Anne Boleyn's, the next morning.'[64] More seriously, *Harper's Weekly* argued that America was the only country in the world that Britain could count on. 'She can never find a friend so valuable or so staunch as the United States, if only she can secure our friendship. And there is no way so simple – in view of the character of our people – to secure that friendship as by having her Prince marry an American.' *Harper's* concluded, a little optimistically, that in a democratic age the marriage of the Prince with an untitled girl would be a great hit with the British public.[65]

The girls of Boston missed their chance when the Prince came to town, though not for want of trying at the ball held in his honour at the Academy of Music. The Prince was 'evidently in a higher social atmosphere', remarked Engleheart, who thought the dance in Boston better 'in every respect' than the one in New York.[66] Not only was the event a great success, but the two days in Boston were also a high point of the visit. Engleheart, who hoped to see his New England friends back in '*old England*', observed that the welcome in Boston was more cordial and genuine than elsewhere in the United States, for it 'was borne of a feeling towards England as towards *a home, the* home of their forefathers, the home of some of their warmest feelings'.[67]

10. The Grand Ball at the Academy of Music in Boston, 18 October 1860, *Harper's Weekly*.

This warmth of feeling was clearly on display in Boston, where the Prince met, among other luminaries, Longfellow, Ralph Waldo Emerson, and Oliver Wendell Holmes. At Harvard, he was taken to various buildings and shown the curiosities, but with the exception of Louis Agassiz's snakes, he paid scant attention to them, for he was by then 'too tired to care for anything or anybody'.[68] Still, after breakfast at two o'clock, the Prince drove to Mount Auburn cemetery, then, at his own request, stopped at Bunker Hill, where he spoke to the last survivor of that symbolic battle, the 104-year-old veteran Ralph Farnham. The old soldier had heard so much in praise of the heir to the throne that he feared Americans 'would all turn royalists'.[69] The memorable, highly publicized gesture to meet Farnham was, like the visit to Mount Vernon, a brilliant stroke intended to erase any lingering doubts about the royal family's attitude to the once rebellious Americans.

Palace officials, with advice from the British government, carefully scripted the Prince's itinerary, which included rather a lot of church going. A photo session in New York with Mathew Brady marked an important milestone in making royalty more accessible to a wider American public. The script did not

11. Albert Edward, Prince of Wales, 1860.

include spending much time in the slave states. A committee of citizens from the southern states had invited the Prince to visit the South in a letter to Lord Lyons, the British Minister in Washington:

The plantations of the South, with their peculiar system of labour, and their abounding wealth, may well be looked upon by the future sovereign of the British empire with deep interest. The cotton fields of that fertile and extensive region supply the material from which much of the wealth and power of the British empire is derived, and we are confident that, nowhere in this Republic does there exist a higher appreciation of that great nation than in the plantation States.[70]

In a gracious reply, Lord Lyons regretted that the Prince was so pressed for time that his travel to the South must be restricted to a brief trip to Virginia. The British party may even have regretted that visit, for in Richmond an irreverent crowd taunted the Prince with jibes that Washington 'socked it to you at the Revolution' and 'gave you English squirts the colic'.[71] Powerful voices in England suggested that the visit to Virginia should never have taken place. An editorial in the London *Times*, circulated in the northern states, called the excursion to Richmond the 'only unpleasant incident' of the Prince's tour: 'If there be a place justly odious to the feelings of Englishmen and their Sovereign, it is that mart where the human animal, which is now almost the only produce of Virginia, is ruthlessly sold for consumption in the dreary plantations of the South.'[72]

The tensions between the northern and southern states over slavery, which bedevilled relations between Britain and America, were never far from the surface during the tour. The abolitionist newspaper the *Liberator*, founded by William Lloyd Garrison, reminded the Prince that, while Americans boasted of their freedom, millions of slaves remained in bondage.[73] But the mainstream United States press, which preferred to take a positive line, largely ignored the slavery issue, as it did the Irish protesters. It was perhaps not surprising to see that the municipal authorities excluded African Americans from the festivities, or that the press ignored their absence.[74] Still, many of what the British party called 'ebony faces' saw the Prince during his travels. Several of his aides took the trouble to visit the African Baptist Church while in Richmond, which did not go unnoticed.[75]

In Boston, the Prince received an 'Address' from the 'Colored Citizens of Boston':

Beg leave to place in Your Royal Highness's hand this expression of their profound and grateful attachment and respect for that Throne which you represent here, under whose shelter so many thousands of their race, fugitives from American Slavery, find safety and rest: and of their love for that realm which, noblest among modern nations, first struck off the fetters of her slaves . . . God bless England, while her law is Justice, and her sceptre secures Liberty![76]

Whether the officials accompanying the Prince responded to this petition is unknown, but they carefully monitored such messages from the American public lest they be caught unaware of United States sensitivities. Tributes to British 'Justice' and 'Liberty' and to the Prince's 'democratic air', whatever the source, pleased the royal family, especially when these virtues were seen as emanating from the Crown. After his conquest of New York, one American writer declared that the Prince 'may consider himself a lucky lad if he escapes a nomination for President before he reaches his homeward-bound fleet'.[77]

The tour was undoubtedly a triumph for the Prince, and set him on a diplomatic course for which he would become renowned. Even hardened critics who deprecated the visit admitted that the Prince had found his *métier* – spreading goodwill. As the Prince recognized, spreading goodwill also meant spreading largesse, and like a medieval king moving among the peasantry he left a trail of gifts and cash in his wake. To Mayor Wentworth of Chicago, who took the Prince on a tour of his farm, he sent two fine buck sheep; and to Mr Spencer, who entertained him during his shooting trip in Illinois, he sent two pointer dogs.[78] His generous tips – $500 to the White House staff alone – left pleasant memories among American hoteliers and servants. The *Dallas Herald* speculated that the Prince's visit cost the British government $2,000,000.[79] It was rumoured that he was willing to write a description of his tour if an American publisher would pay off England's National Debt![80] But what about the American debt? It was estimated that the United States spent $1,525,000 on the visit.[81]

In the burgeoning democratic world of the mid-nineteenth century the appreciation of largesse and sentiment was not to be underestimated.[82] If nothing else, the tour illustrated that Anglo-American relations had a basis in sentimentality as well as trade. But it was to a large extent a sentimentality of race, as one English correspondent noted: 'It is to be feared that American society, adulterated as it now is with Irish and German ingredients, has much more forgotten the brotherhood of race than we have, but the cordiality shown to the Prince proves that it has not quite fallen into oblivion.'[83] The tour was a gauge of national identity and social differentiation. It suggested that Americans, especially the educated classes in the Northeast, still looked to Britain for their cultural origins. But the pull of ancestry was also strong among the Irishmen and Germans who had flooded into the country in the 1840s and 1850s. Could Britain and its monarchy sustain such a purchase on American sentiment given the changing social and ethnic makeup of the United States?

Despite the build-up of diplomatic tensions, the trip was widely thought to have been a turning point in Anglo-American affairs.[84] As the Prince sailed home, it was noted that politicians of all hues vied with each other in their attentions to him, from the President and state governors down to local mayors.[85] Indeed, the obsessive interest in the Prince threatened to overwhelm the coverage given to the presidential election campaign taking place that autumn. There were occasional complaints that dancing and shooting interested the Prince more than responsible government or commercial statistics,

12. Prince of Wales in a carriage with entourage, Portland Maine, October 1860.

but the press and the pundits in the United States were generally positive about the political implications of the royal visit. As a reward for his diplomatic success, the Prince Consort gave his son permission to smoke, though only in private.[86]

The Prince did not meet Lincoln during the tour. Had he done so it would have been a remarkable encounter of inherited fame with the self-made man, the heir to an ancient throne and the rail-splitter from the backwoods. Shortly after the 1860 election, the *New York Herald* published an article with the headline 'Did the Prince of Wales Elect Lincoln'? Americans in Paris, it was reported, attributed Lincoln's victory to the effect produced by the Prince's visit and noted that the election was decided by the state of New York, a scene of great enthusiasm for his Royal Highness:

Upon former occasions election contests in New York wavered; and it was known that jealousy of England had much to do with the indifference manifested towards the anti-slavery candidates. It was believed that England felt strongly on the subject; and it was fancied that the English people meddled too openly with blunt expressions of opinion. Along with the Prince's presence, a reaction set in, and feelings of sympathy with English feelings arose, so that it seems no strained conclusion to attribute Mr Lincoln's return upon anti-slavery principles to the genial effect produced by the Prince's visit.[87]

The effect of the royal tour on the presidential election, if any, will never be known.[88] But that it was even suggested at the time illustrates just how influential the Prince was seen to be by parts of the American press. Various commentators said that the possibility of war between the two countries had diminished as a result of the visit.[89] The *New York Times*, for example, saw the royal tour in imperial perspective: 'We trust that nothing will happen to mar its effect; and that the people of both countries will more clearly understand in the future that the "manifest destiny" of the two great Anglo-Saxon Empires is not antagonistic, but points to the accomplishment of the same high purposes – the extension of freedom and the spread of civilization.'[90]

The British, for their part, were no less sanguine. Lord Palmerston commented that the visit had 'awakened the deepest interest in the mind of every Englishman' and anticipated improved ties between the two nations.[91] The *London Daily News* thought the Prince was also a beneficiary of the visit, for the vitality of the new civilization would have sharpened his intellect.[92] In an exceptional gesture, Minister Dallas received an invitation to Windsor Castle the day after the Prince's return, which he took as an acknowledgement of the handsome treatment accorded the Prince of Wales in America. On inquiry, Dallas discovered that no Minister of the United States had been called to Windsor for 28 years. Lest there be any doubt of the reason for his invitation, the Queen, the Prince Consort, and the Prince of Wales all spoke to him of their pleasure at the success of the royal tour.[93]

In an exceptional public tribute, the Queen asked her envoy in Washington to write to President Buchanan in December 1860. It was a further instalment in the monarchy's diplomatic offensive, a telling sign of its changing attitude towards the United States:

I am commanded to state to the President that the Queen would be gratified by his making known generally to the citizens of the United States her grateful sense of the kindness with which they received her son, who has returned to England deeply impressed with all he saw during his progress through the States; but more especially so with the friendly and cordial good will manifested towards him on every occasion by all classes of the community.[94]

These lines were more than 'mere words' to the *New York Herald*, which argued that Americans, bound to Britain in Anglo-Saxon unity, 'now feel almost a personal interest in the fortunes of the royal family of England'.[95]

* * *

The American journalist Stephen Fiske, who wrote for English magazines in the 1860s, said 'the Prince of Wales was to Americans – a show, a curiosity, a guest; something to be stared at, and followed about, and treated with Anglo-Saxon hospitality'.[96] But why all this fuss over the heir apparent of a foreign sovereign, when America had rejected the hereditary principle and prided itself on its republican virtue? Why all the fawning over an adolescent Prince, who had little to recommend him apart from his station? On his return to London, Engleheart concluded his record of the tour with the observation that Americans of all classes admired the Queen because she represented the ideal of motherhood:

> In some measure, also, it may be attributed to that innate craving for the exercise of veneration and loyalty, which finding but little to satisfy at home, looks abroad for the worthiest object.
>
> Superadded to these motives there exists a strong feeling of kinship. A common ancestry, language, and literature, and a common freedom, must be productive of a strong feeling of sympathy towards England, if allowed its natural bent, – a sympathy which is glad to express itself in overt acts. It wants but a fitting opportunity, and the result is seen in the magnificent reception given to the Prince by the 'Empire City'.[97]

In explaining the Prince's reception, American commentators emphasized those familiar nostrums of a common culture, the blood of the Anglo-Saxons, and a shared attachment to liberty. So powerful were the links of race patriotism and a common Christianity that Americans celebrated monarchy itself, as practised in English hands, as a defence of the rights and liberties of mankind.[98] A religious magazine opined: 'Had we been colonists of any other country, speaking any other language, reared under any other laws, – had there not been the element of freedom in the British nation and the English heart, our history had had far other record. She is our mother by no mere figure of speech'.[99] Others, less loftily, argued that the bachelor Prince simply captivated the female sex, mothers and daughters alike, although some observers said that he was not even handsome and others that the brazen behaviour of American women during the visit sullied the nation's reputation.[100] Among the most common explanations for the Prince's triumph was that it was a mark of respect for the Queen's unblemished life. Fiske argued that

Americans might not appreciate the blessings of a monarchy, but they did know a good woman when they saw one.[101] The *Saturday Evening Post* observed that in the Prince, America honoured not so much the individual as his position as heir to the throne.[102] Gone were the days when the spectre of a perfidious George III hung over the royal family's reputation in the United States. To most Americans, Queen Victoria was a benign head of state and a symbol of motherliness, who had introduced a new generation of royals dedicated to international accord and family values.

In his diary, Strong confirmed such views, but with a twist: 'Under all this folly and tuft-hunting there is a deep and almost universal feeling of respect and regard for Great Britain and for Her Britannic Majesty. The old anti-British patriotism of twenty years ago is nearly extinct. . . . No community worships hereditary rank and station like a democracy'.[103] The last observation was a variation on Engleheart's point that the Prince's success was due to the 'innate craving' for an object to venerate, which looked abroad because there was little to satisfy it at home. Such comment was reminiscent of Tocqueville, who thought the young republic was lacking in social refinement and needed the diversions of rank to break the monotony of egalitarianism. The lavish hospitality betrayed a sense of American insecurity when exposed to an ancient aristocratic culture. The 'thin skinned' American, as Trollope observed, took offence at any criticism of his country. 'Any touch comes at once upon the net-work of his nerves and puts in operation all his organs of feeling with the violence of a blow.'[104] Behind the rapturous welcome for the Prince was the American need to be loved.

Americans clung to the royal magic from abroad for want of republican magic at home. Was their relentless self-serving praise of new-world democracy and republican virtue a charade? The Prince's tour illustrated that Americans, who took such pride in their independence and self belief, could bow to rank and privilege just like Britons. The royal tour revealed that something was missing in the promised land of the republic, and that something was class. The callow Prince, whose presence would have turned few heads in America had he not been the son of the Queen, was a harbinger of the American culture of celebrity. Once asked how he would make a living if the crown were abolished, the Prince replied: 'I think I could support my family by giving lectures in the United States on "How it feels to be Prince of Wales".'[105]

CHAPTER 5

AMERICA'S QUEEN

Had Queen Victoria been on the throne, instead of George III, or if we had postponed our rebellion until Queen Victoria reigned, it would not have been necessary, and had there been any rebellion at all, it would have been on the part of England.

William M. Evarts, Secretary of State, 1878

The Prince's visit heralded an *entente cordiale* between the American people and the monarchy at a critical juncture in history. In her speech at the opening of Parliament in 1861, which was widely reported in the United States, Queen Victoria alluded to the Prince's visit and to American affairs generally, which were increasingly fraught with the rise in tensions between the North and South. She referred to the growing differences between the states and of her fears that further developments might 'affect the happiness and welfare of a people purely allied to my subjects by descent and closely connected with them by the most intimate and friendly relations. My heartfelt wish is that these differences may be susceptible of satisfactory adjustment'. On a more positive note, she said the visit of the Prince of Wales had brought the two nations closer together and that her interest in the well being of the American people had been increased by the cordial reception given to him.[1]

The outbreak of the Civil War was a near disaster for Anglo-American relations, for it placed the British government in the awkward position of neutrality in the civil struggles of a friendly nation with which it had historic and commercial ties. Not a few Britons saw the schism in America as retribution for 1776 and vaguely sympathized with the 'chivalrous' South as the underdog. The issue for British diplomacy was how to deal with the crisis without alienating one or other of the powerful combatants. 'To recognize the Confederacy', remarked a leading historian of Anglo-American relations, 'would have fanned to a new white-heat the latent embers of Northern anti-British feeling.'[2] But as the military conquest of the South by the North looked doubtful, the British Government tread a precarious diplomatic path while waiting upon events on the battlefield. On that diplomatic path the monarchy played a modest part, which, blown out of proportion by United States observers, intensified America's admiration for the Queen.

In the uncertainty surrounding Britain's 'strict neutrality', both North and South were bidding for British support. The *Times* of London reported that northern politicians were telling Britain 'that it does not become us to be indifferent', while southern leaders 'are half inclined to become British once more'.[3] Both parties in the struggle saw Queen Victoria as a possible ally. Though this is little remembered now, elements in the Confederacy called for her to come to their rescue. The *Richmond Daily Dispatch* cited a letter, published originally in the British press, from a Scottish-born citizen from Alabama in January 1861, three months before the outbreak of hostilities at Fort Sumter. It suggested that one of the Queen's sons should become a constitutional sovereign for the South and predicted that it would happen within three years.[4]

In the days after the battle of Fort Sumter the *Richmond Daily Dispatch* asked the British to attack the North and declared 'that we would rather be a subject of Queen Victoria . . . than the beastly and brutal despotism of a mob, represented by its chief blackguard and ruffian, Abraham Lincoln'.[5] In its rage against 'the contemptible Yankees' the *Richmond Whig* also looked to the British sovereign in the summer of 1861: 'To be under the dominion of a lady like Queen Victoria, distinguished by every virtue, would constitute a favorable exchange for the vulgar rule of a brutish blackguard like Lincoln.'[6] As the war took its toll, the expedient monarchism of the southern loyalists became more desperate. In November, another editorial in the *Richmond Daily Dispatch* pronounced that the Queen's rule over the Confederacy 'would be glorious'.[7] To some of Lincoln's supporters the rebellion originated in the determination of the leading secessionists to establish a 'slavery nobility' under a monarchical regime.[8]

*   *   *

Not long after the attack on Fort Sumter, the Queen formally welcomed President Lincoln's new Minister to Britain, Charles Francis Adams, the grandson of John Adams. Like other members of his illustrious family, Adams was an admirer of his host country and its monarchy. Unlike his predecessors Buchanan and Dallas, Adams was not a slave to the American demos and discarded his plain black suit in favour of court dress, which is said to have led the Queen to remark that she was 'thankful that we shall have no more American funerals'.[9] Adams found the Queen unprepossessing but dignified and spoke to her of 'amicable relations' and the 'personal regards' of the American people.[10] He had his work cut out for him in the tense diplomatic atmosphere, but he soon established a working relationship with Lord John Russell, the British Foreign Secretary. But politically and socially isolated, he found his posting in Britain often trying and forlorn.[11]

Adams had a high regard for the Prince Consort, who in late 1861 had been trying to resolve issues arising from the Civil War. The North, which suspected Britain of favouring the Confederacy, widely credited the Prince with reducing the animosity between the two nations at the time of the crisis over the *Trent*, a British mail packet boarded by an American warship that proceeded to remove Confederate envoys on their way to Europe. In what Queen Victoria called 'the *last* thing he *ever* wrote', the Prince had moderated the language of the British government's formal response to the incident, which contributed to the eventual resolution of the controversy.[12] The Queen's role in the *Trent* affair was peripheral at best, though she would have been aware of Prince Albert's intervention and his desire to preserve friendly relations between Britain and the United States.[13] In America, however, stories spread that she had played a more active role in the government's decision not to recognize the Confederacy.[14] And with the passage of time, Americans gave her much of the credit for the restraint shown by the British government.[15] It was a tribute to the royal mystique in America.

Many Americans saw Prince Albert's death in December 1861 as a tragedy for Britain and the Queen but also as a loss to the United States.[16] At the legation, Adams feared that a conciliatory policy towards America would be abandoned with his passing.[17] Beyond the legation, other Americans cherished the Prince's prudent diplomatic counsel, which they felt was in keeping with his benign domestic influence. To the pious guardians of the American family, not least the widows, the Prince Consort had been the paragon of faithful husbands. On his death, editors of American religious and women's magazines took the widowed Victoria ever closer to their hearts: 'Her great loss, her deep grief, these have darkened the British Empire, and shadowed the Christian world.'[18]

Throughout North America there were observances of the Prince's death: ships' flags flew at half-mast; British societies held commemorative events; clergymen delivered sermons on the significance of his family life; and church bells tolled, distant echoes of the great bell of St Paul's in London.[19] Royalty establishes trends and traditions, and among the Prince's legacies in the United States, apart from the revival of Christmas, was a change in the character of mourning rituals.[20] In the weeks after his funeral, the 'Republican Court' in Washington, led by Mary Lincoln, set the tone by going into 'half mourning' at presidential parties and receptions.[21] In the midst of it all, one tactless wit wrote that Lincoln should immediately seek a divorce from his wife 'for the purpose of marrying Queen Victoria and thereby secure the interests and assistance of Great Britain in suppressing the rebellion'.[22]

Among the large number of letters of condolence received by the Queen on the death of the Prince Consort, now bound together in attractive volumes in the Royal Archives, is one from President Lincoln, who had been informed of Albert's death by the Prince of Wales. In his letter he sought not only to console the Queen but also to foster improved relations at a critical juncture in United States history. 'The offer of condolence in such cases is a customary ceremony . . .' he observed, 'and may sometimes be even insincere.' But he wished the Queen to apprehend that on this occasion real sympathy and honesty between nations could exist:

The People of the United States are kindred of the People of Great Britain. With all our distinct national interests, objects, and aspirations, we are conscious that our moral strength is largely derived from that relationship. . . . Accidents, however, incidental to all states, and passions, common to all nations, often tend to disturb the harmony so necessary and so proper between the two countries, and to convert them into enemies. It was reserved for Your Majesty in sending your son, the Heir Apparent of the British Throne, on a visit among us, to inaugurate a policy destined to counteract these injurious tendencies, as it has been Your Majesty's manifest endeavour, through a reign already of considerable length and of distinguished success, to cultivate the friendship on our part so earnestly desired. It is for this reason that you are honoured on this side of the Atlantic as a friend of the American People. The late Prince Consort was with sufficient evidence regarded as your counsellor in the same friendly relation. The American People, therefore, deplore his death and sympathize in Your Majesty's irreparable bereavement with an unaffected sorrow. This condolence may not be altogether ineffectual, since we are sure it emanates from only virtuous motives and natural affection. I do not dwell upon it, however, because I know that the Divine hand that has wounded, is the only one that can heal: And so, commending Your Majesty and the Prince Royal, the Heir Apparent, and all your afflicted family to the tender mercies of God, I remain

Your Good Friend,
Abraham Lincoln[23]

The Queen may have recalled this letter at the time of Lincoln's assassination in 1865. On hearing the news, she wrote a letter of condolence to Mary Lincoln, in which she expressed her 'heartfelt sympathy' on her 'dreadful misfortune'. She compared the tragedy to her own terrible loss of Prince Albert, 'who was the light of my life'.[24] Bagehot, writing soon after Lincoln's assassination, believed that 'Americans were more pleased at the Queen's letter to Mrs Lincoln than at any act of the English government. It was a spontaneous act of intelligible feeling in the midst of confused and tiresome business.'[25] So, too, was Mary Lincoln's widow to widow reply to the Queen, to 'a heart which from its own sorrow, can appreciate the *intense grief* I now endure'.[26]

The Queen's views on America had been influenced by Prince Albert, and her kindly gestures allayed the North's mistrust of British policy during and after the Civil War. In 1865, Adams wrote from the American legation that the English throne had never been filled 'by a more honest, conscientious and scrupulous individual in the performances of her duties'.[27] The Queen's American correspondence suggests the value she placed on political propriety and conventional piety, which deepened with her isolation after the death of Prince Albert. Her reputation for respectability and keeping the memory of her beloved husband alive helps to explain why many Americans followed her activities so closely. They were among the most enthusiastic readers of her book, *Leaves from the Journal of Our Life in the Highlands* (1868), which they admired for its 'healthful simplicity' and 'high family affectionateness'.[28]

Americans often presented the Queen as a potent symbol of tradition and stability in an era of political and social change. The upheaval of the Civil War had intensified the sense of American insecurity, causing 'a mushroom growth of artificial social criteria which appeared to be more absurd, as well as less elastic, than any which existed in Britain'.[29] By comparison with the traumatic experience of the United States, British social progress had been orderly in the mid-Victorian years. Was it to Britain's advantage that it was a society of permeable gradations headed by a hereditary sovereign, in which social hierarchy was widely accepted? The Prince of Wales, who kept informed about life in the United States after his tour in 1860, found American society so baffling that he used to tease Americans about who was 'in' and who was 'out'.[30] One of the reasons the Prince had been so popular in America during his visit was that in a nation of social climbers he was the social summit and consequently could not be accused of snobbery.

Troubled by social instability at home, Americans of British ancestry found in Queen Victoria an illustrious symbol for the survival of their most cherished values.[31] After Lincoln's death, the United States reverted to the norm of

uninspiring presidents – witness Andrew Johnson's impeachment trial and
the miserable failure of Grant's administration. As head of state, the Queen
was, by contrast, a paragon of virtue. Her taste may have been 'inherited' and
startlingly middle-class, as Henry Adams observed, but that recommended it
to many Americans.[32] And despite the death of Prince Albert, she continued
to exemplify, as the weight of press clippings made clear, the promotion of
family life. As a historian of American Victorianism put it: 'Despite 4th of July
republican rhetoric increasingly numbers of established Americans regarded
Victorian Britain as a society that had successfully weathered the storm of
industrialisation, to emerge a progressive quasi-republican society led by the
ideal, family based epitome of Christian motherhood, Queen Victoria.'[33]

∗   ∗   ∗

In the early 1870s the Queen's isolation, Irish discontents and a sharp rise in
urban unemployment contributed to an upsurge in anti-monarchism in
Britain. But in America the anti-British sentiment of the Civil War years was
now largely a matter of history.[34] There were royal critics, among them
European political exiles, who lampooned the Queen as fat and extravagant.
Others disliked her views on female suffrage. But in America, as in Britain, the
Queen was by now widely seen as outside politics, a sovereign of largely
symbolic purpose, a mother figure and imperial icon. The public were not in
a position to know that she often meddled and intervened, not least in foreign
policy and appointments. This is not to say that she took executive decisions,
or even exercised her residual prerogative powers; but the prestige of the
Crown gave her more discretion as an arbitrator in the political system than
outsiders supposed.

The British monarchy as an institution no longer resonated among
American constitutional writers as it had during the Revolution and early
republic, despite the 'monarcho-republicanism' embedded in the United
States Constitution by its architects. But the belief that the country was dete-
riorating into an elective monarchy because of expanding executive powers
and the re-eligibility in the Presidency remained current, if not widespread,
during and after the Civil War.[35] William Seward, while serving as Secretary of
State under Lincoln, told Louis Jennings, a journalist on the London *Times*,
that 'we elect a king for four years, and give him absolute power within certain
limits, which after all he can interpret for himself'.[36] Nor were mayors and
governors excluded from accusations of elective kingship, as in Illinois in the
1870s over a bill to remove state officials.[37]

While America's rulers were sometimes described as kings or elective
monarchs, there was little in the way of historical scholarship to support such
assertions, which were usually insults hurled at partisan presidents. An American

critic reviewing Bagehot's *English Constitution* in 1874 observed that monarchy and aristocracy were of 'minor interest to us'.[38] This was so, but writing on constitutional issues had entered a period of complacency in America after the heyday of the Founding Fathers. There was no equivalent of England's Bagehot in mid-Victorian America, much less an Alexander Hamilton or James Madison. Although the Civil War had illustrated the Constitution's defects, Americans, at least those in the North, widely believed that it provided the closest thing to political perfection the world had ever seen, which did not encourage dispassionate analysis. But to Englishmen like Bagehot, who exalted in their own parliamentary system headed by a hereditary sovereign, the belief in the genius of the American Constitution was highly questionable.

While the British monarchy played a declining role in discussions of the United States Constitution, royalty continued to divert the public, especially middle- and upper-class citizens of English ancestry living in communities with historic links to the mother country. The humorist J. M. Bailey of the *Danbury News*, who travelled to England in the 1870s, revealed the schizophrenia that beset many of his fellow Americans when thinking about royalty. 'I suppose every one of us who comes here has an unquenchable longing to look with our own eyes upon a member of the royal family. It is not to admire them that we have this desire; but we want to abhor them.'[39] Such a view would have surprised another American visitor, however: 'The Queen of England . . . is so much esteemed personally in the United States, that to hear her Majesty referred to slightingly, and even scandalously, by her own professedly loyal subjects . . . is one of the first shocks that an American receives when sojourning in England.'[40]

Apart from a contingent of Irishmen who had migrated to the United States after the Famine, most Americans had no wish to see the Queen removed from office, though some of them assumed that Britain would eventually follow America's lead and jettison monarchy. In 1873, Emily Faithfull wrote in a United States magazine that Americans held Queen Victoria in great esteem, but assumed that Britain was about to become an uncrowned republic.[41] Given the rhetorical anti-monarchism of the Revolution, many Americans found it difficult to comprehend that Britain was, as various commentators had been saying for a century or more, already a republic, with the Queen serving as a hereditary president.[42] A constitutional sovereign, free of political taint, was compatible with their democratic aspirations. But what did they think in reading Trollope's *North America*, in which he declared that the British form of government was 'the most purely republican that I know'?[43]

The Queen's American admirers rallied to her defence, whether they thought Britain a republic or not. In New York, the Anglophile George

Templeton Strong, who sympathized with Queen Victoria in her grief and seclusion, denigrated her enemies. 'It is fortunate for the public peace that the English republican (and atheistic) agitators seem to be, without exception, curs of low degree.'[44] The mainstream American press, repelled by the stridency of Irish nationalists in the United States, also rallied to the Queen.[45] The virtuous Queen, seemingly removed from politics, was a difficult target. Her very distance endowed her with what the New York *Evening Post* called 'mythic glory'.[46] As she grew older, she endeared the Crown to both Britons and Americans alike through good works and royal spectacle. In the words of an American magazine, she had become the 'first lady of the World'.[47]

If many Americans assumed that Victoria had an uncertain future, some had fun imagining her as Queen of the United States. About the time of the outbreak of anti-monarchism in Britain, an American wit dedicated a new song to *Punch* in London: 'The Yanko-Britannic National Hymn'. It was to be sung by the formerly rebellious, but now repentant and loyal Yankee subjects on the inauguration of the statues of Queen Victoria at the late seat of government of the United States, in the places now occupied by the figures of Washington, Jefferson and Jackson:

Republicans and Whigs
And all old Federal prigs,
    Sleep the last sleep!
Up Aristocracy!
Down with Democracy
(Slavish hypocrisy)
    To darkest deep! . . .

Monarch in every zone!
On lone imperial throne.
    O, hearkening, lean,
While we implore you, aye,
And sing— Victoria!
Reginae Glora!
    All hail our Queen![48]

Though less playful, Emily Faithfull provided a liberal view of English loyalty to the Crown to her American readers in the early 1870s, which made telling comparisons with the United States. She was no believer in the divine right of kings, but having lived in the United States for some months she became less discontented with Britain's 'crowned president', who was without presidential powers but whose moral stature raised the tone of politics. 'Dare I say in this free country that Great Britain stands at the present moment in far less danger of the much-to-be-dreaded "one man power" than America, and that, even now, "we the people" virtually rule.' Nor was she impressed by the establishment of an aristocracy of wealth in America, which she found more obnoxious than the European aristocracies of rank.[49]

In the 1870s, Americans themselves were voicing criticism of vulgar American wealth, and its attendant snobbery, and decried the great private fortunes being created in the United States that dwarfed the magnificence of European princes. In this 'most favored of all favored lands', observed Richard B. Kimball, the American writer and friend of Dickens, 'we have erected and are doing our best to strengthen an aristocracy more powerful than were the feudal lords of old, and more dangerous to the republic'.[50] He added that unlike the sense of moral responsibility attending the actions of English noblemen, American plutocrats were not troubled by historic obligations. Britain's class distinctions were at least founded on aristocratic tradition, while America's fit ill with the egalitarian refrains in the Declaration of Independence. As Faithfull and Kimball suggested, comparisons between a traditional aristocracy and an upstart plutocracy worked to increase respect for British institutions in America, which helps to explain the reverence for Queen Victoria, who put a cap on the social ambition of the moneyed class.

* * *

Despite her long, self-imposed isolation, Queen Victoria often greeted visitors from abroad and from time to time invited Americans to Windsor or Buckingham Palace for discussions about life in the United States.[51] She seemed to take particular pleasure in oddities from the new world. (She had entertained the six-year-old midget Tom Thumb at Buckingham Palace in 1844, but things got out of hand when he was attacked by her pet poodle.)[52] In May 1873, she attended a performance by the African-American Jubilee Singers of Fisk University at the home of the Duke and Duchess of Argyle. To the troupe, several of them former slaves, the thought of performing for the Queen was awe-inspiring. One of their number kept asking herself beforehand whether it could be true 'that I was really away out in that world of water . . . bound for England and with the hope of seeing Queen Victoria, . . . the grandest and noblest queen of them all, under whose flag . . . thousands of our race had sought and found liberty in the dark days of bondage'.[53] The Queen, impressed by the performance, noted in her Journal that the troupe were 'real negroes', and excellent singers.[54]

In April 1872, the Queen asked Miss Nellie Grant, the only daughter of President Ulysses S. Grant, to a private reception, as opposed to a general

13. Queen Victoria at a performance by the Jubilee Singers, 1873.

levée. It was taken as a particular mark of cordiality, something of a quid pro quo for the reception of the heir to the throne in the United States some ten years earlier. It was also a gesture of thanks for the reception given to the Queen's third son, Prince Arthur, the Duke of Connaught, whom the Grants had entertained in Washington in 1870.[55] The London *Times* thought the audience of considerable import, noting that Miss Grant would enjoy the advantages of her position and would return to America with useful information much needed by the people of both countries.[56] As it turned out, on her way home Miss Grant fell in love with an Englishman, Algernon Sartoris, the son of the actress Fanny Kemble, married him in the White House and returned to England, where she lived for many years.

From her lofty social pinnacle Queen Victoria continued to take a keen interest in world affairs. Though secluded in her outposts at Balmoral and the Isle of Wight, she became increasingly attentive to the United States in the second half of her reign, a period of relative 'quiet' in Anglo-American relations.[57] This was a tribute to the growing presence of the United States in the world. Unhappy memories of the former colony had faded in royal and aristocratic circles, and the reality of the ever more powerful and competitive republic had to be addressed. With the growth of tourism and easier communication – the transatlantic cable was laid in 1858 – the Queen's direct contact with American presidents, diplomats and visitors to Britain, and through them the wider American public, increased.

From time to time she received news from America from friends and family, which supplemented the normal diplomatic communications. During his tour of the United States in 1870, Prince Arthur wrote to the Queen of his reception in Washington, remarking that Americans were vulgar but wished to please, immodest but had little thought of expense. He liked the young ladies.[58] Such scraps of information about American manners, or lack of them, did not always please her. She was no friend to women's rights and once wrote to her daughter Victoria, the German Crown Princess, that the loss of modesty in English girls was attributable to transatlantic influences: 'Young people are getting very American, I fear in their views and ways.'[59]

Various American newspapers and journals, led by the *New York Sun*, wished the Queen to be invited to the United States for the Centennial celebrations in 1876.[60] Whether she received a formal invitation is unclear, but she did send several of her finest paintings to the Philadelphia Exposition, a gesture that helped to keep the monarchy in the minds of Americans in that festive year.[61] A clergyman at the Boston Centennial closed his remarks with the 'profoundest homage and respect to Queen Victoria, not our Sovereign – except that, as the highest lady in the world, she should be such to all men – but as our ally and our friend'.[62] The Queen and her advisers would have been startled by the homage paid to her by the Secretary of State William M. Evarts, a man with presidential ambitions, at the Centennial celebration of the Battle of Bennington: 'I believe . . . that had Queen Victoria been on the throne, instead of George III, or if we had postponed our rebellion until Queen Victoria reigned, it would not have been necessary, and had there been any rebellion at all, it would have been on the part of England.'[63]

Though Anglo-American relations had been sorely tested during the Civil War, the Centennial celebrations were a further illustration that Queen Victoria was above the political fray. Republicans and Democrats alike spoke warmly of her virtues, just as the great majority of Liberals and Conservatives did in Britain. By the late nineteenth century Americans, like Britons, had largely separated her from politics, which allowed them to integrate her into the patriotic mainstream. Irish Catholics, who found her a compelling target for their resentments, were notable exceptions. But it was a tribute to the power of British culture in America that those outside its ethnic ranks often took on board its ideology. By the late nineteenth century the term 'Anglo-Saxon' had broken through the confines of race and stood as often as not for 'a civilization, for ideas and institutions, originating indeed with a certain ethnic type of mankind, but no longer its exclusive property'.[64]

Victoria was the Queen of an expanding Anglo-Saxon empire, but she was still able to attract a degree of devotion from those outside the American mainstream, including African Americans and Native Americans. Racial minorities had many more pressing issues to consider than the British monarchy, but if the Fisk Jubilee Singers and the 'Colored Citizens of Boston' are anything to go by, some African Americans identified the Queen with the spread of justice and the end of slavery. Her sympathy for the oppressed, wherever they were found, was not in question. After Jonah Henson, the original of Harriet Beecher Stowe's Uncle Tom, visited Windsor Castle in 1877, the Queen wrote to her daughter Victoria in Germany that he was 'a fine, good old man – who has gone through such untold hardships. He was 46 years a slave and wished to thank me for all I had done for the poor, suffering slaves'.[65]

The tendency to credit the Queen with the spread of justice was a tribute to her benevolent nature and her mythic status above party. Native Americans, frustrated by United States military power and Indian policy, were known to look to Victoria as Queen of Canada for redress. In 1877, Sitting Bull paid a glowing tribute to her Majesty when he moved his band of Sioux to Canada to escape from what he called American 'treaty breakers, thieves and murderers'. When told that she had, through her servant in Ottawa, provided a home for him on the Deer River, he swore his 'unending fealty' to the Crown. The Queen, he declared, would not break her treaties or treat him like 'a dog' as had the Americans.[66]

Just as Sitting Bull was on his way to Canada, General Grant, who had recently left the Presidency, made a world tour. It began with a month in England where he and his wife were fêted by the Queen, the Prince of Wales and various municipal bodies. As President, Grant had been desirous of better relations with Britain. Like most of his predecessors, he thought the two countries natural allies because of their common language and history. For the Grants there were family ties as well, and they spent some time in Southampton with their daughter and her English husband. The London visit, supported by the State Department, did not disappoint. The outing to Windsor for dinner and an overnight stay was a high point of the tour, although it did not go quite as smoothly as the Grants might have hoped. They took the liberty of bringing along their irrepressible nineteen-year-old son Jesse, even though he had not been invited. Such informality made a less than favourable impression on the court, which was not accustomed to social irregularities.[67]

In the later decades of her reign the Queen stepped up her contact with American leaders. Sometimes it was in the form of gifts, as in the case of the desk built from the timbers of the *Resolute,* a British ship abandoned in Arctic exploration, which she presented to President Hayes (and which was later used by President Kennedy).[68] Letters of congratulations and commiseration became routine. A personal telegram to Mrs Garfield on the assassination of President Garfield in 1881 was widely reported, and did much to endear her to the American public.[69] She sent for the American Minister, James Russell Lowell, to express in person her concern for the President's recovery. On Garfield's death, she approved that the court should wear mourning for a week and had a wreath in her name placed on the President's coffin in Cleveland.[70] Palace officials delighted in the news from New York that the kindnesses to Mrs Garfield were much appreciated even among the Irish who mentioned the Queen's name 'with respect, not from affection on the part of the Irish, but from their fear of alienating their American sympathisers'.[71]

The monarchy wished to please and Americans longed for royal recognition. The Queen scrupulously avoided picking sides in American politics, treating Democrats and Republicans alike with solicitude. Meanwhile, tragic disasters in America brought her concern for suffering humanity to public notice. After the Chicago fire of 1871, she dispatched a personally inscribed biography of the Prince Consort to help initiate a free library.[72] Just as she sent messages of sympathy to India during famines, she sent messages to America at the time of the Charleston earthquake and the Johnstown flood.[73] According to the American Ambassador, Joseph Choate, the Queen pored over the details of these events as if they had happened in Britain.[74] Such gestures of royal condescension were not forgotten by American citizens, who saw them as personal acts of kindness that transcended class differences and brought the pride of sovereignty down to the level of the common people.

Not a few Americans repaid such royal acts in loyalty. In the 1870s, British associations in Virginia and elsewhere held annual celebrations of Victoria's birthday, with religious services and festive dinners.[75] From the American legation in London, James Russell Lowell wrote a gallant sonnet to the Queen in the early 1880s. Was he the only American to pay 'grateful homage' to Victoria's 'Right Divine' and compare her crown to the thorns of Christ? Few Britons, however monarchical in their sympathies, would have paid such fulsome tribute:

Empress and Queen, to thrones by birthright thine
Thou add'st a nobler, o'er the giant brood
Of States, thy grandsire's rebels, making good
The claim to tribute of thy royal line;
All fates that hallow woman wove the fine

And sober tissue of that womanhood
Whose tears, with ours commingled, tamed our mood
To grateful homage of such Right Divine:
Two crowns there are secure from mortal taint, –
Of virtue one, of thorns that other borne
By those He loves: so, doubly glorified,
Thou shalt arise triumphant, far-descried,
'Mid the white robes of Earth's last Easter-morn,
By him who waits in Heaven for thee, thy Saint![76]

*   *   *

The Queen's 'mythic glory' turned her Golden Jubilee of 1887 into a world event, widely celebrated in the United States. It set a new benchmark for royal commemoration, with all the dazzling pageantry that enthralled the British dominions and America alike. Medieval kings had celebrated their respective jubilees with acts of piety, but as a celebration of a substantial period in the life of the nation, the first significant royal jubilee took place in the reign of George III. As noted, it was not without celebrants in the United States, though they were relatively quiet about it. By 1887, however, unhappy memories of royal perfidy had largely disappeared. Americans no longer thought Britain's constitutional monarchy incompatible with their democratic ideals, while advances in communications and travel made the festivities much more accessible to the Queen's admirers across the Atlantic.

The *New York Times* called the pageant in London 'the greatest assemblage of human beings that has ever been collected anywhere' and estimated that 20,000 Americans were among the onlookers.[77] President Cleveland sent a letter of 'sincere felicitations' to the Queen in the name of the American people.[78] The Queen's courteous, though perfunctory reply, countersigned by the Prime Minister, Lord Salisbury, but probably written by an aide, was widely circulated in the United States. Its tone did not go down well in some circles. The *New York Times*, like other newspapers sensitive to seeming slights from Britain, took offence at the letter's 'vulgar' language, which offered nothing more than 'best thanks for this proof of friendship and good-will'.[79]

As the *New York Times* predicted, the Jubilee proved a 'colossal' event across the Anglo-Saxon world, but in America, the large influx of Irish immigrants after the Famine ensured that there would be spirited opposition. In cities with significant Irish populations there were counter demonstrations that kept the authorities on edge and the police on patrol. At Faneuil Hall Square in Boston, a large crowd of Irish sympathizers gathered to hiss the arrival of guests at the banquet of English and Scotch societies. In the ensuing tussle, mounted police trampled a boy, who was critically injured.[80] Tickets of admission to the demonstration at Cooper Union in Manhattan were edged in black and contained the following inscription: 'The English Queen's Jubilee, to commemorate the death of the Irish race, who have perished on the scaffold and in the dungeon and by famine and eviction during the fifty years of Victoria's murderous reign.'[81] The authorities largely kept Irish demonstrators under control and out of the mainstream press, just as they had done during the visit of the Prince of Wales in 1860.

Across America there were celebrations of various descriptions, from public dinners to commemorative sermons, with the proceeds often going to local charities. In New York, 20,000 guests enjoyed the pyrotechnic displays, which included a colossal portrait of Victoria, encircled by the royal garter. A choral service and eulogy began the festivities, followed by ceremonies at the Metropolitan Opera House, at which various dignitaries vied to give the most gracious encomiums to the Queen and the decidedly special relationship between the two nations. 'Great Britain and America', observed ex-Mayor Low,

> now see how the tangled threads of Anglo-Saxon greatness have become the warp and woof of human progress over a large portion of the globe. The vigorous daughter has become an empire herself. The sturdy mother has dominated the globe to its farthest shore, developing civilizations and sowing the seed of empire. Before the advance of both human slavery has disappeared. Everywhere mother and daughter have carried the atmosphere of free speech, free thought, and freedom to worship God, according to conscience. The two nations have had their differences; but behind them all beat, as I believe, two kindred hearts.[82]

Abram Hewitt, then New York's Mayor, who had defied the Tammany Irish by flying the flags at full staff on the city's public buildings, was not to be upstaged. Following the playing of Meyerbeer's 'Coronation March' and the reading of Robert Winthrop's 'Jubilee Ode', he rose to pay personal tribute as an American citizen in whose veins blood was thicker than water. America had many reasons to feel grateful to 'our Queen', he insisted, but most especially because she prevented the recognition by England of the Confederacy. 'In the hour of our trial, when it was my fortune to resort to the mother land, I learned that it was to the Queen of England that we owe the non-interference of foreign powers.'[83] The encomium was an example of the American tendency to inflate the Queen's powers and to credit her with a greater support for the North during the Civil War than was actually suggested by the evidence.

While New Yorkers paid tribute to the 'mother land' and 'our Queen', the London papers filled their columns with congratulatory telegrams from

America. News from Britain filled the United States papers over Jubilee summer. Americans learned of the recipe for the great Jubilee cake, weighing half a ton, which was on display in Buckingham Palace, and the 'American suckers' – gulls in Cockney slang – who paid $50 each for a single balcony seat without a murmur.[84] According to the *Albuquerque Morning Democrat*, many Americans secured front-row seats in Waterloo Place and joined the enthusiasm as warmly as the English.[85] In Arizona, the *Daily Tombstone Epitaph* announced that the Queen refused the offer of a Jubilee cheese made from the milk of 5,800 Canadian cows.[86] When Andrew Carnegie, a critic of monarchy, refused to subscribe to a Jubilee fund and publicly attacked the American celebrations he was roundly condemned in Texas.[87]

In celebrating the Jubilee, Americans confirmed Bagehot's insight that royalty sweetens politics through pleasing events. The Queen was not insensitive to such views, and among her outings during the Jubilee festivities she paid a well-publicized visit to Buffalo Bill's Wild West Show, which delighted Americans. As reported in the *Wheeling Register*, the Queen 'actually talked to a real, live, flesh and blood North American Indian, who called her a squaw'.[88] Across the United States, the royal anniversary gave cities, towns and hamlets an escape from

14. Queen Victoria's visit to the Wild West Show at West Brompton, 1887, *Illustrated London News*.

routine, an opportunity to connect to the wider world, if only with a special church service or a meeting of British citizens to toast their distant sovereign. Apart from Boston and New York, those bastions of Anglophilia, Dallas, Philadelphia and Los Angeles were among the leading cities to host festivities, staging an assortment of balls, banquets, parades, concerts, firework displays, fund raisers and sporting events. Chicago, the city of big shoulders, held a tug of war contest between teams of American, English, Scottish and Irish descent, in which the Irish defeated both the English and the Americans.[89]

If we are to believe the *Atlanta Constitution*, Atlanta was an exception to the festive mood in the country at large. The editor may have been Irish, for the paper reported no local tributes and predicted that Victoria would be 'the last queen England shall ever have'.[90] Very different sentiments were heard in Dallas, where the citizens cabled the Queen with the message of 'loyal respects and sincere congratulations'.[91] The English cricket club in the city changed its name to Jubilee Cricket Club. The First Congregational Church, decorated for the Thanksgiving Service with flags and a blue silk banner bearing the words 'God Save the Queen', extended an invitation to all the city's citizens, but especially the British residents of Texas. The Revd. C. I. Scofield, the pastor of the Church, spoke for Anglo-Americans across the country in his meditation on the event:

> We take note of this event because we are part of Great Britain – that earth-encircling family of English speaking nations, the planting and nurture of which is the most remarkable of God's modern miracles. One hundred years ago He broke the bond of authority which bound us to the mother land, but He left unbroken and unbreakable five gentle and unfretting links of union – the link of race, the link of law, the link of language, the link of literature and the link of liberty.[92]

*   *   *

The later years of Queen Victoria's reign marked the apogee of Anglo-American cultural relations. With easier communication and travel, cultural exchanges between the two countries, from tourists to professional elites, widened longstanding ties. The international disputes between the two nations in the decades after the Civil War, though often heated, were settled by arbitration, which defused tensions. With the old resentments diminished, the subservience to British opinion was now fading in the United States. This is not to say that Americans had entirely broken free from their enslavement to British culture. Senator Henry Cabot Lodge remarked that 'the first step of an American entering upon a literary culture was to pretend to be an Englishman in order that he might win the approval, not of Englishmen, but of his own countrymen'.[93] But as a burgeoning power with the confidence of maturity, America looked to Britain for a reciprocal regard born out of language, history and common interests.

Many Americans, linking themselves to the ancient Anglo-Saxons, assumed they had a special mission in the world, based on blood and culture. The origins of 'Anglo-Saxonism' can be traced in America to the seventeenth century, but as a doctrine of racial superiority it reached its peak in the last decades of the nineteenth century.[94] It simply assumed that the English-speaking peoples, characterized by enterprise, intelligence, courage, and a talent for self-government, were more advanced than any other racial grouping.[95] For the British, appeals to Anglo-American kinship served a particular purpose in an era of growing Irish consciousness.[96] Whatever an individual's ancestral background, the spread of Anglo-Saxon civilization had become part of the cultural conversation and provided a rationale for foreign and imperial policy on both sides of the Atlantic. Inspired by the British Empire, the era resonated with the 'destinarian nationalism' of the republic with its ambition to redeem the world's benighted.[97]

A historian of nineteenth-century American foreign policy observed that the positive influences that shaped Anglo-American relations in the 1890s were respect for the Queen, race patriotism, transatlantic family ties, and intermarriage between important families.[98] Such influences often worked below the surface of government action. But in the sphere of politics and international relations, as in social life, the two countries were drawing closer together. In an era of Anglo-American rapprochement, the vital interests of the two countries were less often in conflict. Relations improved as Americans came to see Britain as less threatening to United States interests.[99] Senator Lodge reflected the prevailing mood in his remark that 'the downfall of the British Empire is something which no rational American could regard as anything but a misfortune to the United States'.[100] Sir Edward Grey, the British Foreign Minister, later spoke of an 'Anglo-Saxon feeling' that had its basis in language and a kindred point of view, in which the majority on both sides of the Atlantic 'has a hatred of what is not just or free'.[101]

Proponents of a distinctive Anglo-American friendship saw the rule of law and the liberty of the individual as supreme contributions of the English-speaking people to mankind. They found a priceless focus of sentiment in the Queen, who was hailed for her seminal role in spreading Anglo-Saxon civiliza-tion, with its consoling narrative of steadiness, decorum and Protestantism. The Liberal Member of Parliament Charles Dilke, who visited the United States in the late 1860s, wrote in his travel book *Greater Britain*: 'In America, the peoples of the world are being fused together, but they are run into an English mould. . . . America offers the English race the moral directorship of the globe, by ruling mankind through Saxon institutions and the English tongue. Through America England is speaking to the world.'[102] As often as not, he might have added, England was heard in America through Queen Victoria.

*   *   *

It was against the background of race patriotism, mutual respect and the cross-fertilization of ideas that Queen Victoria's Diamond Jubilee so enthralled America in 1897. For this Jubilee, the White House upped the ante and dispatched Whitelaw Reid, a millionaire from Ohio who had been Ambassador to France, as a Special Ambassador for the occasion. The resident Ambassador, John Hay, a reluctant courtier, watched with amazement and gave a half-hearted cheer from the sidelines, bemused that 'the monarchical religion has grown day by day till the Queen is worshipped as more than mortal'.[103] He took some small pleasure from the antics of his co-Ambassador: 'I have seen my friend Whitelaw sitting between two princesses at supper every night, a week running, and I now may intone my *nunc dimittis*. His rapture had the *aliquid amari* that the end must come, but the memory of it will soothe many an hour of ennui.'[104]

President McKinley spoke on behalf of his fellow countrymen when he wrote to the Queen to recognize her friendship for America and to wish her long life and her people peace and prosperity.[105] Americans from disparate parts of the country sang the Queen's praises, though those of British ancestry were the most vocal. At the Jubilee dinner in Boston, the master of ceremonies, with the mayor and governor in attendance, saluted Americans of British lineage as 'the genuine type of Americans', a remark bound to alienate any Irishman within earshot.[106] The *New York Tribune* christened Victoria 'a Queen of our own race and blood, the head of a sister nation, the titular ruler of the elder half of our own people, who are one with us in spirit, in sympathy, in ambition, and in destiny'.[107] For many Anglo-Saxon Protestants in the United States, Victoria was the Queen not simply of Britain but of the Anglo-Saxon people.

American political commentators saw the Jubilee as an opportunity to discuss the links between American and British democracy. In so doing they were able to celebrate the United States while celebrating the mother kingdom. The Speaker of the House of Representatives, Thomas Reed, a Republican from Maine, saw a synchronism between the Queen's anniversary and American independence. In a Fourth of July address, he declared that 'England is as much a republic . . . as the United States', and that 'it was to our example that the British Empire is indebted for its present greatness. We won liberty, not for ourselves alone, but for all the colonies of the Empire'. In this analysis, the glorious political history of Britain, with its succeeding extensions of the suffrage, came 'not from within the realm, but from without. It came, of course, from us'.[108] The notion that the universal principles in the Declaration of Independence ultimately liberated Britain was a self-serving American conceit that had little basis in reality and would not have found favour with the granddaughter of George III, who could hardly be accused of favouring egalitarian ideas.

Such encomiums to the United States were not on the Jubilee agenda of Mark Twain, who was given the unique privilege of covering the event for the archives of the City of London by the Lord Mayor. (He published his observations in a privately printed booklet, *Queen Victoria's Jubilee.*)[109] Writing with his customary panache for the *Chicago Tribune*, he saw the procession to St Paul's as 'the human race on exhibition'. From his seat in the Strand he watched the passing parade, the ornate costumes of African soldiers and Indian princes, European royalty on horseback and the American Ambassador in a modest carriage. Then, after hours of waiting, a landau, lavishly upholstered, drawn by eight cream-coloured horses

came bowling along followed by the Prince of Wales, and all the world rose to its feet and uncovered. The Queen-Empress was come. . . . It was realizable that she was the procession herself, that all the rest of it was mere embroidery; that in her the public saw the British Empire. She was a symbol, an allegory of England's grandeur, and the might of the British nation.[110]

The Queen's Diamond Jubilee left a powerful impression on Twain. Not for him Marx's dictum that 'the tradition of all dead generations weighs like a nightmare on the brain of the living'.[111] British history – unlike French, German, or even American history – provided a happier historical narrative that royal ceremonial honoured. 'A procession', Twain concluded, 'has value in but two ways – as a show and as a symbol; its minor function being to delight the eye, its major one to compel thought, exalt the spirit, stir the heart and inflame the imagination.' What set British pageantry apart from a 'meaningless' show like a Mardi-Gras was the symbolic, moving history behind it. Even without banners and music or rich and showy costumes, the Jubilee would have been profound and memorable for those who viewed it with sympathy, for it stood, in Twain's words, 'for English history, English growth, English achievement, the accumulated power and renown and dignity of twenty centuries of strenuous effort'.[112]

In America itself, the Jubilee celebrations surpassed those of a decade earlier. From Philadelphia to San Francisco, cities competed for top billing, while local worthies and rival institutions jostled for public recognition. Even distant Hawaiians, who had their own Queen until she was deposed in 1893, sang Victoria's praises.[113] The *Boston Globe* declared that Boston sought to eclipse any previous jubilee held in America. As predicted, the city put together an elaborate programme of events, capped by a grand banquet, a vaudeville show and dancing in the various halls of the Mechanic's building. The funds raised established 'Victorian' beds in Boston hospitals.[114] Lynn, Massachusetts sent delegates to the Boston festivities, while residents toasted the Queen across the water and invited veterans of the English army to join the ceremonies.[115] In Georgia, even the *Atlanta Constitution*, so sour in Golden Jubilee year, recognized the significance of the Diamond Jubilee and carried the news from London.[116] It also noted the celebrations in Savannah and in Tampa, Florida, where the Governor had persuaded the United States Navy to send a warship to mark the festivities.[117]

As in 1887, Chicago's publicity machine geared up. It declared that the City, founded in the year of Victoria's accession, would commemorate the Queen 'on a scale which will be eclipsed by no other city outside the British domains'.[118] Following the Queen's wish that Jubilee funds be raised for the hospitals of London, the city's dignitaries organized an appeal for the hospitals of Chicago. Five thousand British-American citizens gathered in the Chicago Auditorium to honour a ruler they had left but not forgotten. After a sharp debate, the Chicago Council voted 48 to 12 to attend the celebration. Alderman Duddleston, an Englishman, spoke on behalf of the motion with the remark that 'England is the greatest nation on earth or which ever will be', to which the Celtic contingent in the Council took 'violent exception, declaring America the greatest with Ireland a close second'.[119] There were no Irish outbursts at the banquet itself, where the speakers warmed to the blessings of the Queen's reign, which dignified motherhood and family life. The event raised $8,000 for the Chicago hospitals.[120]

As the Chicago celebrations demonstrated, the Jubilee was widely seen as a triumph of womanhood, a celebration of the Queen's loyalty as wife and mother. Churches across America, especially Episcopal ones, took the lead in this line of reasoning, drawing on texts such as Proverbs ix. 16: 'A gracious woman retaineth honour'. The Revd. Dr Henry Lubeck of the Church of Zion and St Timothy in Manhattan closed his Jubilee sermon by saying that Victoria enjoyed 'universal respect and love not alone because she has been a good Queen, but because she has been a womanly Queen and a Christian'.[121] In the triumph of conservative social aspiration over revolutionary principle, the Daughters of the American Revolution sent a resolution to Buckingham Palace: 'Great Queen, Great Woman. The noblest exponent of queenly womanhood the world has seen.'[122]

Not all the Jubilee celebrations in the United States were an unmitigated success. Irish discontents in America mirrored those in Britain, and Irish Catholics boycotted the celebrations in various cities across the country as they had done during the Golden Jubilee a decade earlier. Kansas City boasted a 'Victoria Diamond Jubilee Association', but the Catholic Bishop declined to attend the mass meeting and refused to offer prayers: 'I shall order no prayers for England's Queen in our churches. . . . Our people have no occasion to invoke special blessing on Queen Victoria. As a good woman we admire her; as a Queen we have no prayers to offer her.'[123] In Chicago, an Irish judge refused to adjourn the Criminal Court and remarked that he would serve a sentence on Queen Victoria for contempt if she were present.[124]

In New York, the United Irish Societies resolved to hold a meeting in 'commemoration of our patriotic dead and the millions of victims of plague and famine during her reign of sixty years'.[125] Across the city, posters appeared with the words 'Americans, Americans! Down with the Anglomaniacs.'[126] When the Seventh Regiment Band organized a Jubilee music programme to be held in Central Park, a group of Irish patriots put up an inflammatory poster condemning 'British Flunkeyism' and warned the citizenry to stay out of the park on the day. But the warning did little to dim the enthusiasm of the large crowd that turned up. As in the Queen's Jubilee a decade earlier, the mainstream press largely ignored, or dismissed, the Irish agitators, who found it difficult to make much headway in the face of widespread pro-British sentiment.[127]

Americans in Britain at the time of the Jubilee had their own issues, which were unrelated to Irish opposition. United States citizens resident in Britain bristled on discovering that the only Americans invited to the Queen's Garden Party at Buckingham Palace were married to English aristocrats.[128] But the tensions in London did not diminish the sense of transatlantic kinship that such marriages had promoted by the time of the Jubilee. Many a daughter of the American plutocracy was hunting for a title or an aristocratic connection. Between 1870 and 1914, there were over one hundred marriages between the eldest and younger sons of peers to American women, a tradition that underscored the relationship of royalty with wealthy United States families.[129] In her novel *The Anglomaniacs* (1890), Constance Harrison wrote that the intermarriage of rich girls with British aristocrats created 'for their families the high place Americans begin to crave when they begin to think. . . . Every little sprig of nobility they send over to us from the other side is made much of in New York, and then passed along through the other cities. Blame it, those fellows walk on flowers'.[130]

Royalty clearly walked on flowers. To those who have it is given, and Americans lavished gifts on the Queen, which contributed to the vast display of Jubilee presents on exhibition at London's Imperial Institute. These included articles of imperial necessity such as pen-wipers and tea-cosies, as well as many bound addresses, including those from the Trustees of Mount Holyoke College, the Daughters of the American Revolution, and the Citrus Colony Club of Placer County, California. The members of the Masonic Veteran Association of Illinois even presented the Queen with a photograph, framed in gold, of themselves.[131] Such inconsequential news filled the American prints. In reaction to the tidal wave of royalist gush, the *Irish World and American Industrial Liberator* concluded that the nation's capital was 'gradually passing from an American city into a colonial capital of the British Empire, assuming in many respects a striking resemblance to Ottawa'.[132]

More sympathetic columnists remarked that the Jubilee had notably strengthened the relations between Great Britain and the United States. The sentiment had an echo in Britain, where the American celebrations were noted with approval. The *Chicago Daily Tribune* published a dispatch from London, which observed that the display of affection for the Queen across the United States would have positive diplomatic results. America, it was said, had departed from her desultory style of diplomatic intercourse and had taken her place among the world's powers with dignity and distinction. 'Good feeling has been promoted by this exceptional demonstration of American courtesy and appreciation, and the way may have been opened for the adjustment of several questions vitally affecting the United States.'[133]

The Jubilee celebrations in the United States were both cause and effect of improved Anglo-American relations, a powerful demonstration of the power of the monarchy in binding nations together through ritual. America could view the triumphs of the reign without fear or jealousy and could even claim to have participated in them. As the *New York Times* put it: 'An American in London could not have felt himself quite a foreigner on Tuesday. Americans at home, reading of the celebration, felt that they had some share in it, and that in a true sense it celebrated themselves.'[134] The comment helps to explain why Americans, who were not taught to revere monarchy – if anything rather the reverse – found royal events so engaging. It was a striking feature of the Golden and Diamond Jubilees that they united the people of Britain and the United States, and, like religious rites, induced Americans to worship themselves.

* * *

On 22 January 1901, less than four years after the Diamond Jubilee, the memories and the memorabilia faded, the Queen died. Across the globe, the tributes were deafening, 'a real debauch of sentiment and loyalty' as the Fabian socialist Beatrice Webb observed in London.[135] Across the United States bells tolled; flags lowered; churchmen prayed; the House of Representatives adjourned.[136]

Flying the flags at half-mast on the White House and government office buildings was exceptional. A member of the Cabinet remarked that it was not meant to set a precedent but was a special tribute to the Queen's memory for her personal qualities and for her efforts on behalf of peace in 1861.[137] In Virginia and North Carolina, the legislatures tendered their sympathies and adopted resolutions. In Arkansas, the legislators took the day off out of respect.[138] President McKinley consoled the new King Edward VII, writing that Queen Victoria's 'sterling qualities ... endeared her to the people of this country scarcely less than to those of her own'.[139]

Leading Americans made preparations and offered tributes. In London, Lady Randolph Churchill, the former Jenny Jerome of New York and mother of Winston Churchill, wrote that 'high and low, rich and poor, the whole English-speaking race realize that they have lost in Queen Victoria the greatest of their sovereigns and the best of friends'.[140] Meanwhile, Ambassador Choate agonized over whether he could wear a dress suit while on horseback, but was spared the potential embarrassment when the authorities confined the funeral procession to the royal family and a military escort.[141] Former President Benjamin Harrison, the Secretary of State John Hay, and presidential hopeful William

15. 'Lowered Flag'. Clipping from *Boston Globe*, 23 January 1901.

Jennings Bryan joined the ranks of those who sent messages of condolence.[142] Just before her death, Robert Todd Lincoln, the son of President Lincoln and the American Minister to Britain in the early 1890s, called the Queen 'probably the wisest woman that ever lived. I do not mean to say she is a genius, but her great gift of common sense, reinforced by her vast store of knowledge, has enabled her to counsel men and women of all classes and conditions with wisdom that could not be exceeded.'[143]

While America's great and good paid their respects, the citizens of Chicago named a street in the Queen's honour and raised funds to erect a permanent memorial.[144] Around the country department stores dressed their windows with British flags and pictures of the Queen. Thousands of lowered flags could be seen from the Brooklyn Bridge.[145] Financial institutions draped their buildings with mourning symbols. The New York Stock Exchange closed for the funeral. Queen Victoria always had a special meaning for American women, many of whom saw her first and foremost in the light of their sex. Across the country, women's clubs held memorial meetings and dinners. 'She has had no wonderful achievements in art or literature', recalled a speaker at the ladies' day dinner of the Twentieth Century Club in Boston. 'Instead she has left the memory of a queenly life, the record of a true woman, wearing the triple crown of maid, wife and mother.'[146] In Atlanta, the Federation of Women's clubs cabled a message of sympathy to the new King, Edward VII, which elicited a reply from Buckingham Palace.[147]

In places as diverse as Chattanooga, Milwaukee and Portland, Oregon people attended memorial services or mentioned the Queen in their prayers. Churches and chapels overflowed. In Washington, the President and his Cabinet, joined by the chief officers of the Army and Navy and the British Ambassador, attended a service at St John's Episcopal Church, timed to correspond with that of the pageant in London as 'the mother of rulers was borne to Windsor'.[148] In New York's Trinity Church, 23 clergymen took part in the semi-official service that included representatives from the British Consulate. 'America is bereaved as no other land out of England', proclaimed a Boston clergyman, 'and she mourns the departure of the queen mother who, all her life, was America's faithful friend.'[149] The poet Edward Octavius Flagg wrote of the 'flood of grief . . . that surges through our land / A grief that joins with Albion's hand in hand.'[150]

There were few dissenting voices, apart from 'wearers of the green'.[151] In Boston, the Irish were invited to join the mourners, though the Irish nationalists in the city, echoing republican language in Britain, said they saw little to mourn. As one of their number put it: 'Ireland has lost a ruler, but not a friend.' Another accused the Queen of failing 'to contribute a cent to relieve the suffering of famine-stricken Ireland in "46–47" '.[152] (She had in fact contributed £2,500 to Irish Famine relief in that year.)[153] In New York, the Irish firebrand Maude Gonne, speaking at a meeting sponsored by Clan Na Gael, observed that 'A woman died in England last month (hisses) over which the Anglo-maniacs expressed great sympathy and went into mourning. She is put forward as all that is best and most representative in the English, but so far as we are concerned they are welcome to her.'[154] Years later, New York officials rejected a plan to erect a statue to the Queen in Central Park. Theodore Roosevelt observed that it would furnish 'a steady occupation for the police force in protecting it from celtic enthusiasts whose life ambition it would be to blow it up'.[155]

* * *

Few, if any, Americans wanted a hereditary monarchy at home, but Queen Victoria did more than any other British sovereign to encourage royalist sympathies in the United States. Empresses are easier to love than emperors. That she was a benign woman who reigned in a world of male rulers surely heightened the imaginative sympathy. On watching the funeral procession, the British novelist and later Hollywood screenwriter Elinor Glyn remarked that 'a sublime spirit of chivalry must be innate in a people whose highest response of loyalty and valour is always made to Queens'. Glyn, who saw the Queen's passing as marking the end of an epoch of British glory, noticed the 'little, little coffin, . . . the smallness, the feminine frailty, of the greatest ruler in the world'.[156] In her best-selling poem *The Queen's Last Ride*, the American poet Ella Wheeler Wilcox intoned: 'Uncover your heads, lift your hearts on high, The Queen in silence is driving by.'[157]

The worldwide expression of chivalry and silent emotion at Queen Victoria's death was a tribute to her status above politics, which had endured for over 60 years, binding the generations together in a way that no elected politician could rival. As the embodiment of a global empire, she was better known than any ruler on earth. As a flesh and blood hereditary sovereign she was better understood than the United States Constitution, which Bagehot called 'an old-state paper'.[158] Given America's undistinguished political leadership over most of her reign, she was more admired in the United States than any president, with the possible exception of Lincoln. 'It is not for mere show', reported the *Los Angeles Times*, 'that the Americans have received the news of the death of Queen Victoria as a bereavement of their own and commented upon it in terms such as they would employ in the case of an honored President dying in office.'[159]

James Bryce, echoing Bagehot, noted in *The American Commonwealth* (1888) that the Crown was an object of absorbing interest because 'it touches the imagination whereas assemblies excite ... criticism'.[160] During her long reign, the Queen touched the American imagination more than any British sovereign before or since. She was arguably Britain's single greatest asset in reuniting the severed sympathies of the two great English-speaking nations. It may be thought ironic that Americans, who once rejected the British monarchy as antagonistic to American freedom, had taken Queen Victoria to their hearts. But that would be to see the republic as having rejected English culture, which it had not. Americans, who took such pride in their British origins, had, for half a century, called Victoria their mother, friend, and Queen and in a great gush of sentiment, at once remote and sincere, mourned her passing.

CHAPTER 6

CEREMONY AND CELEBRITY

Is it not a noble farce, wherein kings, republics, and emperors have for so many ages played their parts, and to which the whole vast universe serves for a theatre?

Michel de Montaigne, *Essays*, 1580

The day after Queen Victoria's death, the 59-year-old King Edward VII took the oath of office at St James's Palace. The American papers described in minute and moving detail the arcane and ancient rituals associated with the oath and the formal proclamation of the new King in the capital the following day. For those susceptible to the allure of ceremonial it was an education in the magic theatre of monarchy. Few Americans would have been acquainted with the College of Arms or the Norroy Herald of Arms, who read the proclamation that prefaced the procession through Trafalgar Square and along the Strand to Temple Bar in the City. Few Americans would ever have seen the Lord Mayor, sheriffs, and mace bearers, attired in cocked hats and scarlet robes, borne along to the sound of trumpets in their Cinderella coaches on streets lined with 10,000 soldiers – Life Guards, Horse Guards and Foot Guards – who had been brought in overnight from their barracks to safeguard the route.

Kings may be made by 'universal hallucination', as Bernard Shaw once quipped, but Edward VII's renown at the beginning of his reign cannot be explained simply by reference to illusion. The King inherited a Crown that was identified with material and social progress and served as the unifying symbol of the Empire. In contrast to Queen Victoria's court, Edward VII's was colourful and cosmopolitan, marked by assured patriotism, lavish hospitality and elaborate ritual. It was also less forbidding to those outside looking in.

Taking after his father, the King did not have a contempt for 'trade'. And free of the anti-semitism that characterized many aristocrats, he opened up the monarchy to foreigners and the 'smart set', who had been ignored by his mother. Edward VII was perhaps the only man in England who was not a social climber. Nor was he a snob, though he attracted snobs like a magnet, not least American ones.

Many Americans, especially recent immigrants from Central Europe and beyond, were indifferent to the British monarchy, or saw it as a distant presence. But most United States citizens came from countries with monarchical traditions. It left many of them with a residual sense of deference to royalty and perhaps, by extension, to the American presidency. Those who had left Europe after the revolutions of 1848 often brought with them radical views, but this did not necessarily translate into hostility to the British monarchy, which was seen to be much more liberal and democratic than monarchies on the continent. In an era of transatlantic harmony, critics of British royalty were few and far between in the United States, outside Irish circles. Americans generally may have had little stake in the monarchy's survival or demise, but if the attention devoted to royalty in the press was anything to go by, they craved royal news or at least found it a welcome distraction from their day-to-day lives.

Older Americans remembered the King's successful visit to the United States as a young man. He too remembered it, and ever after sought to sustain the friendly relations that the tour created. He was on excellent terms with American presidents from Buchanan onwards, and he welcomed cultured Americans to his social circle, especially the women who had married into the peerage. Though out of touch with life in the United States, which had changed dramatically since his visit in 1860, he nonetheless kept informed of American opinion through his friendships and contacts with the American Embassy. In 1889, he became the first member of the royal family to attend a baseball game, played in London by a team from Chicago.[1] At the beginning of his reign, he was quick to thank the President and the American Cabinet for attending the memorial service for Queen Victoria in Washington, and took the trouble to express his gratitude to members of the New York Stock Exchange for closing the financial markets on the day of Her Majesty's funeral.[2]

Royalty continued to interest Americans far more than the politics of the British monarchy, which had seen its prerogatives steadily eroded in the wake of democratic reform. Edward VII, unlike presidents Jackson, Lincoln, or his contemporary Theodore Roosevelt, did not have the power to make war or peace. His biographer Philip Magnus, drawing on Bagehot, observed that he would have had to sign a bill for his own execution had the government put one before him.[3] The American President and the British Prime Minister now had the authority once wielded by monarchs, a point not lost on citizens of the two kindred countries. It was deeply ironic that while the British King, a descendant of George III, was now a political cipher, the United States President enjoyed the power and trappings of a ruling monarch.

While the authority of the British monarchy had faded, reports of presidential power bordering on kingship had not died away in the United States. Indeed, the view that America was a monarchy in its own right was again gaining currency in the late nineteenth century. In the 1880s, the widely read constitutional writers Bryce and Maine had compared the President's office to that of George III. A leading American legal scholar observed in 1889 that each president was:

> A chief magistrate who wields the whole military and no inconsiderable share of the civil power of the State, who can incline the scale of war and forbid the return of peace, whose veto wills the course of legislation, who is the source of the enormous patronage which is the main lever in the politics of the United States, exercises functions which are more truly regal than those of an English monarch.[4]

In 1896, a Tennessee newspaper introduced an article on 'The Power of Presidents' with the declaration: 'Great Britain is a republic with a hereditary president, while the United States is a monarchy with an elective king.'[5] Two years later, the *Dallas Morning News* quoted an article from the *Spectator* that described President McKinley, who had just prosecuted a successful war with Spain, as an elective monarch.[6]

Some American commentators took heart from the growth of executive authority, which they traced to the administration of 'King Andrew' Jackson. During McKinley's administration, the political journalist and later Princeton professor Henry Jones Ford wrote that since Jackson's time the office of President had revived 'the oldest political institution of the race, the elective kingship. It is all there: the precognition of the notables and the tumultuous choice of the freemen, only conformed to modern conditions'. But unlike the Whig critics of expanding executive power in the mid-nineteenth century, Ford approved of America's elective monarchy. In his view it was a unique development, compatible with democracy, which 'indicates the highest degree of constitutional morality yet attained by any race'.[7] If the advance of representative democracy had undermined royal authority in Britain, it was starting to be linked to expanding presidential power in America.[8]

While the American monarch ruled, the British monarch simply reigned. But reigning without ruling had its compensations for a king who took his role seriously, especially in regard to foreign relations. Although he never set foot on American soil after 1860, Edward VII cultivated the United States very effectively for the monarchy. While his reputation as a voluptuary preceded him, there was a tendency to overlook the King's failings in the United States, though there was some criticism of 'the unbridled license in his life'.[9] With easy manners and a dignified bearing he was a natural 'head of society' to those for whom society mattered, especially the upper classes, who were particularly friendly towards Britain.[10] If poorer Americans saw the King as a fount of distraction, affluent Americans rallied to him because of his vast wealth and his headship of the international set of millionaires. It was a measure of the change in the relationship between the monarchy and the United States that to many Americans the King was first and foremost the impresario of the plutocracy.

In an era of waning aristocratic power, the King recalibrated the social conventions of monarchy for a secular audience agog at wealth and title. Royal advisers may have wished it had been different, but in America the King was seen as a flesh and blood creature of society, a sportsman and *bon vivant*, not a quasi-religious symbol of middle-class rectitude like his mother. Not one to fade into the background, Edward VII relished his social pre-eminence and international role. As Prince of Wales in an era of 'King Capital' he had been an ideal British complement to America's Gilded Age. As King, he navigated the Progressive era with all its reformism and distrust of traditional institutions without mishap, buoyed by his international reputation for voluntary work and spreading goodwill.[11]

The King's links with America were no small matter to Britain, for the United States had become an ever more prominent competitor by the beginning of his reign. With a population which was by 1900 twice the size of Britain's, a widening sphere of influence and a powerful navy, the United States had become one of the Great Powers. Accordingly, Americans received due regard from the British sovereign, who had long seen himself as a statesman and man of the world. Like his mother before him, the King took pains with American citizens and dignitaries alike, which, however inconsequential, received attention in the United States papers. He and his advisers gave special notice to wealthy Americans resident in England, who often saw themselves as a set apart from their fellow countrymen.

The growing number of American girls presented at court – about 30 each year in the reign of Edward VII – had an exalted status in the American quality press.[12] They were taken less seriously in Britain, for the aristocracy thought them a little common, especially those who came from families in business.[13] A request through the United States Embassy was usually sufficient for girls

1 Portrait of George III, with a view of soldiers through the window, by the Anglo-American artist Benjamin West, painted at the height of the American Revolution, 1778.

2 Washington's arrival in New York in a decorated barge, 23 April 1789, by the French artist Arsène Rivey. A choir on an attendant sloop sang an ode to the President-elect to the tune of 'God save the King'. Collection of The New York Historical Society.

3 Mrs Washington's drawing room in *The Republican Court in the Time of Washington* by Daniel Huntington, 1861.

4 'We owe allegiance to no crown', a banner slogan popular in America after the War of 1812.

5 A replica painting of the portrait of Queen Victoria by the American artist Thomas Sully, commissioned by the Anglophile Society of the Sons of St George of Philadelphia.

6 The American marketing of British royalty. Queen Victoria and Prince Albert paperweight manufactured by the New England Glass Company, 1850. Collection of The New York Historical Society.

7 Commemorative plate, 'Welcome to Our Friendly Land', commissioned to celebrate Queen Elizabeth II's visit to America in 1957. Collection of The New York Historical Society.

8 Peter Cohen's poster of President Nixon, in the guise of King George III, with the Capitol building in ruins in the background.

9 Queen Elizabeth, accompanied by President Ford, speaking at the arrival ceremony at the White House on the occasion of her visit to the United States during the Bicentennial celebrations, July 1976.

10 At a White House reception in July 1976, President Ford introduces Queen Elizabeth to the ultimate in Hollywood glamour, her fellow countryman Cary Grant.

11 The famous picture of Princess Diana dancing with John Travolta at the White House,
9 November 1985.

12 A celebrity encounter as Princess Diana meets Clint Eastwood at the London film premiere of *The Fugitive*, 23 September 1993.

13 Princess Diana speaking at the Red Cross Day, Washington D.C., 17 June 1997.

14 During her tour of Jamestown in May 2007, Queen Elizabeth visits the replica of the *Susan Constant,* the flagship of the fleet that carried the first settlers to Virginia.

with the appropriate diplomatic or social connections. When President Theodore Roosevelt's niece, Miss Corinna Robinson, made her debut at court the society pages back home were full of it, just as they were when a bevy of Yankee peeresses, along with President Roosevelt's sister, opened a stall at the Queen's summer fête in 1907. The *Boston Globe*, with the customary American deference to titled nobility, added that 'three royal princesses will be in charge of stalls'.[14]

As the King and his aides recognized, royal courtesies, like royal indignities, are meat and drink to the popular press. When the King entertained J. P. Morgan and 22 representatives of the New York Chamber of Commerce at Windsor, the American papers reported it.[15] They also covered his audiences with American politicians, like that in 1901 with the former Speaker of the House of Representatives David Henderson, in which the King assured the Congressman that America had 'no more cordial friend in the world'.[16] When Marconi successfully transmitted a message from Cape Cod to Cornwall in 1903, the King sent felicitations to President Roosevelt on behalf of the British Empire.[17] The first telegram received from a foreign head of state on the death of John Hay in 1905 came from Buckingham Palace.[18] The King made repeated inquiries about Grover Cleveland when he fell critically ill in 1908. He even got in on the act when Jamestown celebrated the 300th anniversary of the birth of the American nation, a site that would later become favoured by Queen Elizabeth II.[19]

Form matters more to monarchs than to lesser mortals. Good public relations abroad solidified the King's position at home, and the rewards were disproportionate to the effort expended. This was particularly true of Edward VII's relations with Americans. The King and his aides were well aware of the democratic and Irish sensitivities across the Atlantic, which sat uneasily with Britain's aristocratic traditions. In a world in which news travelled back to Britain from America with great rapidity, to be known in the United States as a friend of democracy was part of the Crown's strategy to subvert anti-monarchical republicanism at home.[20] In an uncertain and increasingly threatening world for monarchs, the King's friendship with some of America's wealthiest citizens provided insurance. He never had to call on their services in a royal emergency, but he ensured that his family would always have a bolthole in Newport or the Hamptons if needed.

Like his mother, Edward VII had an exceptional, if absentee, presence in the United States. More Americans than Britons knew that the King had a taste for ragtime, that his hearing aid was made in America, that he donated gifts to the New York Yacht Club, the Metropolitan Museum and the Bruton Parish Church at Williamsburg, Virginia. His purchase of $35,000 worth of furniture from Evansville, Indiana, resulted in his honorary membership in the local furniture maker's society.[21] In Britain, so many applicants, from orphanages to potato growers, requested to use the King's name that the Home Secretary became alarmed.[22] In 1902, the year of his Coronation, the King Edward potato appeared, which, like the Prince Albert potato before it, soon became an American staple. King Edward Cigars were another favourite and remain so today. By such indirection, the royal brand resonated across the United States.

The King collected tributes and honours the way his plutocratic friends collected dividends, but with decidedly less investment of capital. With little more than an effortless nod on his part the royalties flowed in his direction. His patronage of Americans and American institutions had an effect not unlike his patronage of British subjects and charities. But everything was not always as it seemed. The King was well known as a supporter of voluntary hospitals, and in 1871 a group of playful Princeton undergraduates informed the Prince of his unanimous election to the Princeton Medical Faculty as an honorary fellow. In accepting the honour, the Prince's Private Secretary Sir Francis Knollys wrote that 'His Royal Highness will ever remember with pride and satisfaction the mark that he has received at the hands of the Princeton Medical Faculty.'[23] But Princeton had no medical school.

Unlike Queen Victoria, King Edward enjoyed the limelight, and he lived out Bagehot's dictum that the monarchy needed to be visible: 'It is the essence of the showy parts of the Constitution to acquire importance and popularity by being seen.'[24] From time to time there were celebrity encounters with Americans to amuse the spectators and delight reporters. Mark Twain's attendance at a Buckingham Palace garden party was a priceless moment, a Connecticut Yankee in the court of King Edward. The guests broke into applause as the famous author approached the King, who was standing on a raised part of the garden. Asked whether he enjoyed the experience, Twain said in his drawl that he thought the King enjoyed it:

> I knew we were the centre of all eyes, and I felt my oats. When I approached King Edward, he extended his right hand, and as I took it he placed his other hand on my shoulder. I thought to myself if the King could put his hand on my shoulder I could put mine on his, and so I did. There we two great men stood before all the people 'laying on of hands'.[25]

For all his visibility and charm, King Edward never achieved the august status of Queen Victoria in the United States. This was partly because of his reputation for licentiousness and partly because the traditional Anglo-Protestant culture was being diluted by the rapid expansion of the population.

For immigrants from central, eastern and southern Europe, without historic or familial attachments to England, the royal family was not a link with the ancestral past but at best a diverting curiosity. In the decade of King Edward's reign, over eight million immigrants arrived in the United States, more than in any previous decade, most of them from Austria-Hungary, Greece, Italy, and Portugal.[26] Such humble people did not connect with British royalty as did those of British extraction, whose Anglophilia seemed only to intensify with the onset of greater ethnic diversity. But the recent immigrants, most of whom came from countries with monarchies, were susceptible to the tabloid allure of royal glamour, which was transforming members of the royal family into international celebrities.

*   *   *

 No spectacle enthralled American royal watchers more in the reign of Edward VII than his Coronation in Westminster Abbey, which, after some delay because of the King's appendicitis, took place on 9 August 1902. It represented the pinnacle of the King's imaginative hold over his expectant audience, confirming Bagehot's belief that people bowed down before the '*theatrical show*' of their rulers.[27] In various American cities, British societies held special services and commemorative dinners. President Theodore Roosevelt appointed Whitelaw Reid, who had been the American plenipotentiary at Queen Victoria's Diamond Jubilee, as a special ambassador to the Coronation. Representatives of the United States Army and Navy and J. P. Morgan Jr, who was well known to the King through charitable campaigns, joined the American contingent. Such an event required not only an official delegation from Washington but also a princely gesture, and Reid duly arrived in England with America's Coronation gift, a picture of George Washington in Masonic regalia by the American artist Robert Gordon Hardy.[28]

 When the British government announced the programme in May, the American papers filled their columns with details of the ceremony. In distant Omaha and San Antonio, as well as New York and Boston, readers studied the arcane rituals of the 'Anthem', the 'Litany', the 'Presenting of the Spurs and Sword', the 'Inthronization', the 'Communion' and the 'Recess'. On the day, it was quite a 'show'. In the Abbey choir, the American Ambassador Joseph Choate sat in his 'democratic black coat', in striking contrast with the brilliant dress of those around him. Such radical garb did not detract from the mix of royal mystification, festive music, lavish costumes and priceless jewels, so much medieval mummery greeted by wildly enthusiastic crowds. Unlike Queen Victoria's Coronation, all went smoothly, apart from the tottering Archbishop of Canterbury, who had to be helped back to his seat after the crowning. 'Simply amazing in its perfection', reported the *New York Times*, 'whether compared with the generality of State festivals elsewhere or with the spectacles of the theatre, which it inevitably suggested.'[29]

Such reports were just what the monarchy ordered, and fostered, through its growing contacts with the press. Edward VII's advisers believed that the projection of ancient ritual into modern life was part of the royal magic. They took the view that coronations, like other royal pageants, were fixed constitutional landmarks, which, in a rapidly changing world, provided institutional continuity, making change easier to accept.[30] One of the subconscious attractions of royal pageantry to Americans was that it reflected their own aspirations for the United States. 'The paradox of American history', it has been said, is 'a faith in the inevitability of progress coupled with a desire to see America remain unchanged.'[31]

The Coronation seems to have unsettled a few American commentators, reminding them of the shortcomings of the United States social and political order. One anonymous United States witness observed that all the settled belief of Americans in the sovereignty of the people should lead to a condemnation of such pageantry as false to the spirit of the age. Yet no one who experienced the show in Westminster Abbey could avoid a 'sympathetic emotional thrill', a feeling that monarchy may be 'wise and salutary'. Without a royal family as a focal point of society, he suggested, America was prey to a plutocracy scrambling for the regalia. Were Americans being true to republican principles and democratic simplicity? 'The idea all over the Continent of Europe is that money counts for everything with us; that it is the only true bulwark of our liberties, the only source of our pride. ... The truest American, after contemplating this latest splendid royal exhibition, the coronation of King Edward VII, will be less likely to exclaim "I thank thee I am not as other men", than "be merciful to me a sinner".'[32]

Another American observer of the Coronation thought it was a source of 'endless wonder and amusement' that the monarchy should be taken so seriously in England. But he was a man who saw Montaigne's 'noble farce', in which kings and emperors played to a universal audience, from both sides of the constitutional aisle:

The forms of democracy seem so much more reasonable than the tradition of royalty presiding over a 'veiled republic.' But our British cousins smile at us in their turn and point to the sceptre of real power which we leave in the hands of an uncrowned autocrat of the financial world – who may be hobnobbing at the moment with an emperor on the deck of a royal yacht. ... The English will go on crowning their kings and reverencing their princelings, living their lives of individual liberty, and paying national homage to a sovereign who represents in his person both the dignity of office and strict limitations of power. Are they the poorer for their traditions, or we the richer for ours, as the world goes?[33]

*   *   *

After the spectacle of the Coronation, Edward VII may have seemed a distant presence to most Americans. But the British monarchy always sustained a following in the United States in the years between popular set-piece royal events. The large number of Queen Victoria's descendants – there were 536 of them by 1990 – increased the scope for seeing a member of the royal family in person.[34] And with the growth in tourism across the Atlantic, more and more Americans came into contact with the culture of royalty. Apart from the presentations at court, tens of thousands of ordinary Americans had recollections of the Tower of London, Buckingham Palace Mews or Windsor Castle, which they shared, along with photographs and the associated royal memorabilia, with their friends and families back home. Meanwhile, the United States papers featured royal news of the King's habits, travels and diplomatic efforts, though they were prone to concentrate on the glamour, lavish dinners, and any American association, however slight.

Although Theodore Roosevelt was wary of Britain, which he saw as a rival, he also felt 'a sincere friendliness toward England'.[35] Edward VII was not unaware of the President's dividedness of mind. In his first term, the *New York Times* reported that the King was especially cordial to American diplomats and expressed the warmest admiration for the President, and pleasure that his influence was cementing relations between Britain and the United States.[36] References to the mutual admiration of President Roosevelt and King Edward increased American impressions that the King was a friend of the United States and a presence on the world stage. Some even saw a likeness between the two men.[37] Did they know that Roosevelt descended from the kings of Scotland? The *National Magazine* proudly announced that since the President's mother 'was lineally descended from the royal house of Scotland, President Roosevelt is as truly of royal lineage as Edward VII of England, also descended from kings of Scotland'.[38]

Despite his drop of royal blood, Roosevelt was deeply conscious of the difference between the Presidency and the role of a constitutional king like Edward VII. Yet he saw the Presidency in the light of the classic definition of monarchy: the rule of one. He wrote to the historian George Otto Trevelyan in 1904 that while fools would misunderstand the terminology he could best express to a foreigner the power of a president by describing him as an 'elective King'.[39] The growing power and prestige of the Presidency under Roosevelt was in keeping with the expansion of American interests. Not surprisingly, those former calls to republican simplicity and modesty in dealing with the wider world were on the wane in his administration. In the transformation of the American Presidency, his monarchical tendencies did not go unnoticed, which led Henry James to call him 'Theodore Rex', the title of Edmund Morris's biography of Roosevelt.[40]

Over the years, the two 'kings' became correspondents. In a world in which the world powers 'were increasingly at odds, both men had reasons to wish to strengthen relations across the Atlantic. Roosevelt, the stoic who relaxed by killing animals, made no secret that John Bull was unwelcome in the western hemisphere, but he did not wish to alienate the King. Edward VII, the epicurean who more often found his pleasures indoors, befriended the President as part of the monarchy's strategy for survival in an era of growing British uneasiness about its place in the world. American diplomats, who were increasingly significant players on the world stage, were thus his potential allies, not least in moderating Roosevelt's suspicion of Britain. Whitelaw Reid, who was appointed Ambassador in London in 1905, became an intimate of the King and acted as a go-between, sending enthusiastic accounts of his royal host back to Roosevelt in Washington. 'The more you know him, the better I am sure you will like him, and the more you will come to the prevalent English, and in fact European belief, that he is the greatest mainstay of peace in Europe.'[41]

In early 1905, the King wrote a personal letter of congratulations to the President on his re-election:

You, Mr President, and I have been called upon to superintend the destinies of the two great branches of the Anglo-Saxon race, and this fact should in my opinion alone suffice to bring us together.

It has indeed often seemed strange to me that, being as I am on intimate terms with the Rulers of Europe, I should not be in closer touch with the President of the United States. It would be agreeable to me, and I think advantageous to both countries that this state of things should in future cease to exist.

As a slight indication of the feelings which I have endeavoured to express, it gives me great pleasure to ask your acceptance of the accompanying miniature of a great Englishman, Hampden, who was once a landowner in America. I do so in memory of the old Country and as a mark of my esteem and regard for yourself. . . .[42]

The gift of the miniature of John Hampden, who had led a rebellion against the monarchy in the seventeenth century, was another calculated royal nod to the American republic.[43]

The President graciously replied:

On the eve of the inauguration Sir Mortimer handed me your Majesty's very kind letter and the miniature of Hampden, than which I could have appreciated nothing more. . . . I absolutely agree with you as to the importance, not merely to ourselves but to all the free peoples of the civilised world, of a constantly growing friendship between the English-speaking peoples. . . . To foster it, we need judgement and moderation no less than the good will itself. The larger interests of the two nations are the same; and the fundamental, underlying traits of their characters are also the same'.[44]

In exchange for the miniature of Hampden, Roosevelt sent the King his book, *The Winning of the West.* But as he wrote to Ambassador Reid, he did 'not expect the King to read the book – merely to receive it'.[45] The King later sent Roosevelt a book on the Sevres porcelain in the Royal Collection, which the President, who had an interest in china, may have actually read.

The bond between the King and the President, like the bond between the two countries, had a basis in their pride in the English-speaking people. The strength of the prevailing Anglo-Saxon ideology was such that Roosevelt did not see his name and background as an obstacle to promoting an Anglo-Saxon interpretation of American history.[46] Given all the talk of the communion of the English-speaking peoples, a wit in the London *Review of Reviews* called for the annexation of Great Britain by America 'to make common cause against the all-encompassing arms of the trust octopus'.[47] A common language and culture had long been at the heart of the distinctive relationship between the two countries, but now the issue of immigration was welling up in their respective dominions. Roosevelt wrote a letter to Edward VII in February 1908, which touched on the voyage of the American fleet around the world and the question of immigration:

I feel very strongly that the real interests of the English-speaking peoples are one, alike in the Atlantic and Pacific; and that, while scrupulously careful neither to insult nor to injure others we should yet make it evident that we are ready and able to hold our own. In no country where the population is of our stock, and where the wage workers, the laborers, are of the same blood as the employing classes, will it be possible to introduce a large number of workmen of an utterly alien race without the certainty of dangerous friction. The only sure way to avoid such friction, with its possible conse-quences of incalculable disaster, is by friendly agreement in advance to prevent the coming together in mass of the wage workers of the two races, in either country.

But for the moment our internal problems here are far more pressing than our external ones. With us it is not as it is with you; our men of vast wealth do not fully realize that great responsibility must always go hand in hand with great privilege.[48]

The King replied:

We have watched with the greatest interest the cruise of your fine Fleet in the Pacific and have admired the successful manner in which your Admirals have so far carried out this great undertaking. . . .

I entirely agree with you that the interests of the English speaking peoples are alike in the Atlantic and the Pacific, and I look forward with confidence to the co-operation of the English speaking races becoming the most powerful civilizing factor in the policy of the World.

The question of the immigration and competition of coloured races in other Countries is one which presents many difficulties, and especially to me, who have so many coloured subjects in my Empire. It is one, however, which has, so far, proved capable of adjustment by friendly negotiation. . . .[49]

Such issues would have been on the agenda of the two men had they met. One of the last acts of Edward VII was to approve the arrangements for a dinner that was to have been given for the Roosevelts at Buckingham Palace on 20 May 1910. It was the day of the King's burial at St George's Chapel.[50]

*   *   *

When beggars die, there are no comets seen;
The heavens themselves blaze forth the death of princes.[51]

Edward VII left kingship as he entered it – in style. The King's funeral, like his Coronation, was a triumph of showmanship. It is unknown just how many Americans joined the quarter of a million people who filed silently through Westminster Hall where the body lay in state. But for the thousands of Americans who witnessed the King's coffin borne through the London streets, followed by the German Emperor and eight kings, the spectacle was another unforgettable royal event, more memorable in its solemn grandeur than the funeral procession of Queen Victoria a decade earlier. But like most of the spectators from around the world, the American visitors would have been largely oblivious to the impending dangers to the royal houses of Europe from imperial and dynastic rivalries. When the muffled bell of Big Ben tolled as the

King left Buckingham Palace for the last time, they did not divine, in Barbara Tuchman's words, that 'the sun of the old world was setting in a dying blaze of splendour never to be seen again'.[52]

Ex-President Roosevelt, who rode amidst the princes of Europe in the magnificent funeral procession as special envoy of the United States, saw the King's death as a blow to the cause of world peace. In a widely-reported statement he sent condolences on behalf of the American people:

> We in America keenly appreciated King Edward's personal good will toward us, which he so frequently and so markedly showed, and we are well aware of the devotion felt for him by his subjects throughout the British empire, while all foreign nations have learned to see in the King a ruler whose great abilities, and especially his tact, his judgment, and his unfailing kindliness of nature, rendered him peculiarly fit to work for international peace and justice. . . .
>
> I have a personal feeling about the King's death. I know from having been President that he had an earnest desire to keep the relations between Great Britain and the United States on the closest and most friendly terms. King Edward's death removes an influence that tended strongly for peace and justice in international relations. His own people and those of other lands must feel that loss.[53]

For all King Edward's magnetism, there was less sadness and sense of loss in the United States than there had been over Queen Victoria's death. Americans found it difficult to see Edward VII, unlike his mother, in a quasi-religious light. Still, he had built up a devoted following in the United States by his charm and reputation as a conciliator. He would have taken wry enjoyment from the tribute in the *Hartford Courant* that said he 'was both an aristocrat and a democrat at the same time'.[54] A comment by a Boston clergyman suggested that the racial language of the nineteenth century persisted: 'Not as Americans and not as Englishmen, but as Anglo-Saxons do we gather to worship the god of our fathers. Today two nations kneel at one bier.'[55] In the days after his death, memorial services were held across the country, diplomats paid their respects, and the House of Representatives adjourned, but few American flags were lowered. Appropriately, the Broadway theatres marked his passing by playing 'God Save the King' at the end of their performances. It was a fitting tribute to the greatest royal impresario in British history.

*   *   *

The prestige of Edward VII seamlessly transferred to his successor, the 45-year-old George V, who asked his Consul General in New York to thank

16. Photo of King Edward VII with son Prince George (later George V) and grandson Prince Edward (later Edward VIII), 1908.

Americans for their 'many tokens of sympathy and sorrow'.[56] There seems little doubt that King George was a dutiful, if old-fashioned patriot, with more than a passing resemblance to his grandmother, Queen Victoria. Like her, he was censorious and intolerant of dissenting opinion; and though devoted to domestic life, he mistook parental responsibility for a variation on naval drill. Ill-educated, unimaginative, and rarely contradicted in social intercourse, he too easily assumed that his conception of the world was an expression of some hierophantic truth. Like the British, the American people knew little about the

King's personality, or the tensions in the royal family, especially between the King and his eldest son and heir, Prince Edward, who became the Prince of Wales on his sixteenth birthday in 1910, soon after his father succeeded to the throne.

Drawing on British reports, the mainstream American press fed its growing public a steady diet of royal news at the beginning of the reign. King George's Coronation in June 1911, which caused a surge in American bookings for the transatlantic liners, excited the hyperbole and overkill by then associated with any royal ritual. In New York, several theatres showed the latest 'Kinemacolor' motion pictures of the event. Writing for the *New York Times*, the novelist Marie Corelli called it an event 'never surpassed in all history', a ceremony of such seductive grandeur that it would effectively dish socialism for a genera-tion.[57] What she thought about the awesome display of imperial grandeur at the Durbar in Delhi later in the year, when the King-Emperor received the homage of his Indian subjects, is unknown. It was arguably the greatest spec-tacle ever organized by the British monarchy. To the more astute American commentators, it was of great political significance because of rising Indian nationalism. But to most of the Americans who watched the Durbar on news-reel, it was something of a second act of the Coronation.

By the reign of George V, press coverage of the royal family was becoming a double-edged sword. Newsreels and Kinemacolor were recent inventions, but photographs of royalty had been commonplace since Queen Victoria's day, and the monarchy had often taken trouble to help out with the results. But in 1911, the so-called 'snapshotters', who would later be dubbed the paparazzi, provided an example of what was to come in the life of the royal family. The King and the Prince of Wales were at Cowes regatta, an annual event favoured by royalty, Americans, and photographers. The photographers had agreed not to enter the royal bathing place, but one or two of them broke the contract and took some pictures of the royal party. To the King, this was 'an intolerable nuisance'. The *New York Times* took a different line, which would be taken increasingly by the press, that 'royalty needs advertising to make it popular just as much as anybody's soap'.[58] The comment – perhaps the first to associate royalty with 'soap' – suggests that changes in technology were beginning to encourage editors to switch from royal adulation to royal disregard in order to boost sales.

The photographers were much in evidence during the five-day visit to the United States in 1912 of Queen Victoria's son, the Duke of Connaught, who was then Governor General of Canada. Having visited the United States in 1870, he knew that reporters would be waiting in ambush. To avoid the 'snapshotters' at their arrival at Grand Central Station, the Duke and Duchess resorted to a luggage lift to reach their motorcar. As royal celebrities they were cheered in the streets and relentlessly pursued by the press. As they entered the Stock Exchange – that symbol of rapacity to many Americans – a photographer jumped on top of a hearse, which contained a coffin, to get a better view. Despite the private nature of the visit, everyone knew of the royal presence in New York, and a motorcade down Broadway and a visit to Grant's tomb only heightened the public expectation. Playing to the crowd while wishing to remain mysterious would become a feature of royalty on tour in America.

The Duke and Duchess declined 200 invitations from well-wishing Americans, but they could not ignore the plutocrats. The Morgans and the Vanderbilts, who were among their hosts, guided them through their fabulous treasures and marbled palaces, and the ostentatious display of wealth shocked even the Duchess.[59] The visit provided yet further instances of the treatment of British royalty by America's wealthiest citizens. In his novel *Democracy*, Henry Adams called it 'the respect which all republicans who have a large income derived from business feel for English royalty'.[60] The tycoons were generous to a fault, but intrusive and dangerously seductive to a family that claimed a higher purpose than ornamentation. To many Palace officials, accustomed to aristocratic discretion in matters to do with money, the conspicuous display of American wealth was simply vulgar.

American press coverage was generally sympathetic to George V, though tempered by mischievous comparisons with the amiable and cosmopolitan Edward VII. He was, they noted, able and serious, but unlike his father geniality did not come naturally to him. Taciturn by nature, he disliked society, preferring the company of the old nobility to the international smart set. Although he had twice travelled to Canada during his father's reign, he was content never to set foot in the United States. His knowledge of American culture was limited, though he once endured a game of baseball between the New York Giants and the Chicago White Sox at Chelsea – glorified rounders the British press called it.[61] To Americans it was not auspicious that he found his greatest amusement in philately. The new court would be transformed, noted the *New York Times* at the beginning of the reign: 'It is understood that the new monarch is not fond of Americans. . . . It is not to be supposed that there is any prejudice towards Americans as Americans. . . . It is simply that he prefers Englishmen and Englishwomen to foreigners of any nationality'.[62]

In contrast with their view of the dutiful and sombre King, Americans thought the heir to the throne an independent 'democratic spirit'.[63] Though not a brilliant scholar, the Prince of Wales was amiable and popular with people of all ranks. When he began to make regular appearances in society just before the First World War, commentators noticed that unlike his father, but like his grandfather, he had a particular fondness for American women. Queen Mary, who sought to influence the character of her son's entourage, was known to erase the names of American women from the invitation lists of her friends. She would have been puzzled by the view abroad that American women were livelier than their English cousins. 'Possibly owing to their democratic bringing up,' remarked the *New York Times*, 'they do not stand in as much awe of royalty, even when it is incarnated in a stripling, as does the average Englishwoman, whose obsequiousness is calculated to make a youth like the Prince feel uncomfortable.'[64] A pushy American woman, though not notably democratic, would, of course, be Prince Edward's undoing when he became King.

The First World War brought George V and his family face to face with Americans, who impressed the Prince of Wales decidedly more than his parents. The Prince served as a staff officer at the front, mixing happily, it was said, with all and sundry. Reports of his dancing with American nurses attracted attention in the United States press, as did the fictitious story of his being shot by the jealous husband of a French waitress while taking tea at an inn.[65] Initially, he had been critical of the United States for letting the allies do the fighting. But once the Americans joined the war effort, his views changed. On a visit to their headquarters at Coblenz, 25,000 United States troops paraded in the Prince's honour. Impressed by American discipline, the Prince wrote to his father that the United States:

> are a big power in the world now, I might say the next biggest after ourselves, and they are worth while making *real* friends with . . . I'm just crammed full of American ideas just now, and they want me to 'go over to them' as soon as possible, which is another item for consideration and one that should not be 'pigeon-holed'.[66]

The Prime Minister, Lloyd George, is credited with the idea of sending the Prince on a series of tours, the first to Canada and the United States in 1919, for he was worried that pent-up demand for reform threatened the Empire with disintegration. The Prime Minister was perhaps not fully aware just how well his own political concerns dovetailed with the worries of Palace officials, who believed that the monarchy should cultivate the Empire and the United States for its own ends. With Labour on the march, the aristocracy in retreat, and nationalism on the rise in the Empire, the Crown was feeling less secure. The disappearance of five emperors and eight kings at the end of the First World War had concentrated the British monarchical mind. In such a context, it was judicious to carry on the policy of Edward VII and have the Americans on board the royal bandwagon.

There were serious reservations about plunging the untried Prince into the American maelstrom as the ambassador of Empire. As to the itinerary, there were worries about including New York on the tour. The Prince's Chief of Staff, Admiral Sir Lionel Halsey, believed that it would upset the Canadians, who saw the monarchy as a way of differentiating themselves from the United States and frowned on American attentions to *their* royal family. Moreover, New York was seen to be a hotbed of Bolsheviks and Irish nationalists; and, as Halsey put it, with a touch of superciliousness, the reception committee would be made up of 'disgruntled Irishmen and a very doubtful lot of hyphenated Americans'.[67] There were also worries about the incessant demands that Americans would make on the Prince. One British diplomat observed, in keeping with a widespread view abroad, just 'how restless the Americans are and how they have to be on the go the whole time and expect other people to do the same'.[68]

Though officially delighted with the idea of the Prince's trip, George V remained unconvinced that his son was up to the job of royal ambassador. There was royal apprehension about the planned meeting with President Wilson, which was to be the climax of the visit. King George and Wilson had for some years exchanged birthday greetings and wartime messages, in which they stressed the need for friendly relations.[69] In 1918, the King entertained Wilson at Buckingham Palace and toasted the President with a flattering speech in which he paid the customary lip service to the bonds of literature and ancestry that joined the two nations together. But the King and his advisers were not admirers of the President, whom they took to be an unimpressive busybody intent on uprooting monarchism in Europe.[70] When Wilson refused the King's request to send the American Army into Russia to save the country from Bolshevism, the King told a friend: 'After that I never thought very much of him.'[71]

Such views underscored the King's reservations about the Prince of Wales making a diplomatic visit to Washington. But the perceived need for a public relations offensive in the United States overrode his doubts. In a memorandum prepared for the Colonial Secretary, the political adviser Edward Grigg observed that the chief object of the Prince's tour of Canada and the United States was 'to create an atmosphere' by his 'natural tact and charm' and to persuade North Americans that the monarchy was more than a 'feudal anachronism'. Lloyd George, alert to American sensitivities, insisted that the Prince should avoid any remarks that would look 'like a challenge to republican institutions'.[72]

Ironically, as the Prince set sail, complaints could be heard in America that the United States had lapsed into autocracy and monarchy during Wilson's

17. Woodrow Wilson and George V leaving Charing Cross station in a carriage, 1918.

Presidency, a view that has adherents today among Wilson scholars.[73] Wilson was happy to see the collapse of the Habsburgs, but his own monarchical leanings were on display at the peace negotiations in Paris in 1919. The same year the English political scientist Graham Wallas gave a series of lectures at Yale, which he later published in a book titled *Our Social Heritage*. He noted, no doubt with Wilson in mind, that the future of monarchy was of an 'elective' nature, which may 'be found in the President of the United States'. He did not comment on the tour of the Prince of Wales, but concluded that elective monarchy had 'most of the dangers of hereditary power without its advantage of security of succession'.[74]

Prince Edward's American tour was carefully prepared by British officialdom and went off largely as planned, apart from an initial hiccup caused by Wilson's stroke. The Prince dutifully visited the President, only recently returned from Paris, who was propped up in Lincoln's bed in the White House. They exchanged platitudes. Years later, the Prince recalled that 'the ravages of partisan politics' had left Wilson with 'the most disappointed face that I had ever looked upon'.[75] To the Washington Press Club, he made an innocuous speech, which impressed his audience for its democratic air: 'Your institutions, your ways of life, your aims are as democratic as ours, and the atmosphere in which I find myself is the same invigorating and familiar atmosphere which I have always noticed in my American friends.'[76] More to the Prince's taste, for he was a mediocre speaker, were the dances laid on in his honour, at which many a debutante left in a swoon. As one of his aides said of him, 'he holds very strongly that he can influence American feeling even better by dancing with Senators' daughters than by talking to Senators'.[77]

18. Prince of Wales at the tomb of Washington, 1919.

In Washington, the Prince paid his respects to the American wounded at Walter Reed General Hospital and was the guest of honour at a reception in the Library of Congress, where he met members of the Senate and the House of Representatives. Following in his grandfather's footsteps, he visited Mount Vernon, where he laid a wreath on the tomb of George Washington. A few days later he made a semi-private trip to Oyster Bay on Long Island, where he laid a wreath on the grave of Teddy Roosevelt, who had died earlier that year. Among his other official duties he visited the Naval Academy at Annapolis with the Assistant Secretary of the Navy, Franklin D. Roosevelt, an outing made more memorable by the motorcycle outriders, who, drunk on bootleg liquor, grazed the car and veered into the gutter on the way back to Dupont Circle.[78]

Advisers steered the Prince away from Newport, which had a reputation in Britain for frivolity, but he visited New York despite the nervousness about including the city on the tour. His minders need not have worried about the Irish or the Bolsheviks, for the Prince was given a rapturous welcome without any unseemly incidents. In scenes reminiscent of the visit of his grandfather in 1860, a girl broke through the Broadway crowd and kissed him on the cheek. In later life he recalled the ticker-tape parade: 'This masterpiece of acclamation in my honour was thrilling beyond description. Half-asphyxiated by the smell of gasoline, I found myself sitting up on the back of the motor, bowing and waving like an actor who had been summoned by a tremendous curtain call.'[79] The City made him an honorary 'citizen', and the Prince replied in kind, calling New Yorkers 'fellow citizens', a usage that would have shocked his parents.[80]

The American press noted that the Prince bore a striking resemblance to Edward VII: he had the same build, the same mental makeup, and the same taste for brandy and soda, which presented difficulties in a country with prohibition. Like his grandfather's visit in 1860, his presence in the country spurred the Americans to concoct fabulous stories of the different women who might serve as a future wife. 'It is difficult to conceive how newspapers can give way to such vulgarity', remarked Lord Stamfordham, the King's Private Secretary.[81] The British Ambassador in Washington said that the Prince created 'a feeling of personal affection' in New York.[82] For many Americans the affection had to do with the Prince's modernity, and his being the world's most glamorous bachelor. The Prince not only left a trail of adoring women in his wake but also inspired a romantic comedy, *Just Suppose*, by the playwright Albert E. Thomas, which was performed at the National Theatre in Washington a few months after his visit. (It was made into a film in 1926.) It was not without a prophetic quality, for the Prince falls in love with

19. Prince of Wales visits Washington, drawing from *Chicago Daily Tribune,* 1919.

an American girl and offers to give up his right to the throne for her hand.[83] Did Wallis Simpson ever see it?

Back in Britain, the press covered the Prince's every move and reported that he heralded 'a new British line in democracy! He's a good little salesman, with winning smiles, and prepared to put old prejudices aside and open up a good line of credit with his house!'[84] 'A regular fellow', whose smile 'carried him across a continent', remarked the *Sunday Express*.[85] The Prince's resistance to the pre-war brand of royal stodginess was never far from the surface in the British commentary. 'A Prince among Democrats', declared the *Daily Telegraph*, which hailed the trip as 'a conquest of affection'.[86] Like the American papers, the British ones followed any scent of romance. The *Evening Standard* retailed details of his favourite partner while in New York, Miss Millicent Rogers, the pretty daughter of an oil millionaire. 'For the women he has the grace, dignity, and charm of the princes of legend and romance. For the men he has qualities of good sportsmanship and good fellowship.'[87]

Whether the tour persuaded many Americans that the British monarchy was relevant to the modern world is questionable, but it convinced them that the Prince of Wales was at least one member of the royal family who was not a 'feudal anachronism'. The Prince was seen as his own man and not simply as a royal ambassador. Clearly, he did his diplomatic job, laying a wreath on Grant's tomb, graciously accepting a medal from Yale University, and sending uplifting messages to the Boy Scouts and Girl Scouts of America. Throughout the visit he related to Americans as individuals, not simply as potential allies. Here was an heir to the throne who wished to enjoy a private life distinguished from his royal duties, a point of view that Americans found modern and attractive. The seemingly democratic Prince, without that air of superiority that the Americans disliked in British visitors, further shifted American perceptions about royalty. In an America ever more conscious of celebrity, he was widely seen as the ultimate in glamour.

*   *   *

For the royal family, America was becoming a test bed of its popularity, a measure of its social influence and world renown. Successful royal visits to the United States gave the monarchy a patina of democratic respectability that served its purposes back home. At the end of the First World War, with the imperial monarchy on the wane, the royal family and its advisers developed a strategy of forging bonds of affection across the English-speaking world. The Prince was not a social reformer by temperament, despite the propaganda to the contrary; but he was susceptible to parental pressure. Just as the Prince sought to convince the English, Scots and Welsh that the monarchy was sympathetic to their aspirations, he also sought to convince Americans and

20. Prince of Wales in New York reviewing troops, 1919.

Imperial subjects of his sincerity and commitment to democracy. His good-will visits to the mining and industrial areas in Britain, which he came to call his 'provincial forays', were the flip side of his foreign tours.[88]

As the North American tour confirmed, the Prince of Wales was in the vanguard of internationalizing royalty. As heir to the throne, he connected with Canadian subjects in an official capacity and was rarely free from the restraints of his position. In the United States, he took on the role of a roving ambassador and connected more informally with the citizenry, who had relatively little interest in British politics. He could take comfort in the constitutional and political affinities between the two countries, while indulging his own tastes and predilections relatively free from parental supervision. In his view, America served as something of a safe haven, a place where he felt liberated from the constraints of his life at home. As he put it, 'America meant to me a country in which nothing was impossible.'[89] But the Prince's hedonistic private life often got in the way of the public duty pressed on him by his family and the British government.

A return visit to the United States in 1924 made it abundantly clear, at least in Palace circles, that royal dignity suffered from the Prince's lifestyle.

21. Prince of Wales in rowboat at Waikiki Beach, Honolulu, April 1920.

Importantly, this trip marked an irreconcilable breakdown in his relations with his advisers, who did not share the Prince's view that he had a right to a private life. On his return to America, the press coverage was less gentle than previously, with some papers intent on reducing him to a libertine. The headline in the *Atlanta Constitution* suggested the dangers: 'Society Stampedes From Summer Harbors to Snare Chance to Meet Royal Prince.'[90] As his official biographer Philip Ziegler remarks: 'in 1919 society women had gushed about the Prince as a "charming boy". Now he had sunk, or perhaps graduated, to the status of "a gay young man" ', with all the attendant dangers for the heir to the throne, who was under constant scrutiny.[91] The glare of publicity threatened to shed daylight on the royal magic and expose the Prince as just another titled playboy.

As his ship, the *Berengaria*, steamed into New York a female reporter asked the Prince whether he would marry an American 'gal' if he fell in love with one. He answered in the affirmative.[92] In hope, aspiring matrons and expectant debs pursued him relentlessly during his stay, leading to a game of wits in which the Prince had to shift from car to car to avoid their attentions.[93] The hedonistic Prince insisted that he was simply on holiday and spent much of his time on

Long Island dancing, playing polo, and drinking in public with a set of flashy Americans, whom the British Ambassador, Esmé Howard, disparaged as 'oily magnates'.[94]

Among his many worries, the Ambassador had to find a way to transport illegal alcohol to Long Island for royal consumption. But this turned out to be the least of his worries. When the wallet of the Prince's Equerry, Fruity Metcalfe, was discovered behind a radiator in the apartment of an 'actress' on West 72nd Street, New York society gasped and the Hearst papers, unfriendly to royalty, revelled in the scandal.[95] Meanwhile, the United States religious press attacked the Prince for failing to attend church. Ambassador Howard wrote to the King's Private Secretary that the next time the Prince came to America 'he should avoid dances on Saturday nights and go to church on Sunday mornings'.[96]

The peccadilloes remained unmentioned in the Prince's dutiful letters to 'Papa' from America, though he confessed that he had been to a few parties. But 'Papa' was very well aware of his son's racy conduct. The monarchy paid close attention to the reception given to members of the royal family while on tour abroad. In keeping with tradition, George V kept a nervous eye on his son's movements and blanched as he read the American newspaper reports compiled for his attention by Palace officials. He could hardly avoid the conclusion that the Prince's behaviour threatened to undermine the carefully constructed royal relationship with America, which had been built up since the 1860s. The effect of all the uninhibited American journalism, the Prince later wrote, 'was that my father privately broke off relations between America and the members of his family'. It was a 'bitter disappointment' to him that whenever he or his brothers advanced some scheme that would take them to the United States, 'a series of vague but irremovable obstacles always appeared to block us'.[97]

In the years following the Prince's visits to the United States, the American press supplied a rich diet of news about his travels and fashion sense, laced with gossip about his liaisons and marital plans. For Americans, he was the ultimate darling of the mass media, who commanded respect and veneration less because of his actions than because of his royal descent. The Prince enjoyed an extraordinary fame largely because he personified class and style in a materialist democracy in which routine and blandness typified everyday life.[98] Elinor Glyn, now an expatriate in Hollywood, described celebrity as being endowed with the mysterious 'It', the title of one of her 1920s romantic fictions. As an idolater of all things royal, she might have had the Prince in mind when she wrote that the lucky possessors of 'It' had a personal magnetism and effortless superiority built on self-confidence, physical attraction, and a cavalier indifference to the effect their actions have on others, which she compared to the captivating, 'unbidd-able' nature of cats in the animal kingdom.[99]

The unbiddable Prince, idolized at home and abroad, did as much as anyone of his generation to foster the culture of celebrity in the United States. In turn, America's ever more powerful popular culture propelled his fame worldwide. But the pressures and dynamism of America only increased the tensions between the old guard at Buckingham Palace and the trendy Prince. While intending to bring Britain and the United States closer together, the Prince's American visits magnified their cultural differences. When he broke with royal convention by smoking at the cinema or dancing to jazz, courtiers and the respectable classes in England twittered over their teacups. In the United States, where his choice of cravat excited comment, such behaviour was taken as a sign of modernity and progress. To the Prince, an American *manqué*, the United States was a land free of courtly constraint. To the King, it was a republic of whorish women and unseemly friends, who represented a potential danger to the Crown.

The Prince's very popularity in America fuelled his determination to make a distinction between his private life and his public duties. Such a distinction was anathema to his aides, who were beginning to question his suitability for the throne, and to his nitpicking parents, who were prone to censure their son for his lack of *gravitas* or for the cut of his uniform. King George and Queen Mary were acutely aware of their son's failings, and they did their best to steer him in the direction of royal decorum, public service, and a suitable – preferably British – wife. For them the monarchy could only survive if it maintained its traditions, which were being undermined by the behaviour of the heir to the throne, who placed his private life above his public duty. The tensions between the killjoy King and Queen and the errant Prince only heightened when a woman from Baltimore, Wallis Simpson, a 34-year-old divorcée and the wife of a London businessman, appeared on the scene in 1931.[100]

CHAPTER 7

SPECIAL RELATIONSHIPS

There is always in this country a certain amount of criticism of and super-
ficial ill feeling toward the British, in time of danger something deeper comes
to the surface, and the British and we stand firmly together, with confidence
in our common heritage and ideas.

Eleanor Roosevelt, *This I Remember*, 1949

If Prince Edward's distinguishing mark was his social position, Wallis Simpson's
was her social ambition. As her biographer, Michael Bloch, observes: 'She could
not be considered beautiful. . . . She was neither rich nor well educated. There
was nothing outstanding about her manners or conversation. She had no
sporting, artistic or intellectual achievements to her name. Of politics, history,
the great movements of the day, she knew nothing.'[1] The fact that Mrs Simpson
had a flair for cards, fashionable clothes, and interior design does not explain
her allure. Just why the Prince of Wales, accustomed to a Niagara of attractive
women descending on him, fell in love with her remains something of a
mystery, though he may have desired to be bossed and babied by someone less
adamantine than Queen Mary. Perhaps, as a British diplomat observed, the
Prince simply had 'an unsatisfied craving for domesticity'.[2] His first conversation
with Mrs Simpson turned on differing British and American attitudes towards
central heating.

Much has been made of Wallis Simpson's adventurous background, not
least during her time in China. But tales of her highly-developed sexual
prowess, which was said to give her a 'hold' over men, seem far-fetched.[3] A
more likely explanation for her power over the Prince of Wales was that she
resisted his advances. In her ghosted memoir, *The Heart Has Its Reasons*

(1956), she noted the 'sage advice' given to her by her grandmother: 'Never allow a man to kiss your hand. If you do, he'll never ask you to marry him.'[4] One confidante remarked that the Duchess once told a friend that she never permitted a man to touch her 'below the Mason-Dixon line', and that she did not consummate her first two marriages.[5] To the end of his life, the Duke of Windsor, often dubbed a 'lady killer' in the American tabloids, denied any suggestion that he had made love to his wife before their marriage. He once threatened to sue the historian Sir John Wheeler-Bennett for describing Mrs Simpson as having been his 'mistress'.[6] If we are to believe him, he gave up the throne for a woman who had the audacity to say 'no'!

Mrs Simpson, who was presented at court in 1931, became the Prince's chosen companion in 1934. But few in England outside their immediate circle knew anything about their relationship, for the British press, unlike the American, respected the convention that royalty was off limits. The couple's social circle consisted of a smart set of prominent English people and American businessmen, diplomats, and celebrities, not the sort much in evidence at Buckingham Palace. As his choice of friends suggested, the Prince had long admired the American outlook. According to Harold Nicolson, he was 'a good mixer', always eager to talk about America.[7] Though the Prince never sought the company of serious Americans, it was said that he was able to break through social convention and connect with people, which was thought to be an American trait. Anne Morrow Lindbergh, the wife of Charles Lindbergh, noted that the Prince 'seemed quite American' in this respect and paid him the back-handed compliment that he was 'the most "human" Englishman I've met'.[8] The Member of Parliament and diarist Chips Channon also thought the Prince 'Americanised', which was not meant as a compliment, for it made 'him over-democratic, casual and a little common'.[9]

Mrs Simpson, whose London life before meeting the Prince centred on American socialites and her husband's business friends, was less enthusiastic about the English than the Prince was about the Americans. An undated entry in her commonplace book reveals her own personal twist on her country's special relationship with England, which reflected the growing sense among Americans that the mother country was on the slide as a great power:

In spite of your heroic qualities, your endurance, your chivalry, your unselfishness, you cannot last. Your brain is going, and you are going at the knees. The centuries bow you to the ground. Tradition fetters your limits. The past clogs the present. But we nations who have the sap of youth in us are grateful to you for giving us the strength of your stock. Your great-ness will live on in us. America is England's immortality.[10]

The *Chicago Daily Tribune* called Wallis Simpson 'a standardized Anglo-American "society" woman', who had 'not lived long enough in England to become a perfected British snob'.[11] It did not consider that she might have turned into a perfected American snob, looking down on the British from the pinnacle of privilege that her royal connection provided. Channon admired Mrs Simpson but noticed that she had 'the air of a personage, who walks into a room as though she almost expected to be curtsied to'.[12]

*   *   *

Americans broadly welcomed the accession of Edward VIII on the death of George V in January 1936. Despite the inquisitiveness of United States reporters, they had little inkling that beneath the King's surface charm and reputation for good works was a weak, selfish, and petulant individual who doubted his own suitability for the throne. The British government had recruited members of the royal family to fly the flag in the United States for three-quarters of a century, and it was taken for granted that the King would provide valued continuity between the two countries. With his charm, stylishness and admiration for America, Edward VIII seemed well-placed to revitalize the Anglo-American alliance, which was becoming increasingly important to Britain as Europe lurched from crisis to crisis. His American associations were even having an influence on his accent. Several people noticed that an American tinge had crept into the King's speech at the State Opening of Parliament in 1936. The Chicago-born Channon spotted a familiar American inflection in the way the King pronounced the word 'prog-ress'.[13] Harold Nicolson remarked on the royal reference to the 'Ammurican Government'.[14]

On the personal front, King Edward's accession triggered intense speculation about his marital intentions, not least in the United States, where there had been a longing for an American Queen since the visit of the Prince of Wales in 1860. As the reign began, a platitudinous biography, *The Bachelor Prince* by Frazier Hunt, captured the mood of uncritical admiration.[15] Choosing a bride for the sovereign became a national pastime on both sides of the Atlantic. Amateur matchmakers saw the 'dark-haired' Princess Eugenie of Greece as the favourite, with Juliana, the 'plump princess' of the Netherlands, also in the running.[16] Two days after King Edward's accession, the *Washington Post* contained an article that said he had a preference for women remote from royalty and mentioned Mrs Simpson as his 'Friend No. 1'.[17] Other United States papers followed the trail, and expectant Americans began to turn their thoughts to the possibility of an American Queen, which had an irresistible appeal to a nation suffering from royal deprivation.[18]

American press coverage of the King's friendship with Mrs Simpson increased in the summer of 1936, when the couple were seen cavorting together on a Mediterranean cruise. As the yacht *Nahlin* made its way through the waters of the Balkans the Prince was acutely aware, as he later put it, 'of the clouds that were rolling up on the horizon – not only clouds of war but clouds of private trouble for me; for the American press had become fascinated with my friendship for Wallis, and now pursued us everywhere'.[19] When the Court Circular announced in September that Mrs Simpson was to be a guest of the King at Balmoral, the American papers, unlike the British, speculated, with obvious merriment, about a possible transatlantic marriage.

Speculation heightened when rumours began to circulate that the King intended to marry Mrs Simpson. The *Washington Post* ran a story on 17 October under the headline 'King to Wed Mrs. Simpson "at Any Cost" '.[20] In a 'sidewalk survey' in the American capital a week later, every woman interviewed knew about the romance, which was in striking contrast to London, where few but those in correspondence with Americans, or who read the United States papers, had heard about it.[21] The American interest heightened when Mrs Simpson received a divorce *nisi* at the Ipswich Assizes at the end of October. The headline in one United States newspaper ran: 'King's Moll Reno'd in Wolsey's Home Town'.[22] Unlike in Britain, where the press took little notice of the divorce proceedings, uninhibited American pressmen were now unequivocal in their announcements of the King's intentions. 'KING WILL WED WALLY' declared the *New York Journal.* 'KING SETS JUNE FOR WEDDING TO MRS SIMPSON' pronounced the Boston *Record.*[23]

Such headlines did not amuse Mrs Simpson, who would have been privy to a dossier of clippings about her from American papers that were given to the King ten days before her divorce.[24] In an 'exclusive' telephone interview with the United Press on the day of her divorce she vowed never to return to America and accused the American press of 'sensationalizing' her activities: 'The things that have been said about me are almost beyond belief. . . . I feel terribly hurt and humiliated.'[25] She was particularly bitter about intrusive photographers, who followed her every movement. On the same day, a rather disingenuous leader in the *Washington Post* took up her case, saying that the rumours and speculation surrounding the King and Mrs Simpson could have 'very evil consequences' and applauded the restraint of the British press, which was hesitant to jump to conclusions about their relationship on the basis of circumstantial evidence. 'This may sound strange to us. But there is something to be said for such an attitude. Even a king . . . is entitled to his rights.'[26] (The American press clearly thought presidents had 'rights', judging from the restraint it showed over Franklin Roosevelt's and later John F. Kennedy's affairs.)

There was some resentment in official British circles that American newspapers were spreading rumours that might be circulated in the Empire.[27] The more serious American papers, like the *Washington Post*, contributed to the tittle-tattle but also discussed the national and international implications of a marriage between a British king and an American commoner. Some corre- spondents saw the match as having the potential to create an *entente cordiale*: 'There is little to rely on in Europe today with war looming on the horizon, and is it not reasonable to surmise that England would only too gladly welcome a staunch support in the United States – an ally already placed in juxtaposition to her colony of Canada?'[28] On the other hand, the *New York Times* saw the crisis as a potential tragedy for the King and the Empire. 'Probably never in modern times has a great nation been paralysed for such an apparently trivial cause.'[29]

As the *New York Times* suggested, Mrs Simpson was playing her part, however reluctantly, in the ongoing trivialization of the monarchy that the American media propelled. The preponderance of the United States press coverage concentrated on her pedigree, tastes, and former romantic attach- ments, which suggested that personality now mattered more than politics when the subject of British royalty came up. Was she descended from the Kings of the Isle of Man? Was she young enough to provide an heir? Did she dye her hair? Journalists pursued relatives, school friends and prom partners, who testified to her 'imperious charm', wit and sparkle, at least when a man entered the room. At her debut in 1914 to 1915, 'she was the belle of many balls', recalled the society editor of the *Baltimore Sun*, a former schoolmate.[30] A former sister-in-law called her 'a typical southern belle', who 'could no more keep from flirting than from breathing', and rather ungraciously revealed that Mrs Simpson's 'raven black hair' was 'decidedly brown' in her youth.[31]

Most Britons remained ignorant of the royal romance in the autumn of 1936. They remained in the dark, as one American commentator remarked, because Britain did not have any 'Broadway columnists'.[32] It would have been fascinating had some organization polled British opinion about the King's marital plans. The lack of such a survey in Britain astonished the American Institute of Public Opinion, which asked a sample of United States citizens in mid-November whether the King should marry Mrs Simpson. Of those who had a direct opinion, 61 per cent said 'yes', which perhaps was not surprising as the American press had covered the story 'as the biggest romance since Cinderella'.[33] Women were slightly less approving of the match than men. Small town voters, espe- cially from the Midwest, showed the strongest sympathy for the couple, while the strongest objections came from New England and the South, often on reli- gious grounds. Those who knew Mrs Simpson best liked the match the least. The citizens of Baltimore favoured the marriage by only 54 to 46 per cent, and on Biddle Street, where Wallis had lived as a girl, opinion divided 50–50.[34]

In a less scientific poll carried out in early December, Chicagoans voted three to one in favour of the King's marriage. 'Is the king a king or just a mouse?', asked Miss Blanche Nepil. 'The English royal blood needs refreshing,' remarked Mrs John Lang. A further survey of people in Chicago named Simpson predictably showed even more widespread support for an American royal. 'Any Simpson is regal enough to be a queen' remarked one of their number, though another took the view that her namesake did not have 'the right equipment'. A few of the more constitutionally minded Simpsons thought the King should play by the rules and abdicate.[35] This was the view shared by several of Mrs Simpson's friends and relatives. One of them observed that she had been married 'to a Navy Lieutenant, a London tradesman, and now a profligate prince. It is not a very imposing string'.[36]

No doubt many Americans, particularly non English-speaking ones, were indifferent to the royal rigmarole taking place in London, just as were many Britons. Judging from the press coverage, mixed emotions ruled on both sides of the Atlantic, but there may have been more sympathy for the King in America than in Britain.[37] But as no one polled the British public it is difficult to be sure. The general view is that when the news broke that the King wished to marry the twice-divorced Mrs Simpson, his support in Britain slipped away. But in the days before the Abdication it became increasingly clear that the King's followers were turning against him in Britain. As the former Conservative minister Leo Amery believed, 'the country as a whole was getting progressively more shocked at the idea that the King could hesitate between his duty to the Throne and his affection for a second-rate woman'.[38]

We will never know just how many Britons thought Mrs Simpson 'second-rate' simply because she was American. Many of her admirers in the United States assumed that she would be despised in Britain because of her background and supported her precisely because of it. Americans had always been sensitive to Britons who looked down their noses at benighted former colonials. During the Abdication crisis they did not always consider the wider question raised by British commentators: would the King's marriage to a divorcée, whatever her nationality, weaken the monarchy? Some Britons would have taken their directions from the moral compass of Queen Mary, who was known to look upon divorce as she would upon manslaughter. That the King could contemplate resignation over an emotional attachment to a twice-married American led her to remark: 'Really! this might be Roumania!'[39]

The King's Abdication address was broadcast on 300 United States radio stations. Within hours, Macy's was selling a record of the speech for a dollar.[40] The King's sincerity shattered many Americans, who were moved by his declaration that he could not fulfil his duty 'without the help and support of the

woman I love'. From Connecticut, the journalist John Gunther wrote to Margot
Asquith that he was 'thunderstruck' by the talk, which 'was one of the finest
things I've ever heard'.[41] A survey of American opinion the day after the
Abdication revealed a high level of interest and a wide range of opinion.
One office worker called the speech 'heartbreaking'. Another felt thought the
King 'a peach of a fellow and I admire him greatly. He is more like an American
than an Englishman'. Another still called the King a 'perfect fool' who 'forgot
his country his church and his people. I am thoroughly disgusted with him.'[42]
Carter G. Osburn, Mrs Simpson's sweetheart of debutante days, remarked: 'I
think, from the viewpoint of a gentleman, that he did the right thing, and I
resent very much, as an American myself, the idea that an American woman
would not be as good a queen as anyone else – if not better.'[43]

As the former King sailed into exile, the *New York Sun* placed Mrs Simpson
at the top of its list of outstanding women of 1936, saying that she 'affected
more people, more governments and more history than a whole carload of
feminists engaged in international activities'.[44] In an attempt to revive the
King's international reputation a society formed in Manhattan called the
'Friends of the Duke of Windsor in America'.[45] Meanwhile, the Governor of
Virginia offered the uprooted couple a haven in a colonial mansion in historic
Williamsburg.[46] The rumour spread that the couple might purchase the
Merryman estate in the Worthington valley of Maryland. Not to be upstaged,
the Mayor of Baltimore invited 'Edward and Wally' to take up residence
in Baltimore. Members of the Baltimore Advertising Club proposed to
make Mrs Simpson its citizen of the year for putting 'the city on the map'.[47]
Mrs Simpson, who once told Chips Channon that she disliked Americans
because they had 'no air', would probably not have been impressed by the
accolade.[48]

In the days after the Abdication there was a good deal of soul searching on
behalf of the former King and Mrs Simpson in the American papers. 'What
can she give him to compensate for the empire he tossed away for her?' asked
the *Washington Post*. Would not the fashion-plate King come to resent a
woman who had cost him his throne? Gone were his title, his country, and the
respect of his compatriots. These were the grim realities facing the couple as
they contemplated their future together in some vain and pointless refuge.
Would Mrs Simpson, who would find herself fluttering in a world of futility,
be able to cope with these threats to her happiness?[49] The last word on the
Abdication must go to the sceptical sage of Baltimore, H. L. Mencken, who
called the King 'an idiot' for giving up the throne for love and advised him
to move to Hollywood. 'If he is too dumb to make good there, then he could
go to Washington and become a member of the cabinet.'[50]

22. Duke and Duchess of Windsor at Yankee Stadium, 5 May 1953.

As the Duke and Duchess of Windsor's plans did not include moving to Hollywood or joining the Maryland squirearchy, they settled into a restless exile, where the Duke tried, without success, to obtain royal recognition of his wife. Though the Duke had always enjoyed the United States, the Duchess was less enthusiastic about moving permanently to America because of the press intrusion and the expense. In the post-war years, unable to settle down or find employment, they wintered in the Waldorf Towers in New York or in Palm Beach, havens of idle privilege, where they nursed their rancour against the royal family amongst their society friends. They may have wished to shun the press, but it was a tribute to royal celebrity that photographers continued to pursue them, a welcome reminder that they were not dead socially. In 1971, Prince Charles visited the couple in their mansion in the Bois de Boulogne. He described the scene as one of utter futility: 'The Duchess appeared from among a host of the most dreadful American guests that I have ever seen. . . . The whole thing seemed so tragic – the existence, the people and the atmosphere.'[51]

*   *   *

The Abdication was regicide by less sudden means, with the former king lingering in exile for decades. Those who expected that his departure would damage the monarchy were disappointed. George VI soon restored the monarchy in the dutiful and unglamorous style of George V. Loyalty to the monarchy as an institution transcended King Edward's failings and trans-ferred to his successor.[52] Nor did the Abdication much upset the business or tenor of British politics. Here was a political lesson for America, where the Constitution invested the role of both the executive and the head of state in the President. As the Pulitzer Prize-winning journalist Arthur Krock observed, the transition was a tribute to British constitutional tradition:

> The solid foundation of popular democratic government which could bear the crushing impact of such a blow without a fissure appearing from top to bottom elicited the admiring recognition of diplomats, American and foreign, some of whom are aware by experience of what a crumbling there would have been in the governing structures of other states.[53]

With the Abdication, the American press shifted its royal focus, and noted the contrast between the glamorous Edward VIII and his shy successor. On 12 December, the day after the Abdication, President Roosevelt sent a message to George VI of 'sincere good wishes for a long and happy reign' on behalf of the American people.[54] The general view on both sides of the Atlantic was that George VI was a decent family man but nervous and insecure. If it had not been for the Abdication, he would probably have led a quiet family life in the country, leavened by a little light work cultivating his rhododendrons and his charities. His traits would have been the ruin of an aspiring statesman; but in a sovereign without ambition, bounced into kingship by the fates, these obstacles could be overcome by that dogged-as-does-it mentality that the British so admire. Unpretentious and public spirited, he was king-as-anti-hero, a constitutional sovereign in tune with mass democracy. Happily for the future of American–British relations, he had not inherited the anti-American prejudices of his father.

Americans who had looked forward to the Coronation of Edward VIII now found themselves looking forward to the Coronation of George VI. Various cities across America planned celebrations, often in association with British societies. Students at Yale organized a tasteful party at the Elizabethan Club, a hub of the University's Anglophilia.[55] From Hollywood, Cornelius Vanderbilt Jr drove his new Pontiac 'coronation express' to New York, where he put it on a ship to Britain.[56] The steamship companies reported capacity bookings and sailing times were brought forward so that passengers could make it to England in time. Though the 'international set' was now out of favour at court, an estimated 20,000 American Anglophiles turned up in London for the 'big event' on 12 May, 1937.[57] General John Pershing and Admiral Hugh Rodman joined Ambassador Robert Bingham and Ambassador James W. Gerard to make up the official American delegation.

In something of a sartorial revolution, the ambassadors wore knee breeches, for the protocol department in the State Department had ruled that the display of American diplomatic legs was not in violation of the ban on wearing official costumes. President Roosevelt took a relaxed attitude to the issue and decided that ambassadors should wear knee breeches instead of trousers if the Sovereign of the State to which he was accredited wished it. Since the Lord Chamberlain stipulated that knee breeches were required for the London diplomatic corps, Roosevelt obliged, fortified by pictures of the Russian Ambassador in short pants. He wrote to Ambassador Bingham: 'If Soviet Russia can stand it I guess we can too.'[58] The silken splendour of the American delegation was all part of the consoling ritual that erased some of the unhappy memories left by the death of George V and the abdication of Edward VIII in 1936, the year of three kings.

On the day, the pageant was a dash of colour in a drenching rain. In the United States, the radio coverage began at 4:45 in the morning, Eastern daylight-saving time and ran for seven hours, the longest continuous broadcast in radio history. From the sound stage of Selznick International, Douglas Fairbanks Jr, Ronald Colman, Raymond Massey and David Niven hosted a special Hollywood salute to the King.[59] In his syndicated column, Walter Lippman wrote that 'the British are elevating a very human being high above for a moment, as a republic might raise its flag, knowing full well that it is made of cotton and colored dyes'.[60] Americans seemed to enjoy the illusion and manufactured their own symbols of royalism. In Pacific Palisades a replica of the crown was on display, which featured at the Coronation Ball held by the local women's club.[61] At a dinner hosted by the English-speaking Union for a thousand guests in New York, the long-familiar question was asked: 'Who can explain the paradox presented by the descendants of men who rose against the Crown of the third George, now rising to acclaim the crowning of King George VI?'[62]

* * *

In his first Christmas broadcast in 1937, the King emphasized the need for goodwill in a world in which the 'shadows of enmity and fear' were on the rise.[63] With international affairs in crisis, he felt the pull of high politics and the pressure of his own inexperience. The politicians who queued up to have a word with him steered him toward his government boxes and their own anxieties. Americans, who were divided between isolationists and those who wanted a more robust foreign policy, also had their own concerns. For his part, President Roosevelt objected to the policy of appeasement. The turmoil in European politics was an opportunity for him to bring his longstanding interest in royalty and his political concerns into communion. With war looming, he decided to invite the King to the United States.

Roosevelt was no stranger to British royalty – the Delanos, his mother's family, liked to trace their ancestry back to William the Conquerer – and he felt an urge to ingratiate himself with the royal family. As a young man he had met Queen Victoria's daughter, Princess Helena, while on a visit to England. In 1918, as Assistant Secretary of the United States Navy, George V received him at Buckingham Palace, and the following year he had escorted the Prince of Wales to Annapolis. 'He was fascinated by kings and queens', his son Elliot observed, 'half-amused, half-impressed, by the pomp and pageantry that enveloped royalty.'[64] Before his marriage, he had designed his family's crest with three feathers over roses, which to the initiated was an unmistakeable nod to the badge of the Prince of Wales.[65] Not a few of his critics thought his Presidency was heading towards a dictatorial monarchy, especially after he won a third term. Some approved of his monarchical sympathies and leanings. In 1937, students at Yale founded a 'Roosevelt for King Club'.[66]

But Roosevelt had more pressing issues than whether he should don a crown. His invitation to George VI arrived in London at the height of the Munich crisis in September 1938. The underlying purposes in proposing the visit were to stiffen British resolve by assurances of material support, to suggest to Hitler that America would not remain indifferent to Nazi aggression, and to warn the American public of the dangers of isolationism.[67] The letter to the King simply stated that, 'It would be an excellent thing for Anglo-American relations.' The President added a personal note that suggested that the trip might be seen as a private, as well as a public, occasion: 'it would give my wife and me the greatest pleasure to see you'.[68] In a further letter, the President outlined his plans for the trip, which included a stay at Hyde Park, his country estate. He also flattered the royal couple with the remark that 'to the American people, the essential democracy of yourself and the Queen makes the greatest appeal of all'.[69]

According to Elliot Roosevelt, 'Father wanted the welcome he planned for the King and Queen of England to act as a symbol of American affinity for a country whose present political leadership he did not trust.'[70] In her autobiography, *This I Remember*, Eleanor Roosevelt said that her husband invited them to Washington largely because he believed that 'Great Britain would be our first line of defense' in any future 'life and death struggle' with Germany.

'He knew', she added, 'that though there is always in this country a certain amount of criticism of and superficial ill feeling toward the British, in time of danger something deeper comes to the surface, and the British and we stand firmly together, with confidence in our common heritage and ideas'.[71] The remark suggested that the traditional patriotism of the Anglo-American people still had some currency in Washington.

After the Munich crisis, the President's invitation was widely welcomed by those in the British political establishment who saw America as a potential ally against Germany. After consulting his ministers, the King wrote to Roosevelt that a visit to the United States would not only be a personal pleasure but hoped that it would also lead to greater understanding between the two countries.[72] The British Ambassador to Washington, Ronald Lindsay, who described Roosevelt as an 'impish schoolboy', advised the King that 'a welcome of utmost cordiality could be counted upon'.[73] Writing to the Foreign Office, the Ambassador said that he did not expect any immediate political advantage from the trip, but 'to an immense extent the political relationship of the United States to the Empire is government by emotional and psychological considerations' and that 'favourable emotional factors' may be crucial.[74]

The King and Queen were not decisive pieces on the international chess board, but they were influential pawns. British commentators were sometimes at pains to suggest that the visit had no political significance, but was merely the natural result of a series of events. The Labour newspaper the *Daily Herald* commented, a touch disingenuously, that there was no expectation that America would pull British chestnuts out of the fire; but there was a desire for mutual understanding.[75] After Munich, various American commentators concluded that the visit had underlying political implications. Some of them saw it as a British ploy to persuade Roosevelt to commit the United States to an alliance against Germany. Walter Lippman questioned its wisdom at a time when the Congress would be debating the issue of armaments: 'the unprecedented fact of a royal visit in the midst of an unprecedented revision of American policy would infallibly cause popular suspicion throughout the world, and no official disclaimer could allay it entirely'.[76]

The visit of King George VI and Queen Elizabeth in June of 1939, which came at the end of a tour of Canada, was the first by a reigning British monarch to the United States.[77] Given world tensions, it could hardly fail to have underlying political implications. Just as the visit to Washington began, the stage was being set for an intense debate over the proposed revision of the policy of American neutrality. The couple received a warm welcome in the press, which gave as much weight to the personal as to the political. But there were notable exceptions. *Scribner's Magazine* took the view that many

Americans still thought Edward, Duke of Windsor, the rightful inhabitant of the throne, that the 'colorless' King was on probation, and that the Queen was too 'plump' and 'dowdy' for American tastes.[78] Still, British officialdom took comfort from the desire of Americans to be seen as hospitable. Ambassador Lindsay quoted with pleasure a *New York Times* article that stated that 'we like the British because we understand them better than most foreigners – and, after all, why shouldn't we? They gave us our speech, our manners and customs and, after a little persuasion by the Continental Army, our country itself'.[79]

When news of the royal visit became known, the expectant American public inundated the State Department and the White House with requests for autographs and audiences. Disparate institutions dispatched invitations to the King and Queen, from Columbia University to the International Poultry Conference. Meanwhile, entertainers, spiritualists and speech therapists offered their services. Once the authorities announced the itinerary, local worthies requested that the royal couple change their route or slow down when passing through their communities.[80] To the delight of the British party, massive crowds appeared at every turn, numbering half a million in Washington on the day they arrived

23. Queen Elizabeth and Eleanor Roosevelt, 8 June 1939.

from Canada. At Union Station, the King and Queen took heart from the multitude of ordinary Americans sweltering in the summer sun just for a glimpse of their passing.[81]

The royal couple stayed as guests of President and Mrs Roosevelt at the White House, which the British had burned in 1814. A hundred and twenty-five years later, the British visitors ignited very different sympathies. At a formal White House banquet, Roosevelt set aside his former criticisms of the British Empire and England's social structure. Helped to his feet to toast the King, he spoke from a few scribbled notes of the 'bonds of friendship' and 'closer ties'. The King called on the two kindred nations to 'walk together along the path of friendship in a world of peace'.[82] As the *New York Times* reported, their Majesties' stay in Washington was 'a triumph of planned diplomatic moves' and 'an object lesson to the enemies of democracy'.[83] Like his brother and grandfather before him, the King sailed down the Potomac to Mount Vernon, where he laid a wreath of white lilies and irises on the grave of Washington. At Arlington National Cemetery, the royal couple visited the Tomb of the Unknown Soldier, a reminder of the first war in which the United States and the British Empire made common cause.

24. King George at the tomb of Washington, Mount Vernon, 9 June 1939.

In the run-up to the trip, it had been argued that a reigning monarch should avoid a visit to Congress, for it would suggest 'hidden motives' and British meddling in American politics. From the King's perspective, and that of his government, a visit would remind the American people of the historic links between Congress and the institutions of Great Britain. In the event, the royal couple made a 'personal', not 'political', stop at the Capitol, where they shook hands with a parade of 74 senators and 352 Representatives. It was an opportunity for the Queen to show off her remarkable social skills, which were put to the test by the antics of Vice President John Garner and several Congressmen, which to British observers were over-familiar.[84] Some legislators found excuses for not turning up. But when a group of 'Senate ladies' failed to receive an invitation to a garden party at the British Embassy, all hell broke loose at the State Department. 'Personally, I'd rather go to a pig wallow', said one senator, 'but I would like to go home nights.'[85]

The great charm offensive moved on to New York, where the King and Queen navigated the vast crowds of the World's Fair to enthusiastic cheers, the playing of anthems, military salutes, the waving of flags, and a display of fireworks, echoes of royal ceremonial in Britain. The British party thought the

25. King George V and Queen Elizabeth on the Capitol steps, 9 June 1939.

Fair, which exhausted the royal couple, a 'nightmare'. But as the *New York Times* reported: 'On Flushing Meadows, where the redcoats of King George III fought the ragged Continentals a century and a half ago, King George VI reigned for an afternoon.'[86] In a well-judged stroke of showmanship, the Queen, smiling and waving to the crowd, appeared in an ensemble of red, white and blue, which was said to have left even hard-boiled photographers in awe. The British Pavilion, meticulously prepared with the royal visit in mind, depicted the common origin and purposes of the American and British peoples. To reinforce the point, it exhibited a large pedigree of George Washington, which illustrated his direct descent from King John and from nine of the 25 barons who signed the Magna Carta, an original copy of which was on display. Here, it was suggested, was a Founding Father with claims to majesty as worthy as King George himself!

The royal couple concluded their state visit on the Hudson River in the country-house atmosphere of Roosevelt's estate in Hyde Park. Apart from White House functions, perhaps never before had an American family given so much thought to foreign visitors, from the itinerary to the choice of food. There had been a 'great argument' in the State Department over whether it was suitable to serve hot dogs to the King and Queen, but at the picnic in their

26. King and Queen visit the Roosevelts at Hyde Park, 19 June 1939.

honour the royal couple appeared delighted with this 'typical American delicacy'.[87] In her inimitable way, the Queen graciously ate the wieners and worked the guests, conveying the impression that everyone she met had received a personal greeting. According to Ambassador Lindsay, the Roosevelts were 'bowled over by the Queen' and, somewhat to their surprise, by the King as well.[88]

For her part, Mrs Roosevelt, who was less enamoured of royalty than her husband, preferred the King: 'I think he feels things more than she does & knows more. She is perfect as a Queen, gracious, informed, saying the right thing & kind but a little self-consciously regal.'[89] The visit delighted the Foreign Office, which believed that the royal couple were Britain's trump cards in America. To Britain's political establishment, they were not simply celebrities on tour, but subtle agents for the advancement of policy. As one courtier put it: 'That there is a brain underneath Her Majesty's becoming hats, and genuine feeling behind His Majesty's handshake is a discovery that is going to promote a better understanding of Britain's system of government and Britain's problems, and help to consign to limbo legends current since the Abdication.'[90]

In private conversation the night before, the experienced President and the untried but earnest King, who was well-briefed by the Foreign Office, discussed the mutual interests of America and Britain and their ideas on international relations. Roosevelt described what he was doing to reduce American isolationism and promised to send material help to Britain should war break out.[91] The talks did not lead to any immediate result, for they were well ahead of American opinion; but they contained the germ of the Lend-Lease agreement and did much to solidify the two democracies for the coming conflict. Henry Stimson, Secretary of State under President Hoover, wrote to the British Ambassador: 'the trip will have a quiet solid influence towards a good understanding on both sides of the Atlantic which can hardly be overestimated'.[92] In sanguine mood, Lindsay called the trip a total success with no jarring note, which 'made a profound impression on the whole country and has deepened and fixed already existing feelings of friendliness'.[93]

After their talks at Hyde Park, the King, not without a touch of naivety, felt he had a 'special relationship' with the President. He confided to Mackenzie King, the Canadian Prime Minister who joined the discussions at Hyde Park, that 'he had never met a person with whom he felt freer in talking and whom he enjoyed more'.[94] Roosevelt, his fascination with royalty redoubled, reciprocated the regard. He jotted in his notes: 'They are delightful and understanding people, and, incidentally, know a great deal not only about foreign affairs in general but also about social legislation.'[95] In her autobiography

Eleanor Roosevelt said that the visit was more successful than expected and recalled the night of the departure of the King and Queen:

> The royal couple stood on the rear platform of the train as it pulled out, and the people who were gathered everywhere on the banks of the Hudson and up on the rocks suddenly began to sing 'Auld Lang Syne'. There was something incredibly moving about this scene – the river in the evening light, the voices of many people singing this old song, and the train slowly pulling out with the young couple waving good-bye. One thought of the clouds that hung over them and the worries they were going to face, and turned away and left the scene with a heavy heart.[96]

The King and Queen would have reason to feel let down by Roosevelt in the months to come, but the United States tour gave them a broader outlook, increased self-confidence and greater recognition back home. Moreover, the visit gave a boost to Anglo-American relations at a time when anti-British sentiment was an issue in the United States, a tendency exacerbated by Irish discontents and the sensitivities of German emigrants, who now outnumbered those from Britain. The national characteristics of the two great English-speaking powers had long been a source of misunderstanding. Americans, upbeat and hypersensitive, recoiled from British indifference, which could often seem like superciliousness; and they had a fundamental distrust of British diplomacy, which they often believed to be hypocritical.

The royal visit moderated such views. According to George VI's official biographer, it 'disclosed to the American public the essential fact that "Royalty" are "people", and in three days did more to demolish anti-British feeling in America than could have been achieved in a quarter of a century of diplomatic manoeuvring'.[97] If the press coverage of the tour was anything to go by, Roosevelt accomplished his intention of making the monarchy appear more human and democratic.[98] With its informalities and 'hot-dog diplomacy', the visit moderated, if only momentarily, the American obsession with appeasing royal superiority.[99] At the same time, the Nazi threat in the background reminded many Americans of their country's British origins. As one historian observes, the royal visit was a notable success because 'it reflected both continuity and change, a linkage calculated to reassure Americans that their imagined Britain would not vanish in the inevitable process of modernization'.[100] The King and Queen had the charm of being part of the future while recalling the past.

The royal couple did their best to put on a show of their 'essential democracy', and Americans took pleasure from the royal trappings. The visit stirred the emotions even if it did not alter the views of entrenched isolationists. The

Consul General in New York declared that the enthusiastic crowds that turned out 'surprised all the prophets' while the friendly bearing of the royal couple 'delighted the man in the New York street'.[101] The memories were slow to wane among those enamoured of the passing royal cavalcade, who treasured their glimpses of the King and Queen. In December 1939, a Gallup poll asked Americans what news stories of the year most interested them. The royal visit came fifth, after the declaration of war in Europe, the conquest of Poland, the repeal of the arms embargo, and the attempt on Hitler's life, but ahead of the German invasion of Czechoslovakia.[102]

*   *   *

Back home the King had the challenge of bringing around the American Ambassador, Joseph Kennedy, who was pessimistic about Britain's future. The cultivation of the Ambassador and his family was a matter of diplomatic necessity for George VI, who was well aware of the public desire in the United States to avoid war. Kennedy had been annoyed that Roosevelt kept him on the sidelines in the preparations for the King's American tour, but wrote and spoke enthusiastically about it nonetheless. He told the American Society in London that the royal couple had 'made more friends for their nation than any other two people in history'.[103] But during the first week of the war in September 1939, he called on George VI full of gloom, saying that the conflict would bankrupt Britain. Exasperated by Kennedy's defeatism, the King wrote him a sharp letter in which he reminded the Ambassador that Britain was a 'free' democracy 'now fighting against all that we . . . hate & detest', and that while suffering could be expected, 'the British Empire's mind was made up'.[104]

While the outspoken and irreverent Kennedy disparaged Britain and wanted to keep America out of the war, he had a great affection for the King and Queen, unusual in an Irish Catholic. But his behaviour towards them, at least in the minds of his fellow diplomats, bordered on the crude. At a court ball, he blithely walked up to the Queen and asked her to dance. One witness observed that when he had the royal couple to dinner he 'had the awesome nerve to invite photographers there so that the evening would be well publicized, a rudeness in the extreme'.[105] Looking at the war from a financial perspective, Kennedy felt that England would be finished as a nation at the end of it, but saw some hope for the future in Queen Elizabeth. 'I will tell you when this thing is finally settled and it comes to a question of saving what's left of England, it will be the Queen and not any of the politicians who will do it. She's got more brains than the Cabinet.'[106]

The Catholic Kennedys, excluded from high society in the United States, were thrilled to be taken up by the royal family. (They were less thrilled when their daughter Kathleen married a Protestant, William Cavendish, the Marquess of Hartington, and eldest son and heir of the tenth Duke of

27. Rose and Eunice Kennedy presented at court, 18 July 1939.

Devonshire.) As Joseph Kennedy said to his wife after a weekend at Windsor Castle: 'Rose, this is a helluva long way from East Boston.'[107] In her memoir, *Times to Remember*, Rose recalled the visit: 'I lay in bed thinking I must be dreaming that I, Rose Kennedy, a simple, young matron from Boston, am really here at Windsor Castle, the guest of the Queen and two little princesses.'[108] When she was presented at court, along with her daughters Eunice, Rosemary and Kathleen, she enthused about practising her curtsy and wearing a tiara borrowed from Lady Bessborough: 'I felt a little like Cinderella.'[109] In March 1939, the Kennedy's son Jack (JFK), who was on a semester's leave from Harvard, met Queen Mary and Princess Elizabeth and attended a levée in his tails and silk breeches, 'in which I look mighty attractive'.[110] No concessions to sartorial purity from the upstart Kennedys.

* * *

Once the United States entered the war in 1941, many Americans followed the activities of George VI and Queen Elizabeth with renewed interest. Without ceremony or pretentiousness, but with due publicity, the royal couple turned Buckingham Palace into a royal war office. Gas masks at the ready, they ate spam and took target practice, becoming symbols of national resistance. Princess Elizabeth moved effortlessly from the jollity of the Girl Guides to the rigours of the Auxiliary Territorial Service. Queen Mary removed to Badminton, where she visited evacuees and salvaged scrap. Americans were well aware of the royal family's refusal to leave the country during the Blitz and their standing side by side with Churchill – and General Eisenhower – during some of the darkest days of the conflict.

The journalist Edward R. Murrow did as much as anyone else to keep the monarchy in American thoughts. He sometimes followed in the footsteps of the King and Queen as part of his wartime reporting from London. He described them as 'two of the busiest people in these islands', darting from canteens and factories to bomb sites and hospitals on a regular basis. When the bombs struck Buckingham Palace in September 1940, missing the King and Queen by 90 feet, it was headline news in America. According to Murrow, it had a greater symbolic impact on the United States than on Britain, where there was not much energy left to be outraged by the bombing of the Palace.[111]

That Britain and America were allies in the common struggle against Fascism heightened the King's symbolic importance, giving him a unique place in American perceptions of royalty. Still, at the end of the war, American references to England as the 'mother country' were less often heard and calls to Anglo-Saxon racial unity had less charm. But America's political establishment, in which a WASP elite still flourished, continued to fuel royalist sentiment. So too did America's social elite, whose daughters continued to be presented at court. (Queen Elizabeth discontinued the system of presentation parties in 1958.)[112] Critics of royalty were fewer and farther between than ever after the war, silenced by the identification of the King and Queen with national service and their dedication to the Anglo-American alliance. Thus the war to save democracy reinvigorated deference to the monarchy.

There was to be no return visit to America for a King exhausted by the war and his own failing health. At his death in February 1952, President Truman wrote in his diary: 'He was a grand man. Worth a pair of his brother Ed.'[113] For public consumption Truman called the King's 'heroic endurance of pain and suffering during these past few years . . . a true reflection of the bravery of the British people in adversity'.[114] The many American notices included Churchill's eulogy in which 'the king walked with death as if death were a companion'.[115] The National Symphony paid homage with a concert, the

House of Representatives adjourned, and the Massachusetts Senate spoke of a 'beloved monarch . . . sincerely devoted to his subjects, who laboured to the point of exhaustion in showing to them, and to the world, the proper discharge of his royal duties'.[116] Eventually, America set up a fund in the King's honour, which President Eisenhower warmly supported.[117]

In a moving tribute, the *New York Times* described the King as 'an anchor in the great storm'; and it assured the British people that his daughter and heir, who had made a successful visit to the United States only a few months before her father's death, would receive 'the sympathy and warm wishes of many peoples, not least from those who live in the one-time colony of the British Throne, the United States'.[118] The Eisenhowers, recalling a trip to Balmoral in 1946, wrote to the Queen Mother of their devotion to the King, 'a gentle human being' who was also 'an inspirational force'.[119] Eleanor Roosevelt, in

28. Princess Elizabeth's visit to Washington D.C., 2 November 1951.

Paris with the United Nations, expressed shock at the King's death and wrote a consoling letter to the widowed Queen from a unique perspective, one 'First Lady' to another.[120] Meanwhile, in a sympathetic broadcast, Edward R. Murrow observed that George VI 'had that quality that the British admire in horses, bird dogs and monarchs – he was steady'.[121]

American commentators, like their counterparts in Britain, looked forward to a new beginning for the monarchy. 'For a few days,' intoned the *Washington Post*:

> we shall hear the beat of muffled drums from London, but thereafter we may see a lifting of the spirit such as the British have not known in many a year. After all, their 'finest hour' was only a decade or so ago. Is it not possible that under Queen Elizabeth II the British people can enter another Elizabethan age of creative achievement?[122]

The monarchy may have been an 'enigma' to Americans, the newspaper concluded, but it had the charm of linking the British people to their 'glorious past' and conveying a sense that they were members of 'one great family'. The reference to the King as head of 'one great family' echoed Walter Bagehot's insight into the attraction of 'a family on the throne', and his emphasis on the monarchy's capacity to gratify the human need for grandeur and tranquillity.

CHAPTER 8

THE NEW VICTORIA

It seems to me that Independence Day, the Fourth of July, should be cele-brated as much in Britain as in America.

Queen Elizabeth II, 1976

Respect for tradition and family life still had currency in the 1950s on both sides of the Atlantic, and despite all the loose talk of a new Elizabethan age the monarchy would have been delighted with the onset of a new Victorian one. At the accession of Elizabeth II, the Anglo-American world looked on the young, attractive, and dedicated monarch with sympathy and affection. The Queen had inherited an exceptional sense of public service and a set of values that remained Victorian. With a built-in reverence for history and ancestral vocations, she subdued her individuality in the interest of the monarchy's greater good. The Queen set the tone of the reign, but many of her advisers, including her Prime Minister, Winston Churchill, and her Private Secretary, Alan Lascelles, had been born in the nineteenth century. With memories of the Abdication still fresh in the memory, the monarchy and its allies in government fully appreciated the consolations of cultural continuity and royal respectability.

While the monarchy remained popular and secure, the Queen was, as Murrow put it at the beginning of her reign, 'a prisoner of circumstances', unable to influence world affairs, given the collapse of the British Empire.[1] Against the background of Indian independence, post-war austerity, and the onset of the cold war, she had her work cut out anchoring the rickety ship of state. Like her father, the Queen was politically unobtrusive and constitu-tionally correct, befitting a sovereign in an era of imperial disintegration and international tension. Like Queen Victoria, but without an Empire, she would seek to unify the Commonwealth and to serve as a model of public service and family values at home. In the post-war uncertainty, the monarchy would also provide a distraction to Britons coming to terms with their kingdom's diminished status.

To self-confident Americans, now basking in their superpower status, Britain was no longer seen as an equal partner on the world stage. Consequently, the monarchy had lost some of its former grandeur in American eyes. While cultural ties remained strong, the United States, unlike the nations in the Commonwealth, had no formal links to the Crown to cement relations. To the more condescending Americans, the monarchy was little more than a folly, quaint but irrelevant. Long gone were the days when Americans looked to the monarchy for moral leadership or celebrated royal jubilees as if they were displaced Englishmen. But if the monarchy no longer resonated in the United States as it had in the nineteenth century, British royalty continued to dazzle through mystique and ceremonial brilliance.

* * *

The ceremonial brilliance commenced on 2 June 1953, when Queen Elizabeth, the titular head of some 610 million people in the British Commonwealth, became the 39th sovereign to be crowned in Westminster Abbey. Forty thousand Americans, twice the number who attended the Coronation of George VI in 1937, joined the multitudes in London for the ceremony.[2] To most commentators, Americans included, the Coronation was a stunning demonstration of national unity, a great patriotic display that defined British identity. By mid-century, the royal family, like Queen Victoria's family a century before, signified domestic virtue. Some saw the Coronation as an extension of the idea of the nation as one large family, with 'the Crown as a moral cord binding the consensus together'.[3] Whatever interpretation might be put upon the event, it was one of the supreme moments of royal ceremonial in modern history. The *Los Angeles Times* noted that it was 'the most publicized, the most pictured, the most discussed and the most widely seen of any coronation ever held'.[4]

Eight thousand, two hundred and fifty-one guests attended the event, a ceremony rich in political and religious significance that dated to 973.[5] They included the four-year-old Prince Charles, who received a special hand-painted invitation, and the 80-year-old Princess Marie Louise, a granddaughter of Queen Victoria. Notably absent were the Duke and Duchess of Windsor, who watched the ceremony on television in Paris. The official United States delegation with invitations to the Abbey, who stood in for President Eisenhower, consisted of General George C. Marshall, General Omar Bradley, Governor

29. *Big day a comin'*, American cartoon drawing by Hy Rosen, 1953. Albany Times-Union.

Earl Warren of California, and Fleur Cowles, editor and publisher. They were joined in London by an unofficial American delegation, which included the opera star Lily Pons, the Hollywood gossip columnist Hedda Hopper, the diplomat and hostess Perle Mesta, and the future First Lady Jacqueline Bouvier. Eleven American debutantes who had just been presented at court added to the glitter.[6]

The mass of spectators, who camped on the Mall for up to two days, included many Americans anxious to get a glimpse of the Queen as she drove by in the drizzling rain in her Coronation coach. 'It better be good', declared Mrs A. C. Gingerich, the wife of a poultry packer from Iowa, who paid $90 for an upholstered chair on a temporary stand erected on a bomb site in Pall Mall.[7] She could only have envied George Davis from Farmington, New Hampshire, who received a seat in the Abbey thanks to a personal invitation from the Queen, who had met him briefly in 1951 at the gate of Clarence House, when Prince Charles toddled over to him to show off his picture book. His invitation came with 'full instruction on what to wear and how to act'.[8]

In the glare of all the publicity, the organizers left no detail unobserved, from the horses pulling the Coronation coach, one of them a sober grey gelding named Eisenhower, to the secret recipe for the anointing oil, later revealed to contain oils of orange, roses, cinnamon, musk and ambergris. The Queen's Coronation dress, a preview of which had been on display in Kansas City, was made of white satin, embroidered in gold and silver thread with encrusted seed pearls and crystals. The service, which lasted nearly three hours, contained six parts: the Recognition, the Oath, the Anointing Investiture, which included the Crowning, the Enthronement and the Homage. In a moment of hushed expectation, Geoffrey Fisher, the Archbishop of Canterbury, placed the solid gold St Edward's Crown on the Queen's head.[9]

The most sacred part of the ceremony, carried out under a canopy, was the moment when the Archbishop dipped his fingers into the anointing spoon and touched the Queen on the hands, chest and forehead. The American response was much the same as it had been in Queen Victoria's Coronation over a century before, though millions more now saw the ceremony. Watching the show on television from her perch in Piccadilly, Perle Mesta recalled the magical feeling that royal ceremonial evoked in an otherwise rational republican breast, the mysterious silence of the solemn moment, and then the Archbishop's voice ringing out 'God crown you with a crown of glory and righteousness.'[10] Through such mystic initiation, the Queen became 'the vision of an uncounted multitude', one of God's anointed, or so it was believed by traditionalists, who saw the ceremony as 'medieval pageantry in patriotism, transfused with religion'.[11]

To monarchists, the Coronation was convincing proof of the virtue of having a hereditary head of state as opposed to a presidential system. The British writer Rebecca West, hired by the *Washington Post* to cover the Coronation, described the Queen as 'the emblem of the state, the symbol of our national life, the guardian of our self-respect'.[12] Anti-royalist Americans, like their British counterparts, were largely reduced to embarrassed silence on the day, though a few made their feelings known in letters to the press.[13] To the more fervent enemies of the Crown, the Coronation was just so much grovelling and old-world conservatism dressed up in tinsel, 'a curious mixture of medieval feudalistic ritual and an ancient aristocracy brought out of mothballs for a day of "Moss Bros" magic'.[14]

Thanks to the BBC, which carried commentaries in 43 languages, the service could be seen on television for the first time. The Queen, worried that she might make a blunder, had opposed televising the event. She perhaps remembered the stories that the Archbishop put the crown on the King's head the wrong way round at her father's Coronation. When it was announced that television would be excluded from the Abbey ceremony, the press complained and the ban was overruled, though it was agreed that the cameras would turn away during the anointing and the taking of communion. The Queen need not have worried, for the personal images on the silver screen – not least of Her Majesty walking down the aisle in resplendent dignity after the crowning – captivated the audience. Television coverage turned out to be 'the essence of what was happening', as the historian Robert Lacey notes: 'It transcended the old rules and created a new rule of its own. Keep close. Get intimate. Television had no boundaries but the power of its picture.'[15]

The Coronation marked, as the *New York Times* observed, 'the birth of international television'.[16] Not only was television given an enormous boost by the event, it also changed the iconography of royalty forever. For the first time, the American public at large was brought into a Coronation, which led to a sense of active involvement, giving the event the character of an international communion.[17] What critics of the monarchy often failed to grasp was that those who made up the worldwide audience were not simply interested in the formal dress and baroque ceremonial. In celebrating such occasions – one is reminded of Twain's account of Queen Victoria's Diamond Jubilee – the public could feel that something more was on offer than a vaporous royal progress in antique clothes. For those patient, enamoured souls who waited for hours in the rain to see the Queen, royalism was not mindless twaddle imbibed by passive idiots, but provided a positive 'electric charge'.[18]

Whether seen as a sacred event or simply a day off, the Coronation gave pleasure, or at least served as a distraction, to the estimated 55 million Americans, out of a United States population of 160 million, who watched the ceremony on television. (In Britain, an estimated 27 million people watched the ceremony out of a population of 36 million.)[19] In a generous gesture, the BBC gave its exclusive Coronation films free to the television networks in the United States.[20] Live transatlantic television transmission was still not available, so during the day the viewers had to settle for a succession of still photographs accompanied by live radio commentary.[21] Murrow, who reported from a platform outside Buckingham Palace, covered the event for CBS. The Royal Air Force flew the films of the event to the United States, which permitted the proceedings to be seen about twelve hours after they had taken place in London.

On the day, millions of Americans from across the United States set aside their republican principles and fell for the ' "Moss Bros" magic'. Whatever they took from the experience, the Coronation satisfied their desire to identify with a unique institution that transcended the mundane and brought people from around the world into the afterglow of memorable, historic events. Theatricality suffused with history once again proved irresistible, even to seasoned diplomats like the American Ambassador Winthrop Aldrich, who saw the event as 'a manifestation of unity which is an example to the world at large'.[22] Hedda Hopper thought it 'a show to turn De Mille green with envy. . . . The decorations are out of this world in color, design, and execution. All streamers feature "E. R.", Elizabeth Regina. I was amused by an American who said to me, "Dear me, I didn't know they were so fond of Eleanor Roosevelt over here" '.[23]

Americans may have been all the more impressed because the tradition of national celebration in the United States was modest by comparison with British standards. One need only compare the staging of Eisenhower's inauguration in 1953 with the Queen's Coronation. Richard Dimbleby, who did the BBC Coronation commentary, gratuitously remarked that the United States could not conceivably put on such a show for 'a thousand years'.[24] Many Americans agreed. Looking back on the Coronation a half century later, a political scientist who watched the ceremony as a boy in his native Massachusetts recalled the 'sheer magic' of royal tradition:

> However much we valued our republic and celebrated our independence from Britain, Queen Elizabeth represented splendor, tradition, and majesty that our republic did not have and somehow envied – and still does. . . . We sat riveted to our television sets watching the beautiful and radiant new queen being invested with the monarchy in the hallowed setting of Westminster Abbey – a setting we could not reproduce anywhere in our country.[25]

One of the journalists who covered the Coronation was Jacqueline Bouvier, who was working for the *Times-Herald*, an unpretentious Washington newspaper. She travelled from New York 'with a boatload of celebrities' headed for the royal festivities. Among them were the Duke and Duchess of Windsor, who were on their way back to Paris to sit by their television. Once in London, Jackie stayed with friends, frequented fashionable nightclubs, and attended a grand Coronation ball at Londonderry House for 500 people, which brought together many of the bejewelled and bemedalled Americans in town for the occasion. For light relief, she interviewed a few sightseers at Buckingham Palace and Piccadilly Circus. It was a tribute to the unquenchable demand for Coronation stories that the American papers published such vacuous babble, in response to the questions: 'What has been your biggest coronation thrill?' and 'Do you think Elizabeth will be England's last Queen?'[26] Jack Kennedy, who had proposed to Jackie only a month earlier, cabled his fiancée to say that he admired her work.[27]

Taking their lead from shopkeepers and the British Travel Association, the British welcomed the Yanks with open hands, if not open arms. The newspapers reported that Americans, who drove up prices for hotels and Coronation seats, would spend $104,000,000 in 1953 enjoying British attractions.[28] Travel companies and merchandisers had prepared the American marketplace for the celebrations in the months leading up to the event. The press, radio and television dug up everything they could about the royal family. Women's clubs, one network official observed, led the insatiable demand.[29] One result was the serialization of 'Happy and Glorious, the Coronation Story' by Marion Crawford, former Royal Governess to Queen Elizabeth. Another was the appearance of a two-thirds-scale model of the Queen's coach in the sunken centre of Rockefeller Plaza.[30] Elsewhere in New York a department store exhibited a copy of the Queen's size five Coronation slippers, which was in turn copied for sale.[31] In Boston a travelling display of royal fabrics, including a leftover piece of velvet from the Coronation robe, appeared at Paine's Department Store.[32]

Clearly, the Coronation was good for trade. And trade, along with ceremonial and media-driven celebrity, was increasingly the way in which the monarchy maintained a high profile in the United States. Hundreds of stores in 150 major American cities made plans for special sales promoting British goods in connection with the Coronation.[33] Sales representatives across America reported heavy demand, and the shops, decorated with flags and pictures of the Queen, filled with commemorative china, trinkets and fabrics provided by British traders. The manufacturers enlisted Princess Margaret to choose five 'official' Coronation colours. Trade journals pumped out special issues, which listed the many new items on the market, from zircon tiaras and miniature coaches to antique armour and gold-plated anointing spoons.[34] Meanwhile, a busy British Information Service in the United States laid on exhibitions, lectures and special movies to help people understand why they were spending their money on a ceremony alien to the republic.

As at past royal events, some Americans questioned their reactions to monarchical spectacle. Why all the fuss over a ceremony so at odds with American traditions? Why such fascination, the *Los Angeles Times* asked, 'when the monarchy has become almost a defunct institution in the world and when pomp and ceremony have largely disappeared from the human scene'?[35] A letter writer to the *Chicago Daily Tribune* grumbled about the royal overkill: 'The inaugurations of our Presidents have never been given the space and publicity by newspapers and magazines, television and radio, that have been given to ... an event that symbolizes an institution and way of life that we Americans supposedly repudiated long ago'.[36]

One correspondent retorted that the Coronation was a welcome alternative to American politics and baseball. Another wrote that that 'it was wonderful to hear and see such glad and awe inspiring pageantry to divert our minds from the day to day news of war, scandal and corruption'.[37] A woman from

Boston who stood for hours in the rain to get a glimpse of the passing parade asked herself why she had endured such discomfort. She concluded that she valued the beauty and historic significance of the event, but her prime motive was 'love for the Queen and the Royal family as individuals'.[38] Was America's fascination a remembrance of a common heritage, or simply a welcome diversion from daily life, a reflection of the power of pageantry traceable to the anointing of prophets in biblical times? Or was it because there was a genuine enthusiasm in the United States for a young and graceful Queen who, unlike the American President, was above politics?

In the 1950s Americans commonly assumed that there were innate differences between the sexes, and more than a few commentators said that women were the principal drivers of Coronation sentiment. Women, it was said, had a genius for 'make believe', and in their daydreams they revered Elizabeth as the highest-ranking woman in the world, a 'Queen of Queens'. An anthropologist concluded that while men yearn for relief from social pressure, 'women generally believe in social climbing as a way of life and are far more interested than men in distinctions of class and rank'. A psychoanalyst thought it was the first time in history 'that the women of America have found a heroine who makes them feel superior to men'. A woman analyst put it more bluntly: 'In the royal household, Philip takes orders from Elizabeth. . . . What wife doesn't secretly wish she had the same authority?' In America, the land of 'Queen-crazy women, . . . every woman is a Cinderella, daydreaming the satisfactions she does not find in real life. . . . Long live Cinderella!'[39]

While Americans in Britain took in the Coronation attractions and bought the royal merchandise, Anglophiles gathered back in the United States, led by Episcopalians and the many citizens of English extraction. In Washington, the British Embassy hosted a garden party, which was billed as an occasion when cold war frictions would be put on hold. Normally, official Washington society eagerly lined up for invitations from the British Ambassador. But the postman delivered the stiff white cards just as Prime Minister Clement Attlee delivered a stinging indictment of American policies in the House of Commons. The diplomatic cauldron boiled over when several Senate wives linked to Senator Joseph McCarthy's investigating committee boycotted Her Britannic Majesty's embassy on the grounds that British ships had been trading with Red China. Still, 2,000 guests turned up, including the Soviet Ambassador, Vice President and Mrs Nixon, members of the cabinet, the Supreme Court, and an array of Congressmen and White House staff. President Eisenhower also received an invitation but protocol dictated that the President only attend embassy parties when a visiting head of state was the host.[40]

*   *   *

30. Queen Elizabeth, the Queen Mother, at the White House with the Eisenhowers and the Nixons, 5 November 1954.

As memories of the Coronation faded so too did any hope of a new Elizabethan age. Looking back, one American commentator said the show was partly 'put on by the British to give a psychological boost to their somewhat shaky empire'.[41] The collapse of Empire that took place after the Second World War diminished the Crown's splendour, while the decline of British competitiveness led to disillusionment and political faction. In the circumstances it was a doubtful tactic to defend the monarch as a treasure house of consolation. Royal ritual may have given a boost to a nation on the decline, but there were limits to the capacity of pageantry and pomp, however accomplished, to compensate for Britain's poor economic performance and the Suez crisis of 1956. Increasingly, there were fears for the future of a monarchy conceived to represent a great Empire but which had been reduced to symbolizing a second-rate power that had embarrassed itself in a futile war with Egypt. But

fears of the consequences of national decline in a world of competing super-
powers did not mean the monarchy was unpopular or ineffective as a diplomatic tool.

It was against the background of the Suez debacle that the Queen visited the
United States in October 1957, following a brief stop in Canada. The celebrations surrounding the State of Virginia's 350th anniversary provided the
excuse for the trip. The underlying aim of the tour was to revive American
Anglophilia after Suez, to bring the special relationship fostered by George VI
and Roosevelt up to date. Eisenhower could scarcely hide his disappointment
over the shortness of the stay, for he had hoped that it might include a tour of
the West, which he believed would give both the Queen and Americans in that
part of the country tremendous pleasure. The President looked upon the
visit as a significant diplomatic event, which provided an opportunity to
illustrate the natural ties that existed between the two countries.[42] In toasting
the Queen at a state dinner he praised the English-speaking peoples for
their courage and their belief in the rights of man. 'The respect we have for
Britain', he concluded, 'is epitomized in the affection we have for the Royal
Family.'[43]

31. Queen visits Jamestown, 1957.

The Queen was no less sanguine about the tour. Before her departure, she wrote to Sir Anthony Eden: 'I do hope our visit will be of value between the two countries, – there does seem to be a much closer feeling between the U.S. and ourselves, especially since the Russian satellite has come to shake everyone about their views on Russian scientific progress!'[44] Her ten-day visit effectively pushed the Soviet triumph off the front pages. Again and again the Queen stressed the ancient ties between the two nations and the need for unity and closer contacts, not least in science. Her efforts proved effective, as citizens and columnists alike rallied round the Anglo-American alliance that had been threatened by Suez and Russian intrigue. As Max Freedman, the Washington correspondent for the *Manchester Guardian* saw it:

> The sinister men who hurl their thunderbolts of power from the Kremlin will watch with disappointment and chagrin the outpouring of affection and admiration with which the American people will so generously salute Queen Elizabeth and Prince Philip on their pilgrimage of friendship. Unless they are perversely blind, the Russian leaders will see that Britain and America, no matter how much they may differ on solitary issues, are united by an unbreakable community of interest and ideals whenever the treasury of freedom is menaced.[45]

Public interest in the visit was intense. The days were long past when the Mayor of Chicago, the ineffable Big Bill Thompson, playing to his Irish constituency, shouted: 'I wanta make the King of England keep his snoot out of America.'[46] Even in 1920s Chicago, a period of heightened Midwestern isolationism, such views were exceptional. At the time of the Queen's visit in 1957, America's sense of kinship with Britain remained largely intact, fuelled by the wartime alliance, Churchill's rhetoric, memories of the Coronation, and the Queen's graciousness. In keeping with all royal tours, considerable thought was given to gift giving. In a gesture that pleased the President – who was later to be hailed as 'the king of America' on one of his own foreign tours – the Queen presented him with a mahogany coffee table, now in the Eisenhower Museum in Abilene, Kansas, which featured a map of the situation at H-Hour on D Day, 1944.[47]

The demanding schedule set up by the British Embassy left the royal couple little time to travel much beyond commercial and political centres, apart from an excursion to Virginia. But the trip proved yet again that royal popularity was not restricted to the East and West coasts. From the Midwest, there were complaints that the royal couple were spending too much time in the East, with 'the same old tired dignitaries in Washington and New York'.[48] Of the

3,000 American towns and cities named after English towns, the mayors of 70 of them, including Newport, Rhode Island, Cumberland, Maryland, Bristol, Tennessee and Colchester, Illinois sent greetings to the Queen. The letters were bound in a book and presented to Her Majesty by a delegation of about 25 of the mayors.[49]

In Washington D. C., another city that resonated with British associations, not all of them joyful, a million people braved the rain to line the streets as the Queen drove with Prince Philip and President Eisenhower from the airport to the White House. The royal couple met ordinary citizens on a 'walkabout', visited the National Gallery of Art, and attended a college football game between Maryland and North Carolina that reminded Prince Philip of armed conflict. The Queen enjoyed a ticker-tape parade in New York, but told Eleanor Roosevelt that she regretted not having the time to visit the shops on Fifth Avenue.[50] Delighted by the impact she was having, she later mused over the differences between a hereditary monarchy and an elected Presidency, thoughts that did not flatter the United States. On her return she told a friend that the ailing Eisenhower lacked self-confidence. She was likewise shocked 'by the American need to be liked', which expressed itself in details such as her hosts agonizing over whether they should make signs of obeisance in her presence.[51] Most of those who scraped an invitation to one of the royal functions bowed or curtseyed.

Whether out of social insecurity, snobbery or simple curiosity, American citizens had pursued family links with British royalty since the early days of the republic. Genealogical research published in the United States in the 1930s showed that through the descent of her mother, the Queen was one of the nearest living relatives of George Washington, her second cousin seven times removed on her mother's side. She was also related to Washington through her father, as well as to President Franklin Roosevelt. The genealogists traced the royal ancestry of the Queen and the two American presidents to Cerdic, an Angle from what became Schleswig-Holstein, who had invaded Britain and made himself King of Wessex in the sixth century. To put the icing on the American ancestral cake, the Queen was also General Robert E. Lee's fifth cousin five times removed.[52]

The diaspora of royal cousinage in the North and South had its uses. During the 1957 tour, Virginia, the most royalist of the former American colonies, was a principal object of the Queen's attention. The excursion south provided her with the opportunity to see the horse farms around Upperville. At Williamsburg, she delighted her audience with a reference to the fact that Virginia had counties named after every British monarch from Elizabeth I to George III, 'even George III'.[53] The royal biographer Hector Bolitho, who followed the Queen's progress, argued that Virginians, like southerners generally, related emotionally to the monarchy, whereas northerners, with their 'Pilgrim blood', were more remote:

> When the lady from Boston . . . says, 'We love your Queen', she does not mean that she wishes to have a royal dynasty taking over the White House. But when the Virginia lady, with Lely and Benjamin West portraits of her ancestors on the walls of her drawing room, says, 'We just love the Queen', she means that she wouldn't have a photograph of Mrs Eisenhower in the house at any price.[54]

A crowd of some 5,000 people greeted the Queen at the airport on her return to England and another crowd gathered at Buckingham Palace to cheer her home. The British press had carried news of her success in America and the relative informality of the tour. The Prime Minister, Harold Macmillan, hailed 'the warmth and gaiety of the welcome given to the Queen by her subjects and our allies across the sea'.[55] As with the American visit of her parents in 1939, the glowing reports enhanced the monarchy's reputation both at home and abroad. But it also caused some in the British press to complain about Palace precautions and royal stuffiness. 'Why did she have to cross the Atlantic to become REAL?' asked the *Daily Herald*. 'People here have been reading of the Queen going about freely among ordinary people, behaving like a natural person. Canada loved it. America was bowled over by it. Why is it not allowed to happen here?'[56]

For all the hoopla surrounding the Queen's visit, there was little sense in America that she was a major player on the world's political stage. Unlike her father's tour in 1939, there was no equivalent of the highly-charged visit with Roosevelt at Hyde Park. In her various meetings with Eisenhower they were as likely to exchange recipes as views of foreign affairs – the Queen sent him a recipe for scones after his trip to Scotland in 1959.[57] Accordingly, Americans revered the Queen less for her diplomatic skills or political influence than for something less tangible, which boiled down to respect for an ancient, still magical throne inhabited by a woman whose life resonated with the worldwide audience for royal theatre. As a British commentator, Dermot Morrah, argued, the monarchy of Queen Elizabeth II was not so much a form of government as a way of life, the sovereign as bourgeois *mater familias*.[58] Here was Queen Victoria redux, constant and reassuring but less glamorous with the passing years.

*   *   *

A little charisma rubbed off on the Queen during the whirlwind visit of President and Mrs Kennedy to London in June 1961. While Eisenhower and

Truman had both visited Britain, it was the first time a president had been entertained in Buckingham Palace since Woodrow Wilson dined with George V in 1918. According to Gore Vidal's report of the event, Jackie found the Queen 'pretty heavy going', only at ease escorting her guest down a Palace corridor to look at a picture of a horse.[59] Unlike Woodrow Wilson, the Kennedys left the British entranced and expectant, particularly Jackie, who was mobbed by admiring crowds wherever she appeared. A cartoonist captured the moment in a drawing depicting the Statue of Liberty with the First Lady's face, with one hand holding the torch of freedom and the other a copy of *Vogue*.[60]

The British fascination with the Kennedys prompted by the presidential visit of 1961 reversed the normal scheme of things. Instead of Americans

32. The Queen and Prince Philip with the Kennedys, 6 June 1961.

ogling royalty, the British were ogling America's first family, treating the Kennedys like crowned heads of state. Here was Camelot in the making, a princely presidential couple with a dynasty waiting in the wings, whose vitality and style captivated Britons and Americans alike. At the end of 1961, a Gallup Poll asked Americans to name the women they most admired in the world. Eleanor Roosevelt headed the list, with Jackie Kennedy second and Queen Elizabeth third.[61] Jackie's biographer, Sarah Bradford, later titled her book *America's Queen*. It would seem that in Anglo-American culture the highest aspiration, and tribute, is to be seen in the context of royalty.

Comparing the Kennedys and the Windsors became a commonplace on both sides of the Atlantic. In 1963, Lord Hailsham, Britain's Conservative party leader, gave a talk in New York in which he remarked: 'Your system of government is an elective monarchy with a king who rules with a splendid court and even . . . a royal family, but does not reign. Ours is a republic with a hereditary life president, who, being a queen, reigns but does not rule'. The comment raised the familiar theme of America's elective monarchy but with a dynastic twist, which the *Chicago Daily Tribune* made the most of in an article titled 'Kennedys and Coronets'. The newspaper took a dim view of the family ambitions of the Kennedy clan and compared the nepotism in the White House to that of George III: 'The power of the President today is greater than any English king has known for centuries, and the Presidential appetite continues to grow.'[62]

Unlike President Kennedy, Queen Elizabeth's dynastic claims were impeccable, but she played a largely passive role as head of state. This was a reassuring sign of sanity and stability to many in Britain, but in the 1960s the polls suggested a growing indifference to the Crown as an institution. The monarchy was beginning to look out of touch, a view that the popular culture of that decade, much of it imported from America, exacerbated. Apathy was perhaps most noticeable among the young, to whom the monarchy seemed dull and withdrawn. In the era of Andy Warhol and the Beatles, a sovereign who espoused the values of Queen Victoria seemed a little incongruous. Viewing figures for the Queen's Christmas broadcast had slipped, while the playing of the national anthem at cinemas and public gatherings had died away. Such straws in the wind did not go unnoticed in Palace circles. But however much attention the Queen gave to modern life – she sent a message of congratulations to the American astronauts on the first moon landing in 1969 – she was perceived as a pillar of traditional values.

* * *

Courtiers could rely on the royal magic when Prince Charles, accompanied by his sister, Princess Anne, first visited the United States in the summer of 1970.

It was only a year after his investiture in Caernarvon Castle in Wales, a pageant that was seen by a worldwide audience of perhaps 500 million people. It was the first trip to the United States by a Prince of Wales for decades, and its purpose was to shore up the royal foundations of the Anglo-American alliance. Following in his great-uncle's footsteps, the Prince was not simply the heir to the throne, but a world celebrity. President Nixon, who welcomed – some said 'manhandled' – the Prince during a photo opportunity on the White House lawn, treated him accordingly. Hoping a little of the royal magic would rub off, Nixon opened his remarks by saying the personal visit was an indication of the closeness between his family and the Queen's family in London.[63] The President went beyond the call of duty in conspicuously pairing the Prince with his unmarried daughter, Tricia Nixon.

The two-day visit to Washington included the obligatory trip to Mount Vernon, a cookout of steak and beans at Camp David, a tour of Washington monuments, a meeting with the astronaut Neil Armstrong, and a baseball game, at which the Prince, who had been raised on cricket, found the concept of a foul ball difficult to grasp.[64] The crowning social event of the visit was a dance for 700 guests on the White House lawn, with music provided by the

33. Prince Charles and Nixon at the White House, 16 July 1970.

Canadian rock stars, the Guess Who, which did not feature their anti-American lyric 'American Woman'. Throughout the trip, the Prince expressed fascination, smiled a good deal, and made gracious and amusing comments. The American press reciprocated, commenting on his intelligence and sense of fun. But it was less than generous to Princess Anne, who, as the *New York Times* put it, 'made no effort to conceal a mood of incredulity and vague discomfort'.[65]

One purpose of the trip was to extend the Prince's training in diplomacy and American politics. To his delight a courtesy call to see the President turned into an extended discussion. The conversation took place in the days before Nixon routinely turned on his tape recorder. A memorandum to the President by Henry Kissinger, who admired the Prince's 'modesty, intelligence, and wit', laid out the groundwork for the talk.[66] The Prince's Diary and Nixon's later comments refer to the subjects discussed, which included East–West relations, Cambodia, the Middle East and the attitude of the young towards government. The President spoke warmly about the 'special relationship' between Britain and America, based on common traditions, and advised the Prince to be a 'presence' in the world and not be afraid of a little controversy. The Prince, who felt the frustrations of his role, replied that if he became too controversial people would not take him seriously. He wrote in his diary: 'To be just a presence would be fatal. I know lots of Americans think one's main job is to go around saying meaningless niceties.'[67] The President later wrote that he had expected him to be 'a rather callow, superficial youth with no particular interest or understanding of world affairs. His conduct completely dispelled that image'.[68]

Prince Charles's successful American visit may be taken as a sign that the royal family was becoming more outgoing, at least abroad. In the United States deference towards royal visitors, though it could not be assumed, remained widespread. But the democratization of the royal family, which Americans had encouraged for over a century, had its perils. Deference was on the wane in Britain, while the public desired greater royal visibility. The consequent press intrusion put the Queen's family under the spotlight. The selling of the monarchy as the nation's first family, as in the BBC film *Royal Family* (1969), broadcast in the United States, fed the ravenous appetite. The growing press and television interest put ever more flesh and blood on royalty, but the commercial demands of the media in an era of declining respect for public institutions created problems for a monarchy that treasured its right to privacy. Though royalty was becoming less hidebound, the policy of Palace advisers continued to be essentially protective, to present the Queen and her family as a unique example of graciousness and dignified public service.

Those qualities were to the fore when the Queen and Prince Philip arrived in the United States on 6 July 1976, to celebrate the 200th anniversary of the American Revolution. It was said in the American press that the job of a monarch was to make people feel good. (Comparisons with the Vice President's office sprang to mind, but not to the advantage of the Vice President.)[69] The Bicentennial was an ideal occasion for a British monarch to make Americans happy, and it was guaranteed to bring the two nations closer together, if only because it gave both peoples the opportunity to flatter each other and themselves. In rapid succession, the Queen charmed the dignitaries and citizenry of Philadelphia, Washington, Boston and New York, with only a few Irish demonstrators to mar the effect. Highlights of the trip included a royal visit to Bloomingdale's, where the Queen was given an American Indian peace pipe, and a motorcade to Federal Hall, the site of America's first capital in New York, for a mayoral reception and the conferring of honorary citizenship.[70]

In Philadelphia, the Queen presented a Bicentennial Bell as a gift from the British people to the United States. In a simple speech, nicely judged to symbolize the loss of rancour between two nations, she paid tribute to the Founding Fathers, while flattering Britain into the bargain:

> I speak to you as the direct descendant of King George III. He was the last crowned sovereign to rule in this country and it is therefore with a particular personal interest that I view those events which took place 200 years ago. It seems to me that Independence Day, the Fourth of July, should be celebrated as much in Britain as in America. Not in rejoicing in the separation of the American colonies from the British crown but in sincere gratitude to the Founding Fathers of the great Republic for having taught Britain a very valuable lesson. We lost the American colonies because we lacked that statesmanship 'to know the right time, and the manner of yielding what is impossible to keep'. But the lesson was well learned. . . . We learned to respect the right of others to govern themselves in their own way in 1776. Without that great act in the cause of liberty, performed in Independence Hall 200 years ago, we could never have transformed an empire into a commonwealth.[71]

The Queen seemed to enjoy the irony in it all.

*   *   *

No sooner had the Queen returned from America than her mind turned to celebrating her own anniversary, the Silver Jubilee of 1977. Given the oil crisis, the collapsing pound, and the failure of Princess Margaret's marriage, many people, including not a few Palace advisers, expected it to be a damp squib, less an expression of ardent royalism than a bit of merriment under the pretence of flying the flag. Unlike Queen Victoria's jubilees in 1887 and 1897, Britain was no longer the world's superpower. Unlike George V's Jubilee in 1935, there was not even an Empire to celebrate. Bemused Americans, who had forgotten the spirited celebrations in the United States for Queen Victoria's jubilees, could be forgiven for thinking the festivities on 6 June were a belated celebration of D-Day. Many Britons were not even sure what was being celebrated. Some thought it marked her Silver Wedding, although the Prince of Wales was already 28.

Like the former jubilees, there was some colourful opposition, from the proliferation of anti-monarchist badges to the release of the best-selling single 'God Save the Queen' by the Sex Pistols, which contained acrid lyrics taunting the Queen as a heartless stooge. There was also some criticism of the monarchy in the United States, though much of it was tongue in cheek. As Americans noted, Britain had come down a notch or two since the jubilees of George V and Queen Victoria. There was less pomp and majesty to admire. At the *Chicago Tribune*, a paper less sympathetic to royalty than some of its rivals, the journalist and comic strip writer Michael Kilian described the Jubilee as a 'lunatic festival' and called for a revolution: 'The time has come for Britain to recognize that the middle ages are over – that backward, impoverished nations can no longer go around scrounging money from the rest of us while lavishing millions on a family of mindless twits.'[72]

Such criticism was unrepresentative of Americans, who made up a significant part of the large number of people who watched the ceremony live on television and spent lavishly on an array of royal souvenirs, from T-shirts to champagne buckets.[73] Perhaps the Bicentennial celebrations the year before, which evoked memories of George III, made Americans more attentive to the British festival. There was nothing in the United States to compare with the festivities that marked Queen Victoria's jubilees, but most Americans were aware that a special anniversary was being celebrated in Britain, if only from the extensive media coverage. In Boston, the congregation of the Old North Church, where once the lanterns had hung for Paul Revere, linked their services to those being held in honour of the Jubilee at St Paul's Cathedral, which President Jimmy Carter attended.[74]

The new American Ambassador, Kingman Brewster, arrived in London just in time to participate in the ceremonies. As a descendant of renegade puritans, he noted the irony in returning to his mother country to represent the republic at the court of Elizabeth II.[75] But many Americans overlooked the ironies and saw the anniversary revels as a tribute to the genuine renown. To

a restive people frustrated by shady, disposable presidents – Nixon's resignation was still in the public mind – jubilees celebrating the longevity of a non-
political head of state had the intangible charm of a fixed historic landmark.
In an era when television produced 'false intimacy' and 'vulgar celebrity',
declared a leader in the *New York Times*, the Queen 'has maintained admirable
dignity, self-discipline, and good taste. . . . Americans, like free people everywhere, join the celebration: Long live the Queen!'[76]

CHAPTER 9

A WEDDING AND A FUNERAL

All but a few cynics like to see a pretty novel touching for a moment the dry scenes of the grave world.

Walter Bagehot, *The English Constitution,* 1867

Shifting cultural norms were taking a toll on the monarchy by the 1980s. The Queen had imbibed Victorian values, but Victorian values were in short supply in postmodern Britain and America. In an increasingly dumbed-down world of media hype and global vacuity, of pop stars and political cynicism, the staid and ageing Queen looked increasingly out of touch, a sovereign in aspic. Americans enjoyed the aspic, but few had any inkling of the monarch's constitutional or patronage roles; and the Anglo-Saxon culture that once placed British sovereigns on a pedestal was on the defensive. Rallying calls to the unity of the English-speaking people, or to the Protestant ascendancy, which had promoted the monarchy in America for generations, were by now unfashionable, if not absurd. Diversity was in. WASPs were out.

The monarchy's reputation, some would say its fate, was increasingly in the hands of the media, which was growing more international, some would say more Americanized, each year. The expansion of mass culture tended to denigrate elite culture, and it posed a particular threat to the monarchy, which struggled to retain its privacy and privileges. Press intrusion and its deleterious effect on the royal mystique had been a worry for the royal family since the nineteenth century and mounted with each succeeding advance in the media industry.[1] Over the years the ancient institution had been subsumed into popular culture, with a consequent loss of distance and deference. As the royal family became more acutely aware after the Abdication, relatives are hostages to fortune in hereditary institutions. In the 1980s, with the Queen's children subject to unrelenting scrutiny, the monarchy could not take the future for granted. There were fewer and fewer places for royalty to hide.

To America's corporate media, the House of Windsor was of interest primarily as a family saga, a set of princes and princesses with stories to tell, whose claim to fame was inherited and therefore unique. In a society seeking ever more novel distractions, in which deference was in decline and political institutions under attack, any sign of royal misconduct would trigger a media storm. Meanwhile, the public greeted a royal romance as if possessed. What explains the behaviour of normally sane people bursting into tears at the announcement of a royal wedding or a royal death? Was it the media hype, the vacuous culture, or simply madness? Or was it that the public saw royalty as life in idealized form and looked into the monarchy's 'enchanted glass' as an indirect form of self-worship? Americans, the self-proclaimed guardians of classless democracy, with little regard for irony, peered into the royal mirror hardly less than monarchical Britons. In a restless society in which motion passed for progress, the monarchy offered the consoling 'glamour of backwardness'.[2]

* * *

'A princely marriage is the brilliant edition of a universal fact, and as such, it rivets mankind'.[3] On the occasion of the wedding of Prince Charles and Diana Spencer in the summer of 1981, Rebecca West took up Bagehot's theme in the *New York Times*: 'The pageantry of the court exists simply to put beauty into the daily routine. . . . The royal scene is simply a presentation of ourselves behaving well; if anybody is being honoured it is the human race.'[4] As various American royal watchers observed, the heir to the throne's wedding was one of life's rituals writ large, celebrating continuity and the commonplace. In his sermon, the Archbishop of Canterbury, Robert Runcie, set the tone for the marriage as a love story with universal meaning: 'All couples on the wedding day are "royal couples". . . . This is the stuff of which fairy tales are made.'[5] The fairytale was a potent one. It bowled over the million or so people who lined the route, and the 2,500 invited guests at St Paul's Cathedral, who included Nancy Reagan, Margaret Thatcher, and all the reigning monarchs of Europe, except the King of Spain, who had to cancel his plans to attend when the Spanish authorities discovered that the royal couple were to begin their honeymoon from the contested territory of Gibraltar.

The wedding also bowled over the Prince of Wales, who wrote to a friend that it was 'a revelation to find the real heart and soul of the nation being exposed for a moment in good, old-fashioned, innocent enjoyment'.[6] The Prince had always been sensitive to the competing claims of duty and romance, the constitutional niceties, the external constraints, and the need for an heir to the throne. In an interview with the *Evening Standard* in 1975, he had said that love was basically a friendship based on affection and shared interests and added that 'marriage is something you ought to work at'.[7] When asked during the official engagement photo call whether he was in love with Diana he replied famously, 'Yes . . . whatever love means.' Was the sanguine Prince aware of the definition of 'love' in Ambrose Beirce's *Devil's Dictionary*: 'temporary insanity curable by marriage'? On the night before the wedding, Diana Spencer reportedly told a friend: 'I felt I was the lamb to the slaughter.'[8]

Whatever the royal couple felt for each other on the day, the marriage ceremony reminded the worldwide audience, estimated at three-quarters of a billion people, of 'past glories and future possibilities'.[9] As a day of national renewal, it reminded many of the 55 million American viewers of the Bicentennial five summers before. The networks wheeled out Dan Rather, John Chancellor, Tom Brokaw and Barbara Walters to whip up the wedding fever. No fact was too inconsequential for the legion of instant experts, from the size of the cake (over four feet across), to Diana's weight loss (14 pounds in the week before the nuptials).[10] Otile McManus, an editorial writer for the *Boston Globe*, was among the more feverish:

> Laugh, Go ahead, rattle the newspaper. Feel superior. Write me off as just another closet monarchist. Tell your friends that you don't understand why some people act as if they wish America had lost the Revolution. . . . I can't get enough. I have read every word from People magazine to Jan Morris, from the Ladies' Home Journal to the New Republic. I really want to know how many pounds of sugar there are in the royal wedding cake, how many steps the prince will have to take across the altar of St. Paul's Cathedral, how much Nancy Reagan paid for the predictable wedding present of Steuben glass.[11]

In the buzz over the cake and the gifts, few noticed the slaughter of six hundred Canadian brown bears to provide new hats for the Foot Guards.[12]

The royal family, though bad news for bears, was good news for British business, a point now often made by the monarchy's promoters. Before the royal wedding, a tidal wave of 'commemorabilia' hit the market, which was worth an estimated $100 million to the British souvenir industry. At the cheap end of the thousand or so items for sale were towels, linens, T-shirts, scarves, bottle openers, beach balls, buttons, banners, bags, badges, and Bibles. Commemorative trays bearing a photograph of the royal couple rolled off an assembly line from Cleveland Ohio. Some of the stuff was so tacky that the Lord Chamberlain tried belatedly, with little success, to preserve a few scraps of royal decorum by decreeing what was in good taste. Ultimately, some of the restrictions on the use of photographs and personal arms were relaxed. Much of the rubbish and some of the official 'Royal Commemoratives' made their way to the United States. For the discerning royalist scouring Madison Avenue or Wilshire Boulevard for souvenirs, the firm British Collectibles offered two-handled loving cups, busts, plates and mugs.[13]

Given the media hype and commercial exploitation, it was inevitable that American pressmen, torn between adulation and disbelief, would mock the wedding. For the killjoys it was an anachronistic charade staged by a country with nothing to brag about but history. Michael Kilian encouraged 'Charles' and 'Di' to elope, if only to spare the world another celebration of the British class system.[14] The humourist Art Buchwald, who took exception to American toadies lining up to bow and scrape, brought together the world's 'greatest minds' in Washington to form a 'Society to Ignore the Royal Wedding'.[15] In the *Los Angeles Times*, a paper besotted by the wedding, Howard Rosenberg thought a 'salivating' media overdid the coverage, but admitted that the English wore uniforms and paraded better than anyone else. 'Watching all this pomp and pageantry, it was hard to imagine England not being the most powerful of nations.'[16] From Chicago, the splenetic Mike Royko called the Queen a 'frump' and stood up for the unsung girls seen every day on Michigan Avenue, who were not only better looking than Diana but had the brains to make their own livings.[17]

* * *

By the time President Reagan visited the United Kingdom in June 1982 thoughts of the royal wedding had turned to thoughts of the pregnancy of Princess Diana. In his toast to the Queen at a dinner in his honour at Windsor Castle the President remarked that Americans shared 'the excitement about the impending birth of a child to the Prince and Princess of Wales'.[18] But homage to royal fecundity was not the purpose of the visit. Nor was the display of horsemanship in Windsor Park, which led Reagan to compliment the Queen on being 'in charge of that animal'.[19] The visit coincided with the Falklands War, in which Britain had received much-needed American support. It thus presented an opportunity for Britain to pay tribute to the strength of the Anglo-American alliance. Softening up American leaders has not been the least of the Queen's duties as Britain's head of state, and she did her diplomatic turn with the Reagans with panache.

As the biographer Ben Pimlott observed, the Queen aimed to reinforce Reagan's 'ideological sympathy for Mrs Thatcher with a personal relationship between the elderly, not overly-involved, Californian monarch and the British one'.[20] Her toast to the President pulled out all the stops, summarizing the

34. Queen Elizabeth and President Reagan riding horses, June 1982.

links that bound the two nations together over the centuries: shared history, common values, kinship, language, and the rule of law. 'These past weeks have been testing ones for this country', she noted, 'when once again we have had to stand up for the cause of freedom. . . . But throughout the crisis, we have drawn comfort from the understanding of our position shown by the American people.'[21] The President had reaffirmed United States backing for Britain's Falklands campaign in a speech to Parliament earlier that day.

The royal touch worked its magic on the sentimental Reagan, who likened his stay at Windsor Castle to a fairytale. 'We will always remember our visit because of the Queen's and Prince Philip's warmth and welcoming hospitality – they could not have been more gracious.'[22] As a former thespian, Reagan was practised in praising leading ladies. 'She [the Queen] is an outstanding human being', he wrote in his diary.[23] Reagan took pride in being distantly related to Her Majesty, a point that he mentioned in his memoir *An American Life*.[24] He was not alone among post-war presidents in having royal ancestry, for Bill Clinton, who delights in being a descendant of King John, and the Bushes, who are related to the Queen through King Henry III, can also make such claims.[25] (While not every president has a royal pedigree, the cultural origins of 42 of the 43 American presidents can be traced back to England, Scotland, Wales, or Ireland – Martin Van Buren, a Dutch Calvinist, is the exception.)[26]

Reagan was not averse to playing the king himself. He recognized, as the Speaker of the House Tip O'Neill remarked, that Americans wanted 'a magisterial air in the White House'.[27] He was, as Stephen Graubard put it in *The Presidents* (2004), 'a popular and canny monarch who made admirable use of his courtiers'.[28] As a showman, Reagan was more interested in pomp than most presidents; and his flair for putting on the show of state was reminiscent of George Washington, while his court was a successor to Kennedy's Camelot, but without an expectant family eager to create a dynasty. When Reagan died in 2004, his funeral, with its tolling bells, riderless horse, and casket lying in state on Lincoln's catafalque in the Capital Rotunda, was an American version of British royal tradition.

* * *

The Reagan visit to Windsor was a memory by the time the Prince and Princess of Wales toured the United States together in the autumn of 1985. *Time* hailed the two of them as 'the most glamorous couple' on earth.[29] The headline in the *New York Times* read simply: 'The British have landed and

35. Queen and President Reagan at dinner in San Francisco, 8 March 1983.

Washington is taken.'[30] With 7,000 pounds of luggage, the couple were fully equipped for the conquest. Four thousand invited guests greeted them at Andrews Air Force Base on a brilliant November day, joined by hundreds of representatives from the accredited press. The jet-lagged Prince noted in his diary:

> there were a lot of people on the tarmac to meet us – all extremely friendly as Americans so often are. Great batteries of photographers and TV people rose up like the Philharmonia Chorus mounted on white-painted scaffolds and made a noise like a giant sneezing as all the apertures went off in union.[31]

Princess Diana, quickly into her stride, lingered with a group of handicapped people.

A Post–ABC News poll suggested that ordinary Washingtonians were pretty blasé about the visit. Two-thirds of those questioned did not have strong views about the Prince or Princess. Interest in the royal couple was higher among middle-class Americans than those who described themselves as 'working class', and Diana received a more favourable rating, at 38 per cent, than Prince Charles, at 29 per cent. Fifty-two per cent said Britain was better off with royalty, while 24 per cent thought that the country would be better off without them.[32] The figures suggested that most Americans did not have a clearly defined opinion of the royal couple. But as a piece in the *New York Times* observed, the Prince and Princess had a symbolic role and Americans did not need a 'clearly established opinion of symbols to react strongly to them; they are by their nature not well defined, and yet they can be very potent indeed'.[33]

However the mass of Americans viewed the Prince and Princess, the competition for an invitation to their engagements was fierce. Looking down on the United States capital from the social heights of Southern California, the *Los Angeles Times* observed: 'In an upstart city where the only aristocracy is one of power, and "access" is the chief measure of status, the visit of these two symbols of an older hierarchy has somehow become the ultimate test.'[34] The Reagans kicked the visit off with a gala dinner, which served as a barometer of America's royal adulation. The President praised the Anglo-American friendship and toasted the royal couple, though he referred to Diana as 'Princess David'. (A year earlier, in an outbreak of aristocratic disdain for upstart Americans, Diana had described Reagan as 'Horlicks', a Sloane Ranger expression for an old bore, and said Nancy Reagan was only interested in being photographed with the royal family.)[35]

The White House gala brought together a distinctive American mix of businessmen, actors, artists, and assorted celebrities, a social set with lots of glitter but little tone in an unfashionable city in need of a royal lift. William Buckley rubbed shoulders with Neil Diamond, Clint Eastwood with Gloria Vanderbilt, Jonas Salk with Estee Lauder. Leontyne Price sang, Prince Charles fidgeted, and Princess Diana danced, famously with John Travolta, who joined the dinner at her request. In an interview two decades later, Travolta would remark that the Princess was clever and media savvy. 'I thought, she not only knows who she is, she knows what this is – and how big this is.' After the dance he bowed and, as he put it, 'turned back into a pumpkin'.[36] 'There is no other woman in the world who could come to this White House and create this kind of hysteria', pronounced the royal correspondent James Whitaker.[37]

The royal couple spent most of their ten days in the United States racing from one formal engagement to another, seventeen in all, from the Prince's visit to the American Institute of Architects to the Princess's tour of the Washington Home and Hospice. The stop at J. C. Penney's 'Best of Britain' promotion at a Virginia mall, with $50 million of British clothing for sale, was the now customary royal nod to trade.[38] The fund-raising stop at Palm Beach, Florida, the brainchild of the industrialist Armand Hammer, was the customary nod to charity, an event that resulted in a Gadarene rush for social pre-eminence among the tycoons and film stars. The gala at the Breakers Hotel gave new meaning to the word 'exclusive', an '8' on the social Richter Scale, one witness called it.[39] The British Embassy provided a crash course on royal manners, from bowing and curtseying to the prohibition on tiaras, except by those with a claim to nobility. Among the rich and famous lucky enough to conjure an invitation were Ted Turner, Gregory Peck, and Eva Gabor. Joan Collins turned up with so many diamond barrettes in her hair that she might qualify as American royalty.

Armand Hammer had to guarantee $1 million for the United World Colleges just to get the royal couple to the gala at Palm Beach.[40] Through such formal events, the Prince and Princess of Wales raised large amounts of cash for worthy causes and enhanced their celebrity status while becoming press agents for the monarchy. Every time they turned up, said a few words and unveiled a plaque, they chalked up 'another notch in the unbounded sentiment'.[41] Their presence at charity events, particularly Princess Diana's presence, suggested to the faithful that royalty not only celebrated good deeds but also caused them to be done. At the Washington Home and Hospice, Diana moved gently through the crowd of 2,000, blushed, patted hands and consoled the afflicted in a modern display of the royal touch.[42] By such gestures she kindled an acceptance of social hierarchy and reverence for royalty in America bordering on delusion.

As they carried out their worldly duties, more thoughtful American columnists wondered how the world's most successful nation, which worshipped progress and power, came to worship a Prince and Princess who represented an ancient social order without authority, whose significance they likened to an ephemeral cover of *People* magazine. Glamour and wealth could not answer it, nor could celebrity alone. After all, there were American women more beautiful than Diana and American fortunes much greater than the Prince's. 'Youth and glamour and money matter, but so does tradition', noted the *New York Times*:

> It matters that Charles marches in the line stretching back to Victoria and Elizabeth I and William the Conqueror and yes, even George III. . . . In a curious way, Americans feel closest to the country they rebelled against, and the hubbub over the royal visit is one sign of that.[43]

The royal visit served as another reminder of the American mix of self-assurance and anxiety expressed in the simultaneous longing for change and for tradition. To those who would bow and scrape to the Prince and Princess while remaining ostensibly hostile to hereditary privilege, the *Chicago Tribune* advised: 'Just be yourself, America', whatever that meant.[44]

The *Wall Street Journal*, which normally shunned royal news, noted that plebeian America sent George III packing and rejected aristocratic titles, but conceded that whenever British royalty turned up in the United States the citizenry always greeted them with a display of spontaneous fawning. Pageantry without power seemed to have a hypnotic effect: 'Important people gape', wrote the Pulitzer-winning editor Vermont Royster:

> and fight for privilege of breaking bread or sipping champagne with them. Those not so fortunate as to be included have been known to take holidays abroad to explain their absence from the guest list. The rest of us among the masses sit home and watch agog on television. . . . Beneath all this, I suspect, is a lingering attachment to her [the Queen's] country and a sentimental attraction to the panoply of royalty, even among citizens with no ties to Britain's political or cultural heritage.[45]

As it was suggested, royalty's power over the American mind turned on heredity and secrecy, which was another way of putting Bagehot's dictum that the monarchy's 'mystery is its life'.[46] The benign members of the royal family, who were rarely exposed politically, were not subject to dismissal like politicians. But their very permanence, mystique, and unflappability led to schizophrenia in the American prints that mirrored the British tabloids with their relentless pursuit of gossip. During the tour of the Prince and Princess in 1985, the tittle-tattle centred on the tensions in the royal family. Rumours were already in the air that the royal marriage was under strain, that the urban Princess shopped and danced alone to her walkman, while the rustic Prince ruminated and spoke to his plants. As *Time* magazine put it: 'The House of Windsor, imperturbable on the outside, has become a seething "Palace Dallas" on the inside.' The royal tour of the United States turned Princess Diana into a world-class celebrity and an American idol. 'Dynasty Di' now played opposite Prince Charles, the 'mystical crank'.[47]

The royal couple were going their separate ways by the time the Princess of Wales visited New York on her first major solo tour early in 1989. During her three-day stay, her Private Secretary, Patrick Jephson, had to deal with a swarm of hangers-on, inquisitive journalists and Irish protesters. Opponents of British rule in Northern Ireland denounced the tour as a public relations stunt and turned up at events chanting 'Diana go home.' Jephson's recurring nightmare was that lurid headlines such as: 'PRINCESS SNUBBED BY REPUBLICAN GRANNY' or 'REPUBLICAN DOC WRECKS TOUR' were about to appear.[48] He need not have worried, for it was love at first sight when British royalty met New York celebrity. One of the seduced remarked that Diana 'knocked over' New York. She dazzled from the royal box at a performance by the Welsh National Opera at the Brooklyn Academy of Music, which was followed by a $1,000-a-ticket gala dinner at the World Financial Center attended by, among other celebrities, New York's glitzy substitutes for royalty, Donald and Ivana Trump.[49]

During the tour, the Princess met a mix of New Yorkers, from Wall Street bankers to Harlem's homeless. Cheering crowds and intrusive cameras greeted her at every turn. 'I dreamed about this last night and it was better than the dream', declared Wanda Morales, one of the thousands of royal worshippers who waited behind police barricades. The visit took on a wacky quality when a contingent of Diana look-alikes in drag put on an exhibition outside her hotel. In a descent from glittering wealth to abject poverty the Princess visited a paediatric AIDS unit at the Harlem Hospital where she left her distinctive signature, stroking the babies and disarming the staff. At the Henry Street Settlement on the Lower East Side, she smiled, mingled with the crowd, and shook a few hands. A local resident summed up the Diana effect: 'She's left the smell of perfume on my hand.'[50]

The Princess's perfume could not disguise the scent of royal misbehaviour in the late 1980s. As royal renown collapsed into notoriety, palace officials did their best to limit the damage. But the monarchy was no longer able to mask or to cushion shocks to the system. The contrast between the respectable Queen and the misdemeanours of her family was becoming increasingly apparent. Intrusion into the private lives of the royal family had taken hold, which Palace advisers had encouraged by letting down the drawbridge. In London, the *Sunday Times* warned that the 'grotesque appetite of the media for all things royal' would eventually bring down the monarchy.[51] As a younger generation of writers and journalists entered the scene, a tug of war ensued between an invasive press and the royal family's demand for privacy. The tension had less to do with the policies of courtiers or editors than with circulation wars, changes in technology, and the economics of mass communication, which encouraged the media to expose any hint of royal misbehaviour.[52]

Television and the press in the United States were not immune to these changes. They had pioneered many of them. Increasingly, the American media treated the monarchy as part of the entertainment industry, as an institution composed of jet-setting celebrities rather than as a constitutional fixture. Royalty might be worshipped one minute and decried the next, just like so many others in the passing parade of idols consumed by the denizens of popular culture. When American journalists called the Princess of Wales 'Dynasty Di', teased Prince Charles as a 'crank', or labelled the Duchess of York the 'Duchess of Pork', they contributed to the royal exposure and trivialization that threatened the monarchy's future. Over the decades, Americans had done their share to turn royalty into fashionable playthings, which was disquieting for a family whose principal claim to status and renown was based on heredity and the British Constitution. The 'family on the throne', which had nourished the monarchy since the reign of Victoria, was coming unstuck in the glare of publicity.

The market for royal news in the United States, always buoyant, had expanded dramatically with the arrival of the Princess of Wales on the scene. Compared to the staid and sombre Windsors, Diana was sparkling and thoroughly modern. So great was her following that she was changing – some would say distorting – America's relationship with the monarchy, from historic linkages to transient glamour. Not since the tours of Edward VIII after the First World War had royalty been so lionized by the mass media and the smart set alike. Prodigal in their desire for distraction, Diana watchers noted her every change of clothes, her mannerisms and signs of boredom, just as they would have done with a starlet. As the editor of *Majesty* magazine remarked, the royal family were treated 'like a British version of Hollywood'.[53] With Princess Diana, royalty met Hollywood head on.

When the Princess appeared, what passed for an American aristocracy fell into what one witness called an 'Anglophiliac frenzy bordering on Di-lerium. Diana . . . simply provided the excuse. America provided the rest.'[54] A special issue of *People* magazine on the Princess in 1988 sold 900,000 copies in the United States at double its normal newsstand price. The Princess held the all-time record for cover appearances in *People*, many more than her closest rival, Elizabeth Taylor. In the 1980s, *Majesty* and *Royalty*, two British monthly magazines devoted to the monarchy, sold over 40,000 copies per issue in America, a large advance on sales in the United Kingdom. More often than not, a picture of the Princess appeared on their covers.[55]

By the 1990s, the Princess was not only the most accessible and alluring member of the royal family, but also the most talked about and photographed woman in the world – *Life* magazine would eventually feature Diana seventeen times. Increasingly, Americans were picking up their royal news from popular magazines, television, and the tabloids rather than serious books and newspapers. The widespread reporting, with their gossipy interviews and glamorous photographs, contributed mightily to her popularity across the United States. With the help of such organs as *Life*, *Hello*, and *People* magazine, which were on sale in every American supermarket, the Princess had broken through the barriers of class and ethnicity on both sides of the Atlantic.

* * *

In May 1991, while the marriage of the Prince and Princess of Wales unravelled, Queen Elizabeth returned to America on an extended visit. The trip took place three months after the successful invasion of Iraq, which revived ideas of the special relationship and made Americans all the more enamoured of the Queen. A British commentator remarked that the Americans had to coin a new word to describe the response to the visit: 'monarchomania'.[56] In a nation of restless social climbers, the Queen loomed like Everest, a social pinnacle that beckoned to be climbed. Most citizens remembered film stars when they had long forgotten their presidents, and members of the royal family were now more akin to film stars than politicians in the American mind. Compared to a hereditary queen, a president who served for a fixed term and divided the nation along party lines had limited appeal.

The serious newspapers stepped up their coverage to meet the demands of the tour, while sales of tabloid magazines with the latest royal gossip soared. At some of the events there were 1,000 or so representatives of the press. The Queen entered the homes of ordinary Americans, made a return visit to Mount Vernon, and had lunch at the Library of Congress, which the British Army had burned in less cordial times. Attending a baseball game was by now the sporting equivalent of a trip to Mount Vernon for British royalty, and in Baltimore the Queen held the first royal receiving line in a dugout. In Washington there was a newsworthy breach of protocol when a woman wrapped her arms around the Queen in a spontaneous hug. In trying to explain the excitement created by the visit, the *New York Times* observed that here was a diminutive woman who was famous not for fifteen minutes but for nearly five decades, 'a living link with the Britain of Chaucer and Shakespeare and Wellington and Churchill, who has herself been privy to the deepest secrets of the West since 1952, when Harry Truman lived in the White House and Joseph Stalin in the Kremlin'.[57]

The Queen was the first British head of state to address a joint meeting of the United States Congress. It was an opportunity to reclaim some of the royal prestige lost by the failings of her children. The 'special relationship', a phrase in favour with the royal family since the Second World War, was made flesh as America's lawmakers rose to the occasion and gave her a reception that no other national leader could match, though several Congressmen with Irish sympathies boycotted the speech. Applause echoed through the chamber as the Queen thanked the United States for its actions during the Gulf War. And no one squirmed when she added: 'Some people believe that power grows from the barrel of a gun. So it can, but history shows that it never grows well nor for very long. Force, in the end, is sterile ... Unfortunately, experience shows that great enterprises seldom end with a tidy and satisfactory flourish.'[58]

From Washington, the royal party flew on Concorde to Miami, where the Queen knighted General Schwarzkopf, the 58th American to receive the

36. Queen Elizabeth II addresses Congress, 16 May 1991.

honorary award since the Second World War. (Others knighted include Bob Hope, Ronald Reagan and Bill Gates.) Asked if he had been nervous about meeting the Queen, he replied that by comparison 'Saddam was a piece of cake.'[59] Moving on to Texas, the Queen and Prince Philip toured the Alamo, then flew to Dallas, where the Mayor welcomed the royal couple as a band played the theme from the television series *Dallas*. On the Capitol steps in Austin, the Queen made a brief speech on the economic ties between Britain and Texas. There was tumultuous applause when she said, perhaps with her distant cousin President Bush in mind, 'that lesser mortals are pitied for their misfortune in not being born Texan.'[60] In a lifetime dedicated to spreading goodwill, the Queen has had to make many a fatuous remark.

* * *

In the summer of 1992, Andrew Morton's *Diana, Her True Story* confirmed the longstanding rumours that the marriage of the Prince and Princess of Wales was a charade. Within days of publication, Simon and Schuster doubled the book's print run in the United States to 400,000.[61] Morton, with the connivance of Princess Diana, depicted the Prince as a husband whose cruelty and betrayals had driven his wife to attempted suicide. Dramatized stories that the Princess was so miserable that she had thrown herself down a staircase while pregnant and had slashed her wrists with a razor mesmerized readers. Like the British, Americans followed the unfolding public disintegration of the once fairytale marriage with a fascination bordering on the prurient. American press and television, taking its lead from Britain, covered the saga with tabloid intensity, helping to turn Diana into a royal martyr, particularly among women. She was turning the royal family's relationship with America into something very special indeed, but not something that gave the Queen and her advisers any pleasure.

In Britain, the Princess was a symbol of national identity. In America she was now widely seen as a symbol of female identity, a woman scorned, undone by an adulterous husband and Palace intrigue. In Britain, the broken marriage had implications for the monarchy's future. In America, it resonated largely in personal terms. Many Americans thought the abandoned 'Queen of Hearts' might reinvent herself by moving to the United States. As her Private Secretary later noted in his book *Shadows of a Princess*, Diana had a 'natural affinity with much of American life' and the United States offered 'a soothing antidote to the simmering acrimony of her daily life in London'.[62] She once told a friend from the fashion world that she thrived in America because 'there is no "Establishment" there', by which she may have meant that there were fewer rules and so many other celebrities that she could find some privacy.[63]

But in star-studded America the Princess was a celebrity among celebrities, a royal with 'It'. As a Palace castaway she had raised the art of performance on the royal stage to a new level, giving fresh meaning to iconic glamour in the United States. Like Queen Caroline or Marie Antoinette, royalty in distress always finds an audience; and whether defending herself on *Panorama* or visiting a hospice, the Princess knew who 'needed her most, and they felt uniquely valued because she needed *them*'.[64] Vulnerability made her all the more attractive to Americans, not least to women with unhappy marriages. To a generation given to self-examination a 'New Age' Princess who suffered from depression and bulimia and who subscribed to popular culture and alternative therapies was all the more intriguing. And then there was her willowy elegance and doe-eyed beauty. 'No matter how bad she felt inside', as an American observer wrote after her death, 'she always looked so good'.[65]

In an attempt to recover her equilibrium and rejuvenate her international role, the Princess began to visit the United States more frequently in the mid-1990s. She had by now become expert in exploiting the power of royal celebrity and was tapping it to promote her favoured causes and her own image. As Andrew Sullivan wrote in *The New Republic*, 'the unassuming English rosebud slowly unfolded into an Oprahfied, American bloom'.[66] In early 1995, she appeared at the awards dinner for the Council of Fashion Designers at the Lincoln Center. At the end of the year she returned to New York to be named

37. The Princess of Wales and Henry Kissinger at an award dinner, 11 December 1995.

'Humanitarian of the Year' by the United Cerebral Palsy charity for her work with sick and underprivileged children. Among the guests were Donald Trump, Henry Kissinger and Colin Powell, who took unbridled pleasure in announcing that he had discovered that he was a distant relation of the Princess through descent from the sixteenth-century Earl of Coote. When she called him 'cousin Colin' on receiving her award he had something with which to upstage Henry Kissinger ever after.[67]

The social work of the Princess of Wales was therapeutic, if not redemptive like the Duchess of York's. It found a natural outlet in America, where her unique blend of royal glamour and the common touch left observers spellbound. In June 1996, the Princess, now dubbed an 'American Saint', turned up in Chicago to raise money for cancer relief. Four months later, in her first international engagement after her divorce, she returned to Washington to lend a hand with a breast cancer charity. At the end of 1996 she was back again, to attend a gala benefit for the Costume Institute at the Metropolitan Museum of Art in New York. Her presence transformed these local events into international media festivals. 'You might think average Americans had had their fill of the whiny Windsors', remarked a reporter in Chicago during her visit to that city, 'but then Diana shows up on the doorstep, and otherwise rational people suddenly go all goofy.'[68]

*   *   *

An aristocrat by birth, the Princess succumbed, in the phrase of the editor Tina Brown, to 'the aristocracy of exposure'.[69] She paid for it with her life. Her tragic death in a car crash in Paris in August 1997 led to an outpouring of emotion in the United States, as in Britain. The mass media that had given shape to her celebrity now moulded the reaction to her demise by the unceasing circulation of her image. The hype was an essential part of the sacralization of Diana as a Queen dethroned. An anonymous message left at the gates of Kensington Palace captured the peculiar pathos of her memory:

> Queen of the Coloured Hearts
> Queen of the Devastated
> Queen of the Unloved Ones
> Queen of the Unknown
> Love from the Unknown.[70]

Not since Queen Victoria died in 1901 had Americans been so moved by a royal passing. But this time it was being played out in a turbulent era drenched in celebrity, a heartless, star-struck culture that the American media had done

more than its share to create. When Diana's brother, Charles Spencer, accused
the press of killing her on NBC's *Today* show, he found a receptive audience in
the United States, where the press and death were so often fatally joined.[71] And
when he remarked at Diana's funeral that she was classless and did not need a
royal title 'to generate her brand of magic', he reinforced American assumptions about his sister's essential democracy, the hierarchical nature of British
society, and the remoteness of the Windsors.

It was not the media's finest hour. 'We have met the zeitgeist in the Death of
Diana' observed one sceptical commentator, 'the collapse of news into that
ersatz stuff now indiscriminately passed off as news.'[72] In *Time*, the writer Jan
Morris regretted a life 'enlarged for us all by unrelenting advertisement, blown
up like a fictional drama so that it is already entering, before our eyes, the
realm of myth – an apotheosis that in previous ages took centuries to
happen'.[73] In the *New York Times*, Maureen Dowd decried the obsessive media
coverage:

> We can't stop. The photographers can't stop. The reporters can't stop. The
> editors can't stop. And the consumers can't stop. The celebrity culture has
> become a mass psychosis. It has broken out of its former confines in the
> entertainment industry and overrun institutions of authority. It has swamped
> the British monarchy as it has swamped the American Presidency.[74]

The tragedy did not swamp the monarchy, but the Queen's initial restraint
in dealing with it led many to the conclusion that she was out of touch with
opinion. Meanwhile, the British and American media raised the emotional
temperature. The fevered response around the world suggested that the
media-driven transatlantic popular culture – democratic, sensationalist and
synthetic – had taken hold. A royal death has always been good for American
self-advertisement, but Diana's exceeded expectations, as various critics noted
with disdain. Royal pundits and friends of the Princess – the slightest acquain-
tance would do – fuelled the frenzy. In addition to the presidential tribute
from Bill Clinton, Barbara Walters, Katherine Graham, John Travolta, and
Tom Cruise were among those who spoke out publicly. In *Newsweek*, under
the byline 'An American favorite', Nancy Reagan compared the Princess to
Grace Kelly and lamented that 'magic doesn't last'.[75]

Diana may have signified the monarchy's collapse into the ephemeral, but,
as in the past, a royal death was good for trade. Overnight, she became a
legend, an academic subject, and a marketing tool.[76] The media outlets
quickly spotted a commercial market and tacked on to their real object the
pretence of memorializing a popular Princess. The tragedy was so profitable

that a host of magazines rushed to redo their cover stories. *Time* sold 650,000 additional copies in its first issue after her death. A commemorative edition sold over 1.2 million copies, the largest seller in the history of the magazine. American newspaper sales, like their British counterparts, skyrocketed. *USA Today* sold several hundred thousand copies more than normal in the week after her death.[77]

In the marketing of royalty, charity and commerce have long worked in tandem. The use of Diana images was vital in manufacturing her posthumous fame as beatific. Not since the death of Prince Albert in 1861 were so many commercial reproductions of royal imagery created in response to popular demand.[78] Diana's apotheosis was reminiscent of ancient religious cults, with relics and souvenirs shaping memories of a secular Princess. Within days of her death the Princess of Wales Memorial Fund materialized, which raised money worldwide to further her philanthropic interests through the licensing of gifts and memorabilia. The Franklin Mint, a supplier of souvenirs in Pennsylvania, quickly brought out a range of Diana products, with some of the profits going to good causes associated with the Princess. The Memorial Fund and the Franklin Mint soon engaged in legal wrangling on both sides of the Atlantic over the use of her image. Meanwhile, royal relics were much in demand, from autographs to dresses, with websites eventually offering a veritable arcade of tacky keepsakes.

In the global mourning, hundreds of new websites appeared, many of them American, with on-line chat rooms to give vent to the outpouring of 'virtual grief'.[79] Homemade websites nurtured the cross-fertilization of loss. News organizations, Yahoo, and AOL created special internet bulletin boards to allow the admirers of the Princess to gush, or to rant about the paparazzi. 'It is with great sadness I sit here in front of my computer', remarked one American cyber pundit, 'I cannot be at the embassy to sign the condolence book . . . I cannot be at the service to say goodbye to a wonderful human being. For Diana was more than a royal . . . she was real.' A woman from Texas posted the message: 'I felt the need to reach out to Diana's sons hoping that maybe in some small way they would find some comfort in my words.'[80] There was no agenda on the web democracy, but a torrent of collective emotion, touched by fantasy and couched in maudlin prose. As the web pages suggested, Dianamania had something of religion about it, and her death induced a form of reverence that encouraged people to mourn themselves.

Just as the internet hosted a record number of hits, television ratings soared. The cable channels reported dramatic surges in viewers. In the two weeks after Diana died, the American broadcast networks devoted more time to the Princess than to any other story. 'We overdosed on Diana', remarked a former president of the Society of Professional Journalists. Another media expert noted 'that in a country that revolted against the British crown to form a democratic union, many people can give you chapter and verse now on the infighting amongst British royalty, but can't identify their representative to the U. S. Congress'.[81] The pollster Robert Worcester observed that 'Diana's death received more media attention than any event in history'. The BBC carried the funeral to 187 countries with a worldwide audience estimated at 2.5 billion people, exceeding the biggest previous audience of two billion for the World Cup Final between Brazil and Italy in 1994.[82] Twenty-six million United States households, perhaps as many as 100 million Americans, interrupted their schedules to gather round their televisions, rapt in quasi-religious communion.[83]

In her final public appearance, Diana's cortege moved in solemn procession through the heart of London. Over a million people lined the route from Kensington Palace, around Hyde Park Corner, past the Queen and her family bowed in silent tribute at Buckingham Palace, the Union Jack lowered to half mast, to Westminster Abbey, the burial ground of seventeen British sovereigns. The muffled tenor bell of Westminster tolled once per minute as the body of the Princess, borne on a gun carriage, wound its way through the packed streets. Behind her coffin, draped with the royal standard and bearing wreaths of white lilies and tulips, walked, in cadenced step, her two sons, her former husband, her former father-in law, and her brother, four princes and an earl. Behind them, in a departure for royal funerals, filed representatives of each of the 100 charities that the Princess had been associated with in life, some in wheelchairs, others on crutches. A notable array of invited guests – among them Hillary Clinton, Henry Kissinger, Tom Hanks, Tom Cruise and Diana Ross – joined the 2,000 mourners inside the Gothic Abbey.

The service, with its timeless rhythm of anthems, prayers, tributes and hymns, leavened by Elton John's evocative 'Candle in the Wind', was relayed outside the Abbey and around the world, the broadcast pictures breathtaking in their solemn beauty, giving the worldwide audience a sense of both shared and personal loss. Like the funerals of England's kings and queens past, Princess Diana's demonstrated the cathartic and consoling power of royal spectacle, a ceremony of extraordinary allure, polished and brilliantly adapted over the centuries by Europe's grandest surviving monarchy. At one point, Tony Blair, who read from 1st Corinthians, said it was 'something more profound than anything I can remember in the totality of my life'.[84] When the Princess's remains left the Abbey, tens of thousands of mourners crowded the roads to say goodbye as she travelled the 70 miles to her final resting place at Althorp, her ancestral home. They left a trail of tears and flowers in her wake. And like a vapour, 'England's rose' – and America's – vanished.

CHAPTER 10

CONCLUSION

Kings never die.

William Blackstone, *Commentaries*, 1765

In the wash of instant analysis in the days after Princess Diana's death few American commentators questioned the cause of her celebrity, preferring to dwell on its effects. But a Harris Poll taken in December 1997, three months after her funeral, asked a nationwide cross-section of over 1,000 adults in the United States why they admired the Princess. Only 6 per cent of women and 18 per cent of men said they did not admire her. Seven per cent of the sample said that it was because 'she struggled through an unhappy marriage', 11 per cent because 'she lived her life as she wanted to', and 12 per cent because 'she was beautiful and friendly'. The Princess's charitable work had made a significant impact in the United States, for 63 per cent of women and 48 per cent of men said that they most admired her because of her humanitarian activities.[1]

The Harris Poll provided some welcome insight into the foundation of Princess Diana's popularity in the United States, but it failed to ask an essential question: did Americans admire her because she was married to the Prince of Wales and the mother of a future king? Yes, she struggled with an unhappy marriage, but the world was well-endowed with obscure aristocratic women with troublesome husbands. Yes, she was beautiful and friendly, but so were countless women. Yes, she was caring, but Mother Theresa, whose death a week after Diana's made little impact on the American media, was surely the paragon of charity. What would have become of this poorly-educated girl had she not married the heir to the throne? Her fame, at base, was a tribute to the palpable glamour of the British monarchy, which alone among the royal houses of Europe still retained much of its Victorian splendour. For all the abuse heaped on the Prince of Wales and the royal family by Diana's British and American admirers, no one would ever have heard of her without them.

Whatever the cause of her popularity, Princess Diana's death excited a response in America in a way that few other events have done in recent history. Her plight resembled that of Queen Caroline, who had captivated the attention of the American press in the early nineteenth century, with the added allure that Diana was highly visible in the United States. Like the case of Queen Caroline, the death of the Princess created a momentary surge in anti-royalist murmuring on both sides of the Atlantic, but did not seriously threaten the monarchy. The Princess was not only an unlikely radical heroine, but her many admirers knew that she wanted Prince William to become king one day. Compassion for the young princes did not hearten enemies of the Crown. After the catharsis of Diana's funeral, there was no enthusiasm in Blair's Labour Party, with its comforting language of continuity and renewal, for a serious discussion of the monarchy's future.

Americans followed the unfolding drama of the dead Princess as it was played out in Britain with a fascination usually reserved for a favoured soap opera or the latest pop idol. More than any other member of the royal family in living memory, Diana captivated a cross-section of Americans throughout the country. Not since the Abdication had they been so animated by a royal issue, but now they became so involved that the fate of the Princess would colour their views of the monarchy for years. In the decade after Diana's death the Queen Mother passed away, Elizabeth II celebrated her Golden Jubilee, the Prince of Wales remarried and twice visited the United States with his wife the Duchess of Cornwall and the Queen returned to America to celebrate the 400th anniversary of the settlement of Jamestown. These events attracted considerable interest in the United States, but the reporting suggested that many Americans saw them through the prism of their attachment to Princess Diana.

The vivid reaction to Princess Diana's death in the United States, which many thought exaggerated, if not unseemly, was not an aberration as some might suppose, but was in keeping with the interest that royalty has aroused in America since its colonial beginnings. It was a further, dramatic chapter in the saga of royalty's hold over the American imagination. One is reminded of the obeisance to George III before the Revolution, the ecstatic reception given to the Prince of Wales in 1860, the reverence for Queen Victoria at her jubilees, the buzz surrounding Edward VIII and Mrs Simpson, and the warmth shown to Queen Elizabeth during the Bicentennial. The outpouring of joy and sorrow towards members of the royal family over the centuries indicates that the British monarchy has cast a long shadow across American history, leaving a legacy that is both puzzling and profound.

The longstanding emotional attachment to royalty suggests that the break with Britain at the foundation of the republic was less absolute than is widely assumed. It was indicative of something deeper. Americans had turned away from the mother country, but they still retained a sense of family as citizens of an independent but kindred nation. For many nineteenth-century American commentators, the nation's British inheritance – its language and literature, its mores and habits of mind, its respect for the law and representative government – were determinant. 'Say what you will', observed Harriet Beecher Stowe in a letter home from Liverpool in 1853, 'an American, particularly a New Englander, can never approach the old country without a kind of thrill and pulsation of kindred. Its history for two centuries was our history. Its literature, laws, and language are our literature, laws, and language. . . . Our very life-blood is English life-blood.'[2] Such views, though in the minority today, have persisted, most notably among those of English ancestry in those parts of the country with historic ties to Britain.

To some, all the talk about America's cultural diversity simply cloaks the underlying Britishness of American values. A historian of early America wrote in the 1950s that 'Great Britain's influence is still so strong that it subtly determines qualities of mind and character in Americans who cannot claim a drop of Anglo-Saxon blood.'[3] In his survey of British folkways in America (1989), David Hackett Fischer noted that 'in a cultural sense most Americans are Albion's seed, no matter who their own forebears may have been'.[4] Demographic statistics reveal that 49 per cent of the American population in 1990 was attributable to the settler and slave populations of 1790.[5] The conservative social critic Russell Kirk argued in the 1990s that if the British elements were removed from United States society 'Americans would be left with no coherent culture in public or private life.'[6] Such readings of United States history may be seen as against the grain of multicultural trends. But the enduring fascination with the monarchy should be seen against the background of the tenacity of what the political scientist Samuel P. Huntington approvingly calls 'Anglo-Protestant values'.[7]

History is fate. Lincoln's 'mystic chords of memory' from the Revolution did not excise those mystic chords of monarchy that have reverberated through American history since the first English settlers landed four centuries ago. As Harriet Beecher Stowe reminds us, monarchical rule lasted for nearly two centuries before American independence. It is thus not surprising that successive generations have found it difficult to discard the royal inheritance. For all the king-bashing in the Revolution, Jefferson said of royalism in 1789: 'some of us retain that idolatry still'.[8] Over two centuries later, many Americans still do. It suggests that Americans are less exceptional as a people than they take themselves to be, whether in politics or consciousness. To some of the Founding Fathers it was not simply the weight of the colonial past that could not be excised, but human behaviour. Franklin succumbed to the royal mystique while living in England and even after the turmoil of the Revolution thought mankind had 'a natural inclination . . . to Kingly Government'. Likewise, John Adams believed that mankind had an innate affection for monarchy, pomp and titles. The history of the United States does not contradict their views.

Politically, Americans forged a Constitution and a court modelled on the British monarchy, with the panoply of power and patriotism centred on the Presidency. As various commentators noted in the eighteenth century – and as has been intimated ever since – America is a veiled monarchy. But America is a monarchy with crucial differences. Firstly, it is elective and consequently lacks a hereditary family on the throne to give it the extraordinary glamour that United States citizens seem to relish. (Had America adopted a hereditary monarchy it is likely that there would have been a woman head of state by now.) The American press touched on this longing for the dynastic during the visit of the Prince and Princess of Wales in 1985: 'Lacking a monarchy, lacking even an indirectly elected chief of state like West Germany's President, Americans gravitate toward the British monarchy'.[9]

Secondly, America's elective monarchy is unusual among nations, whether republics or hereditary monarchies, in combining the executive and the head of state in a single office. As a consequence the country lacks a non-political head of state who can provide consensus and a focus for national pride in times of crisis or political division. This has been an unresolved issue since the foundation of the nation – witness the administrations of Andrew Jackson and Richard Nixon, to mention only two partisan presidents who divided rather than united the country. Over a century ago, an American constitutional expert noted the dangers inherent in combining the ceremonial and the practical in the Presidency, which he described as an elective monarchy: 'The attempt to compass these two functions is a killing task, fraught with great perils to the individual incumbent and to the public welfare'.[10]

The United States Constitution encourages Americans to revere the President as head of state even when they disapprove of him as the executive or commander in chief. The result is a disconnection between thoughts and feelings in the citizenry, which leads to perplexity while diluting criticism of presidential abuse. One is reminded of the discomfort of some Americans in 1842 when the news appeared that New York dignitaries greeted a toast to President Tyler in silence but stood to applaud one to Queen Victoria. In Britain, with its more elastic Constitution, such discomfort is largely avoided. In times of political turmoil, censure is directed at the Prime Minister, who can be removed from office far more readily than an American President, while the monarch, who 'can do no wrong' constitutionally, serves as an anchor of national unity and identity. In a much-quoted remark the historian Thomas Babington Macaulay observed that the United States Constitution 'is all sail and no anchor'.[11]

The constitutional contrast between the two nations has not been without effect on American perceptions of Britain and its monarchy. Given their cultural origins many Americans have looked approvingly on the dignity and decorum of Britain's head of state, especially at times when those qualities were wanting at home. As the *New York Times* noted recently, Americans have invested in the Presidency 'something of the awe due to royalty'.[12] But in United States politics the presidential norm has been less than inspiring. To paraphrase Anthony Trollope, who remembers Van Buren, Harrison, Tyler, Polk, Taylor, Fillmore, Pierce, Buchanan, Johnson, Hayes, Garfield, Arthur, Harrison, McKinley, Harding, Coolidge, Hoover . . .? And when Americans do remember their presidents it is often for an abuse of power rather than a profile in courage. As an anonymous American commentator observed in 1860: 'The citizens . . . of the United States, in the absence of any prominent object of admiration at home, have, not unnaturally, adopted the image of the queen of England in the place of a national idol.'[13]

The Loyalists lost in the Revolution but had their revenge in the republic. Given the familial, linguistic, religious and commercial ties with Britain, the former colonists chose to make their peace with the mother country. Reconciliation ripened into a robust transatlantic culture in the reigns of Queen Victoria and Edward VII, reinforced by the infusion of American wealth into some of the oldest aristocratic families of Britain. Americans rediscovered their royalist sympathies in the nineteenth century in part because the British monarchy, nervous about its future in a democratic age, wished to have the good opinion of the American people and worked towards that end. Moreover, as benign instruments of foreign policy, monarchs have proved of great utility in Britain's diplomatic dealings with the United States, which points to the advantages of a head of state outside politics with a family of ambassadors spreading goodwill in the wings.

British monarchs, at least since Queen Victoria, have been admired, if not revered, in the United States, where they may be said to have put the 'special' into the 'special relationship'. In an era of unsettling social change large numbers of Americans, though now a minority, have found in the British monarchy a symbol of stability and tradition embellished by a royal theatre of absorbing spectacle. Many Britons cannot remember their prime ministers

38. *The Royalty Trap*, cartoon of Uncle Sam and royal image in mirror, *The Economist*, 12 May 2007.

but know their kings and queens by heart. Americans, without a dynastic head of state outside politics, simply forget their presidents. Royal pageantry, the quaintness of monarchs, and their longevity in office do not altogether explain the continuing fascination with royal tradition. Nor do the shortcomings of all but a few prime ministers and presidents as national idols.

It is said that monarchy is naturally comprehensible because it reflects the human condition in a way that is foreign to politics.[14] As James Bryce noted in the late nineteenth century, kingship 'touches the imagination whereas assemblies excite . . . criticism'.[15] At the time of the Coronation of Queen Elizabeth II, the *Christian Science Monitor* mused that presidents are prose but queens are poetry.[16] 'So long as the human heart is strong and the human reason weak', as Bagehot reminds us, 'Royalty will be strong because it appeals to diffused feeling, and Republics weak because they appeal to understanding.'[17] A seamless narrative of kings and queens, in turn chapters in a family saga honouring universal rites of passage, has the charm of the familiar and timeless. 'Kings never die', observed William Blackstone early in the reign of George III.[18]

Old ties and influences die hard even in republics founded in revolt. Americans have widely shared with the British a devotion to precedent, a love of ancient ritual, a toleration of inherited privilege, a fondness for dynastic families, a regard for titles, and deference to their head of state. Such proclivities allay the weightlessness of life in a nation that both dreads and is drawn to change, committed to the future but uncertain what the future might bring. The past provides consoling ballast in times of uncertainty. Thus most Americans seem to have little difficulty in bowing to the Queen even when it gives them qualms about their patriotism. In doing so they are acknowledging her role as a living symbol of a shared history. For all the nation's experimentation and diversity, and despite the waning influence of a specifically British culture, there remains a residual, time-honoured attachment to the monarchy in the 'monarcho-republic', which continues to shape the way many Americans view themselves and the world. Every parent believes in the hereditary principle.

NOTES

Chapter 1

1. *The Papers of Benjamin Franklin*, ed. Leonard Labaree et al., 38 vols (New Haven and London, 1959 2006), vol. 9, p. 355.
2. Ronald W. Clark, *Benjamin Franklin. A Biography* (New York, 1983), p. 165.
3. Roy Strong, *Coronation. A History of Kingship and the British Monarchy* (London, 2005), p. 394.
4. *The Papers of Benjamin Franklin*, vol. 10, p. 407.
5. Ibid., vol. 14, p. 253.
6. Ibid., vol. 19, p. 259.
7. Brendan McConville, *The King's Three Faces: The Rise & Fall of Royal America, 1688–1776* (Chapel Hill, 2006), pp. 63–70.
8. Quoted in Jerrilyn Greene Marston, *King and Congress: The Transfer of Political Legitimacy, 1774–1776* (Princeton, 1987), p. 13.
9. Louise Burnham Dunbar, *A Study of 'Monarchical' Tendencies in the United States from 1776–1801* (Urbana, Illinois, 1922), p. 9.
10. Marston, *King and Congress: The Transfer of Political Legitimacy, 1774–1776*, p. 35.
11. T. H. Benton, *Thirty Years' View ... of the American Government ... from 1820 to 1850*, 2 vols (New York, 1856–1858), vol. 1, p. 58.
12. On this issue see McConville, *The King's Three Faces: The Rise & Fall of Royal America, 1688–1776*; Marston, *King and Congress: The Transfer of Political Legitimacy, 1774–1776*. On the flourishing culture of Loyalism in British society see Hannah Smith, *Georgian Monarchy: Politics and Culture, 1714–1760* (Cambridge, 2006).
13. *The Papers of Benjamin Franklin*, vol. 17, pp. 161–5. See also Louis Namier, *Crossroads of Power* (New York, 1962), p. 128.
14. McConville, *The King's Three Faces: The Rise & Fall of Royal America, 1688–1776*, p. 8.
15. John Brooke, *King George III* (London, 1985), p. 173.
16. Jeremy Black, *George III: America's Last King* (New Haven and London, 2006), p. 220.
17. Thomas Paine, *Rights of Man, Common Sense, and other Political Writings*, ed. Mark Philp (Oxford, 1995), pp. 15–18.
18. Thomas Hutchinson, *Strictures upon the Declaration of the Congress at Philadelphia* (London, 1776), pp. 16, 28.

19. Black, *George III: America's Last King*, pp. 224–7.
20. *The Papers of Benjamin Franklin*, vol. 37, pp. 194–5.
21. The volume, published in 1769, is among the Franklin Collection at Yale University. I am grateful to Ellen Cohn for showing me this volume.
22. See Sheila L. Skemp, *William Franklin: Son of a Patriot, Servant of a King* (New York, 1990).
23. Louis B. Wright, *The First Gentlemen of Virginia: Intellectual Qualities of the Early Colonial Ruling Class* (Stanford, 1949), pp. 128, 131.
24. Edmund S. Morgan, *The Birth of the Republic, 1763–89* (Chicago, 1992), p. 7.
25. H. C. Allen, *Great Britain and the United States. A History of Anglo-American Relations (1783–1952)*, (New York, 1955), p. 240. Most historians of Loyalism would put Adams's estimate on the high side.
26. On Loyalism see William H. Nelson, *The American Tory* (Oxford, 1962); Wallace Brown, *The King's Friends* (Providence, 1966). On Loyalist slaves see Simon Schama, *Rough Crossings: Britain, the Slaves and the American Revolution* (London, 2005).
27. John Shy, 'The Loyalist Problem in the Lower Hudson Valley: The British Perspective', *The Loyalist Americans: A Focus on Greater New York*, eds Robert A. East and Jacob Judd (Tarrytown, 1975), p. 4.
28. Paul Downes, *Democracy, Revolution, and Monarchism in Early American Literature* (Cambridge, 2002), p. 35.
29. Black, *George III: America's Last King*, p. 227.
30. David Hackett Fischer, *Albion's Seed: Four British Folkways in America* (New York and Oxford, 1989), p. 47.
31. King George to Lord North, 7 March 1780, in *Correspondence of King George the Third from 1760 to December 1783*, ed. Sir John Fortescue, 6 vols (London, 1927–8), vol. 5, p. 30, quoted John L. Bullion 'George III on Empire, 1783', *William and Mary Quarterly*, 3rd ser., vol. 51, no. 2, p. 305.
32. Quoted in R. B. Mowat, *Americans in England* (London, 1935), p. 54. See also Allen, *Great Britain and the United States*, pp. 255–6.
33. RA George Add 32/2010/11. The entire document is included in Bullion, 'George III on Empire, 1783'.
34. Bullion, 'George III on Empire, 1783', p. 309.
35. *The Works of John Adams* (Boston, 1853), vol. viii, pp. 256–7.
36. Ibid., p. 257. See also David McCullough, *John Adams*, (New York, 2001), pp. 336.
37. See www.ellisislandimmigrants.org. See also Thomas L. Purvis, 'The European Ancestry of The United States Population, 1790: A Symposium', *William and Mary Quarterly*, 3rd series, vol. 41, no. 1, January, 1984, p. 98.
38. Samuel P. Huntington, *Who Are We? Challenges to America's National Identity* (New York, 2004), p. 44.
39. Quoted in Fischer, *Albion's Seed: Four British Folkways in America*, p. 831.
40. Quoted in Rufus Wilmost Griswold, *The Republican Court or American Society in the Days of Washington* (New York, 1855), p. 381.
41. B. F. Bache, *Remarks Occasioned by the Late Conduct of Mr. Washington, President of the United States* (Philadelphia, 1797), p. 38.
42. For a discussion of monarchy in the eighteenth century see Black, *George III: America's Last King*, chapter 3.
43. Forest McDonald, *The American Presidency: An Intellectual History* (Lawrence, Kansas, 1994), p. 4.
44. Quoted in Richard N. Rosenfeld, *American Aurora* (New York, 1997), pp. 500–1.
45. For a discussion of American republicanism see Gordon S. Wood, *The Creation of the American Republic 1776–1787* (Chapel Hill, 1969), chapter 2.
46. See, for example, the engraving titled 'The Constitution of England' c. 1774, by an unknown artist, in the British Library.

47. *The Papers of Alexander Hamilton*, 27 vols, ed. Harold C. Syrett (New York, 1962–87), vol. 25, p. 536; Alexander Hamilton, James Madison and John Jay, *The Federalist Papers* (New American Library, 1961), no. 39, pp. 240–1.
48. Paine, *Rights of Man, Common Sense, and other Political Writings*, p. 230.
49. John Adams, *A Defence of the Constitutions of Government of the United States of America*, 3 vols (Philadelphia, 1797), vol. 1, p. 87; vol. 3, p. 159.
50. Quoted in Brooke, *King George III*, pp. 56–7. See also P. D. G. Thomas, 'Thoughts on the British Constitution by George III in 1760', *Historical Research: Bulletin of the Institute of Historical Research*, vol. 60, number 143 (October, 1987), pp. 361–3.
51. Quoted in Black, *George III: America's Last King*, p. 12.
52. Richard Pares, 'Limited Monarchy in Great Britain in the Eighteenth Century' (Historical Association, 1957) p. 21.
53. Quoted in Wood, *The Creation of the American Republic 1776–1787*, p. 561.
54. P. D. G. Thomas, 'George III and the American Revolution', *History*, vol. 70 (February, 1985), pp. 16–31. See also Namier, *Crossroads of Power*, p. 129.
55. Brooke, *King George III*, p. 176.
56. Ibid., p. 175.
57. Alexander Hamilton in *Federalist* no. 69 also overstated the King's authority.
58. Brooke, *King George III*, p. 200.
59. The King strongly opposed William Pitt's proposal for Catholic emancipation in 1801, but as the measure was withdrawn it did not reach the stage where a royal veto might have been invoked. See Black, *George III: America's Last King*, p. 374; Robert J. Spitzer, 'The President's Veto Power', *Inventing the American Presidency*, ed. Thomas E. Cronin (Lawrence, Kansas, 1989), pp. 157–8, 173.
60. Walter Bagehot, *The English Constitution* (Oxford, 2001), p. 53.
61. Edward S. Corwin, *The President, Office and Powers 1787–1948* (New York, 1940), p. 459.
62. James Bryce, *The American Commonwealth* (New York, 1933), p. 14.
63. Vernon Bogdanor, *The Monarchy and the Constitution* (Oxford, 1995), p. 11.
64. Dunbar, *A Study of 'Monarchical' Tendencies in the United States from 1776 to 1801*, p. 128.
65. *The Writings of Thomas Jefferson*, 20 vols, ed. Albert Ellery Bergh (Washington, D.C., 1904), vol. 16, p. 94.
66. See Richard Krauel, 'Prince Henry of Prussia and the Regency of the United States, 1786', *American Historical Review*, vol. xvii (1911–1912), pp. 44–51.
67. *The Writings of Thomas Jefferson*, vol. 17, p. 400.
68. Quoted in Dunbar, *A Study of 'Monarchical' Tendencies in the United States from 1776 to 1801*, p. 45.
69. *The Writings of George Washington*, ed. John C. Fitzpatrick, 39 vols (Washington, 1931–1944), vol. 24, pp. 272–3.
70. Ralph Ketcham, *Presidents Above Party: the First American Presidency, 1789–1829* (Williamsburg, Virginia, 1984), p. 90; McDonald, *The American Presidency: An Intellectual History*, p. 152.
71. John Keane, *Tom Paine: A Political Life* (London, 1995), pp. 283–4.
72. George Bancroft, *The History of the United States: From the Discovery of the American Continent*, 10 vols (Boston, 1864–1875), vol. 8, p. 474.
73. *The Papers of Alexander Hamilton*, vol. 1, p. 487.
74. Ron Chernow, *Alexander Hamilton* (New York, 2004), p. 724.
75. Jefferson to Lafayette, 16 June 1792, *The Writings of Thomas Jefferson*, vol. 8, p. 381.
76. *The Papers of Alexander Hamilton*, vol. 4, pp. 184–6.
77. See, in particular, *Federalist Papers*, nos 67 and 69.
78. Ibid., no. 70, p. 430.
79. Chernow, *Alexander Hamilton*, p. 232.

80. *The Papers of Alexander Hamilton*, vol. 4, p. 194. See also Chernow, *Alexander Hamilton*, p. 232.
81. *The Papers of Alexander Hamilton*, vol. 25, p. 536.
82. *The Autobiography of Thomas Jefferson 1743–1790* (New York, 1959), p. 75. See also Black, *George III: America's Last King*, p. 342.
83. *The Writings of Thomas Jefferson*, vol. 16, p. 93.
84. Joanne B. Freeman, *Affairs of Honor: National Politics in the New Republic* (New Haven and London, 2001), pp. 22, 62–9.
85. *The Papers of Alexander Hamilton*, vol. xii, p. 253.
86. For a discussion of American political views of mixed government, which emphasizes the radical and democratic elements see ibid., chapter vi.
87. Sir Henry Maine, *Popular Government: Four Essays* (New York, 1886), p. 212.
88. Bernard Bailyn, *The Ideological Origins of the American Constitution* (Cambridge, Mass., 1967), p. 71.
89. Quoted in Wood, *The Creation of the American Republic 1776–1787*, p. 236.
90. On this issue see Maine, *Popular Government: Four Essays*, essay 4.
91. *The Papers of Thomas Jefferson*, ed. Julian P. Boyd et al., 33 vols (Princeton, 1950–2006), vol. 12, p. 396.
92. Wood, *The Creation of the American Republic 1776–1787*, p. 237.
93. Bache, *Remarks Occasioned by the Late Conduct of Mr. Washington, President of the United States*, p. 38.
94. Griswold, *The Republican Court*, p. 153.
95. Rosenfeld, *American Aurora*, p. 477.
96. Joseph Ellis, *His Excellency: George Washington* (New York, 2004), p. 193; McCullough, *John Adams*, pp. 405–8.
97. McCullough, *John Adams*, p. 405.
98. Bagehot, *The English Constitution*, p. 53.
99. Ellis, *His Excellency: George Washington*, p. 78.
100. Quoted in ibid., p. 77.
101. Quoted in Rosenfeld, *American Aurora*, p. 500.
102. Bache, *Remarks Occasioned by the Late Conduct of Mr. Washington, President of the United States*, pp. 3, 37.
103. Dunbar, *A Study of 'Monarchical' Tendencies in the United States from 1776–1801*, p. 99.
104. http//:memory.loc.gov/ammem/collections/continental/Randolph.
105. J. Elliot, *Debates in the Several State Conventions, on the Adoption of the Federal Constitution*, 5 vols (Philadelphia and Washington, 1866), vol. iii, pp. 58–9.
106. Ibid., vol. iv, p. 311. See also Dunbar, *A Study of 'Monarchical' Tendencies in the United States from 1776–1801*, p. 99.
107. Quoted in McCullough, *John Adams*, pp. 410–11.
108. Benjamin Franklin, 'Dangers of a Salaried Bureaucracy', 1787. See also Max Farrand, *Records of the Federal Convention of 1787*, 3 vols (New Haven, 1911), vol. 1, p. 83.
109. Chernow, *Alexander Hamilton*, p. 278.
110. Gordon Wood, *Revolutionary Characters: What Made the Founders Different* (New York, 2006), p. 52.
111. Griswold, *The Republican Court*, passim.
112. Quoted in Wood, *Revolutionary Characters: What Made the Founders Different*, p. 52.
113. McCullough, *John Adams*, p. 402.
114. *The Diary of William Maclay and Other Notes on Senate Debates*, eds Kenneth R. Bowling and Helen E. Veit (Baltimore, 1988), vol. ix, pp. 13–16.
115. James Thompson Callender, *The Prospect Before Us* (Richmond, 1800), p. 18.
116. Henry Jones Ford, *The Rise and Growth of American Politics: A Sketch of Constitutional Development* (New York, 1898), pp. 72–3.

117. Wood, *Revolutionary Characters: What Made the Founders Different*, pp. 52–3.
118. *The Papers of George Washington*, ed. W. W. Abbot (Charlottesville, 1989), series 3, June–September 1789, pp. 290–1.
119. Bradford Perkins, *The First Rapprochement: England and the United States 1795–1805* (Philadelphia, 1955), p. 18.
120. *The Life and Correspondence of Rufus King*, ed. Charles R. King (New York, 1896), vol. 3, p. 202.
121. McDonald, *The American Presidency: An Intellectual History*, p. 252.
122. *General Advertiser*, 25 February 1794.
123. *Washington Federalist*, 3 January 1805.
124. *Federal Republican & Commercial Gazette*, 17 August 1810.
125. See, for example, *Aurora*, 2 January 1793.
126. *Hampden Patriot and Liberal Recorder*, 17 July 1822.
127. *New York Journal, & Patriotic Register*, 20 August 1791.
128. *Herald of Freedom, and the Federal Advertiser*, 9 October 1789.
129. *Pennsylvania Gazette*, 5 October 1791.
130. For a description of the levées of George III see Brooke, *King George III*, pp. 293–8.
131. See, for example, a letter from a young gentleman from Philadelphia, *Federal Orrery*, 2 June 1796.
132. Griswold, *The Republican Court*, p. 165.
133. Ibid., pp. 269–70
134. Ellis, *His Excellency George Washington*, p. 193.
135. Griswold, *The Republican Court*, p. 215.
136. *Carlisle Gazette, and the Western Repository of Knowledge*, 6 March 1793. See also *Aurora*, 2 January 1793.
137. *The Diary of William Maclay and Other Notes on Senate Debates*, vol. ix, pp. 70, 342.
138. *The Life and Correspondence of Rufus King*, vol. 3, pp. 549–50.
139. Chernow, *Alexander Hamilton*, p. 278.
140. *National Gazette*, 2 February 1793.
141. Bagehot, *The English Constitution*, p. 41.
142. Bryce, *The American Commonwealth*, p. 23.
143. Maine, *Popular Government: Four Essays*, p. 211. The American political theorist Russell Kirk revisited Maine's analysis and observed: 'the president of the United States is an elected king'. See Russell Kirk, *America's British Culture* (New Brunswick, New Jersey, 1993), p. 64.
144. Bagehot, *The English Constitution*, p. 48.
145. Ford, *The Rise and Growth of American Politics: A Sketch of Constitutional Development*, pp. 61–2.
146. Jefferson to William Short, 8 January 1825, *The Writings of Thomas Jefferson*, vol. 16, p. 93–5.
147. *The Writings of Thomas Jefferson*, vol. 7, p. 312.
148. On this issue see Jeremy D. Mayer and Lee Segelman, 'Zog for Albania, Edward for Estonia, and Monarchs for all the Rest? The Royal Road to Prosperity, Democracy, and World Peace', *PS: Political Science and Politics*, December 1998, p. 773.
149. Arthur M. Schlesinger, Jr, *The Imperial Presidency* (Boston, 1973), p. 213. For an updated study of the imperial Presidency see Charlie Savage, *The Return of the Imperial Presidency and the Subversion of American Democracy* (New York, 2007).
150. See, for example, Nat Hentoff, 'Who Made George W. Bush our King?', *The Village Voice*, 25 July 2003; Jacob Weisberg, 'The Power Madness of King George', *Slate*, 25 January 2006; Michael Isikoff, Richard Wolffe, and Evan Thomas, 'Disorder in King George's Court', *Newsweek*, 26 March 2007; John Hanchette, 'Monarchism Remains Alive and Well', www.niagarafallsreporter.com, 14 August 2007.
151. Sheldon Richman, 'Our Elective Monarchy', *Atlanta Inquirer*, 3 July 2004.

152. Stephen Graubard, *The Presidents: The Transformation of the American Presidency from Theodore Roosevelt to George W. Bush* (London, 2004), pp. 3–4, passim.
153. On Britain as a republic see Frank Prochaska, *The Republic of Britain, 1760–2000* (London, 2000).
154. *The Monthly Religious Magazine and Independent Journal*, 24 December 1860.

Chapter 2

1. Quoted in Beckles Willson, *America's Ambassadors to England (1785–1928)* (New York, 1928), p. 47.
2. Ibid., p. 45.
3. H. C. Allen, *Great Britain and the United States: A History of Anglo-American Relations (1783–1952)* (New York, 1955), p. 287.
4. Quoted in Charles R. Ritcheson, *Aftermath of Revolution: British Policy Toward the United States 1783–1795* (Dallas, Texas, 1969), p. 357.
5. David Hancock, 'Transatlantic Trade in the Era of the American Revolution', *Anglo-American Attitudes: From Revolution to Partnership*, eds Fred M. Leventhal and Roland Quinalt (Aldershot, 2000), p. 38.
6. Bradford Perkins, *The First Rapprochement: England and the United States 1795–1805* (Philadelphia, 1955), p. 13.
7. Allen, *Great Britain and the United States: A History of Anglo-American Relations (1783–1952)*, pp. 56, 59, 299.
8. Christopher Mulvey, *Anglo-American Landscapes: A Study of Nineteenth-Century Anglo-American Travel Literature* (Cambridge, 1983), chapter 4.
9. Scores of citations for the King's Jubilee can be found on the America's Historical Newspapers internet site, www.newsbank.com/readex.
10. *American Watchman*, 27 December 1809.
11. *Salem Gazette*, 26 December 1809.
12. *Newburyport Herald*, 6 April 1810.
13. Quoted in *Vermont Gazette*, 16 February 1830.
14. *The Works of John Wesley*, 14 vols (London, 1872), vol. 11, p. 16.
15. Hilaire Belloc, *Louis XIV* (New York and London, 1938), p. 7.
16. *The Vicar of Bray* (1734).
17. See Marilyn Morris, *The British Monarchy and the French Revolution* (New Haven, 1998).
18. *Arkansas Gazette*, 6 May 1820.
19. *New-Hampshire Gazette*, 1 August 1820.
20. *Ladies' Literary Cabinet*, 6 May 1820.
21. *Salem Gazette*, 28 July 1820.
22. *Carolina Centinel*, 8 August 1820.
23. *Salem Gazette*, 28 March 1820.
24. *The Greville Memoirs*, ed. Henry Reeve, 8 vols (London, 1888), vol. 1, p. 159.
25. See, for example, *Carlisle Gazette*, 5 June 1812. See also E. A. Smith, *George IV* (New Haven and London, 1999), p. 23.
26. Henry Adams, *History of the United States during the Administration of James Madison*, 4 vols (New York, 1930), vol. 3, book vi, p. 19.
27. Quoted in ibid., vol. 4, book viii, p. 314.
28. See, for example, *Alexandria Gazette*, 2 October 1812; *New Hampshire Patriot*, 29 September 1812.
29. A. J. Langguth, *Union–1812* (New York 2006), p. 382.
30. Willson, *America's Ambassadors to England (1785–1928)*, pp. 136–7.
31. Richard Rush, *Memoranda of a Residence at the Court of London* (Philadelphia, 1833), pp. 112–26.

32. Willson, *America's Ambassadors to England (1785–1928)*, p. 137.
33. *New York Sentinel and Working Man's Advocate*, 11 August 1830.
34. *New-York Columbian*, 7 January 1818.
35. Helen Currie, *Poems* (Philadelphia, 1818), pp. 107–8.
36. *Connecticut Gazette*, 27 December 1820.
37. *Connecticut Courant*, 25 September 1821.
38. *Connecticut Gazette*, 27 December 1820.
39. *Middlesex Gazette*, 26 October 1820.
40. *Washington Irving and the Storrows: Letters from England and the Continent, 1821–1828*, ed. Stanley T. Williams (Cambridge, Mass., 1933), pp. 13–14.
41. See, for example, *New York Commercial Advertiser*, 19 July 1820.
42. *Baltimore Patriot*, 20 October 1830.
43. *Providence Gazette*, 15 September 1821.
44. *New York Evangelist*, 14 August 1830.
45. *Casket*, June 1830.
46. *Correspondence of Andrew Jackson*, ed. John Spencer Bassett, 7 vols (Washington D. C., 1926–1935), vol. 4, p. 159.
47. *New-Hampshire Gazette*, 17 August 1830.
48. *Eastern Argus*, 10 August 1830.
49. *The Times*, 16 July 1820.
50. W. M. Thackeray, *The Four Georges* (London, 1861), p. 169.
51. *Diary of Charles Francis Adams*, 6 vols, eds Marc Friedlaender and C. H. Butterfield (Cambridge, Mass., 1974), vol. 5, p. 53.
52. Willson, *America's Ambassadors to England (1785–1928)*, p. vii.
53. Henry Jones Ford, *The Rise and Growth of American Politics: A Sketch of Constitutional Development* (New York, 1898), p. 3.
54. David Hackett Fischer, *Albion's Seed: Four British Folkways in America* (New York and Oxford, 1989), pp. 10–11.
55. Louis B. Wright, *Culture on the Moving Frontier* (Bloomington, 1955), p. 122.
56. On the character and tenacity of 'Anglo-Protestant culture', see Samuel P. Huntington, *Who Are We? The Challenges to America's National Identity* (New York, 2004), chapter 4.
57. Paul Langford, 'Manners and Character in Anglo-American Perceptions, 1750–1850', *Anglo-American Attitudes: From Revolution to Partnership*, eds Fred M. Leventhal and Roland Quinault (Aldershot, 2000), p. 84.
58. Michel Chevalier, *Society, Manners, and Politics in the United States* (New York, 1961), p. 139.
59. Henry Adams, *The Education of Henry Adams: An Autobiography* (Boston and New York, 1918), p. 19.
60. Quoted in Howard Temperley, *Britain and America since Independence* (Basingstoke and New York, 2002), p. 45.
61. Gerald W. Johnson, *Our English Heritage* (Philadelphia and New York, 1949), pp. 237–8.
62. J. B. McMaster, *A History of the People of the United States, from the Revolution to the Civil War*, 8 vols (New York, 1903), vol. 5, p. 287.
63. Basil Hall, *Travels in North America*, 2 vols (Philadelphia, 1829), vol. 1, p. 239.
64. Frances Trollope, *Domestic Manners of the Americans* (New York, 1949), p. 404.
65. Alexis de Tocqueville, *Democracy in America*, eds Harvey Mansfield and Delba Winthrop (Chicago, 2000), p. 544.
66. Calvin Colton, *The Americans* (London, 1833), pp. 160–3.
67. Ibid., p. 160–1.
68. *The Private Letters of Princess Lieven to Prince Metternich, 1820–1826*, ed. Peter Quennell (London, 1937), p. 372.

69. *The Ariel*, 21 August 1830.
70. See, for example, *Salem Gazette*, 15 November 1831; *Eastern Argus*, 11 November 1831.
71. Philip Ziegler, *King William IV* (London, 1971), pp. 38–9.
72. *New York Sentinel and Working Man's Advocate*, 11 August 1830.
73. *The Nineteenth-Century Constitution 1815–1914: Documents and Commentary*, ed. H. J. Hanham (London, 1969), p. 31.
74. Calvin Colton, *Four Years in Great Britain*, 2 vols (New York, 1835), vol. 1, p. 242.
75. Glyndon G. Van Deusen, *William Henry Seward* (New York, 1967), p. 211.
76. Willson, *America's Ambassadors to England (1785–1928)*, p. 188.
77. Ibid., p. 192.
78. Ibid., p. 190.
79. W. Gore Allen, *King William IV* (London, 1960), pp. 32, 45.
80. Quoted in Willson, *America's Ambassadors to England (1785–1928)*, p.195.
81. Ibid. See also *Correspondence of Andrew Jackson*, vol. 4, pp. 351–2.
82. *Correspondence of Andrew Jackson*, vol. 6, pp. 518–19.
83. John T. Morse, *Life and Letters of Oliver Wendell Holmes*, 2 vols (Boston and New York, 1896), vol. 1, p. 135.
84. Oliver Wendell Holmes, *Our Hundred Days in Europe* (Boston, 1887), pp. 51–2.
85. Rush, *Memoranda of a Residence at the Court of London*, p. 141.
86. Charles S. Stewart, *Sketches of Society in Great Britain and Ireland*, 2 vols (Philadelphia, 1834), vol. 1, pp. 107–26.
87. Colton, *Four Years in Great Britain*, vol. 2, p. 307.
88. Charles Dickens, *American Notes* (Gloucester, Mass., 1968), pp. 146–8.
89. *Connecticut Mirror*, 30 January 1830.
90. Dickens, *American Notes*, pp. 149–50.

Chapter 3

1. *Royal Lives*, ed. Frank Prochaska (Oxford, 2002), p. 167.
2. Allen, *Great Britain and the United States: A History of Anglo-American Relations (1783–1952)*, p. 59.
3. See Reginald Horsman, *Race and Manifest Destiny: The Origins of American Racial Anglo-Saxonism* (Cambridge, Mass. and London 1981).
4. *The Diary of George Templeton Strong: Young Man in New York 1835–1849*, ed. Allan Nevins and Milton Halsey Thomas (New York, 1952), p. 71.
5. The *New Yorker*, 29 July 1837.
6. Ibid.
7. Beckles Willson, *America's Ambassadors to England (1785–1928)* (New York, 1928), pp. 205–8.
8. Allen, *Great Britain and the United States. A History of Anglo-American Relations (1783–1952)*, p. 435.
9. *New Bedford Mercury*, 11 June 1838.
10. *Richmond Enquirer*, 31 July 1838.
11. Ibid.
12. Quoted in the *Farmers' Cabinet*, 3 August 1838.
13. *New-Hampshire Sentinel*, 23 August 1838.
14. *New Hampshire Patriot*, 30 July 1838.
15. *Richmond Enquirer*, 31 July 1838.
16. Manuscripts and Archives, Yale University Library, Morse Family papers, ms 358, box 20, folder 2.
17. Willson, *America's Ambassadors to England (1785–1928)*, p. 215.

18. Quoted in Francis Fry Wayland, *Andrew Stevenson: Democrat and Diplomat 1785–1857* (Philadelphia, 1949), p. 163.
19. *Richmond Enquirer*, 31 July 1838.
20. See Christopher Mulvey, *Anglo-American Landscapes: A Study of Nineteenth-Century Anglo-American Travel Literature* (Cambridge, 1983), chapter 1.
21. 170 passports were issued in 1831, 638 in 1845 and 1,167 in 1850. See Willson, *America's Ambassadors to England (1785–1928)*, p. 263.
22. *Atlanta Constitution*, 30 January 1901.
23. Lucy Seymour, 'Queen Victoria', *The Baltimore Monument*, 7 October, 1837; 'Factory Blossoms for Queen Victoria', *The Lowell Offering*, October 1842.
24. Michael J. Sewell, 'Queen of Our Hearts', *Victorianism in the United States: Its era and its legacy*, eds Steven Ickingrill and Stephen Mills (Amsterdam, 1992), p. 215.
25. Willson, *America's Ambassadors to England (1785–1928)*, pp. vii–viii.
26. *New-Hampshire Sentinel*, 14 August 1839.
27. From the *Richmond Enquirer*, quoted in *The Newport Mercury*, 27 April 1839.
28. *Southern Rose*, 4 August 1838; the *New Yorker*, 5 January 1839.
29. The *United States Magazine, and Democratic Review*, July 1839.
30. Ibid.
31. Quoted in *London Court Journal in the New York Mirror: a Weekly Gazettte of Literature and the Fine Arts*, 18 January 1840.
32. *Boston Weekly Magazine: Devoted to Moral and Entertaining Literature*, 29 December 1839.
33. Quoted in *Pittsfield Sun*, 19 December 1839.
34. Walter Bagehot, *The English Constitution*, ed. Miles Taylor (Oxford, 2001), p. 41.
35. Quoted in *Saturday Evening Post*, 4 January 1840.
36. *The Diary of George Templeton Strong: Young Man in New York 1835–1849*, p. 132.
37. Wayland, *Andrew Stevenson: Democrat and Diplomat 1785–1857*, pp. 160, 165.
38. Anonymous, 'To Queen Victoria on her Marriage', *Southern Literary Messenger*, June 1840.
39. Paul Revere Frothingham, *Edward Everett, Orator and Statesman* (Boston, 1925), p. 194.
40. Arthur Cleveland Coxe, *Impressions of England; or, Sketches of English Scenery and Society* (New York, 1860), pp. 1010, 234.
41. Quoted in *Pittsfield Sun*, 19 December 1839.
42. The *New Yorker*, 21 December 1839.
43. Ibid., 14 August 1841.
44. *The Cultivator*, April 1861.
45. James Pope-Hennessy, *Queen Mary 1867–1953* (London, 1959), pp. 55–6.
46. *Old and New*, May 1873.
47. Bagehot, *The English Constitution*, pp. 41, 50.
48. *Christian Parlor Magazine*, January 1845.
49. Quoted in Henry Jones Ford, *The Rise and Growth of American Politics: A Sketch of Constitutional Development* (New York, 1898), p. 180.
50. *Life and Speeches of Henry Clay*, ed. Daniel Mallory, 2 vols (New York, 1844), vol. 2, pp. 378–9.
51. See, for example, *Ohio Statesman*, 7 September 1842; *Milwaukee Sentinel*, 24 June 1848; *Hudson River Chronicle*, 7 November 1848.
52. http://www.worldwideschool.org/library/books/hst/northamerican/UnitedStates PresidentsinauguralSpeeches.
53. Jo. G. Baldwin, *Party Leaders: Sketches of Thomas Jefferson, Alex'r Hamilton, Andrew Jackson, Henry Clay, John Randolph, of Roanoke, including Notices of many other Distinguished American Statesmen* (New York, 1855), p. 331.
54. *Saturday Evening Post*, 10 September 1842.
55. Alexis de Tocqueville, *Democracy in America*, eds Harvey C. Mansfield and Delba Winthrop (Chicago, 2000), p. 190.

56. Anthony Trollope, *North America*, 2 vols (Philadelphia, 1862), vol. 2, p. 216.
57. Norton Long, 'Public Administration and the Goals of Rationality and Responsibility: Further Reflections', *Public Administration Review*, March/April 1996, vol. 56, no. 2, p. 154.
58. James Bryce, *The American Commonwealth* (New York, 1922), pp. 49, 63.
59. Walter Bagehot, 'What *may* be in America', *The Economist*, vol. 19, 17 August 1861, pp. 897–8.
60. Pierre Crabites, *Victoria's Guardian Angel: A Study of Baron Stockmar* (London, 1937), p. 148.
61. G. M. Young, *Victorian England: Portrait of an Age* (London, Galaxy edition, 1964), p. 80.
62. See Tom Nairn, *The Enchanted Glass: Britain and its Monarchy* (London, 1988), p. 195.
63. Willson, *America's Ambassadors to England (1785–1928)*, pp. 281–2.
64. Philip Shriver Klein, *President James Buchanan* (Pennsylvania State University, 1962), pp. 228–9.
65. Willson, *America's Ambassadors to England (1785–1928)*, p. 285.
66. Klein, *President James Buchanan*, p. 285.
67. Ibid., pp. 236–7.
68. RA VIC/Q 9/1.
69. Robert J. Scarry, *Millard Fillmore* (Jefferson, North Carolina, 2001), pp. 268, 290.
70. George Mifflin Dallas, *Letters from London, Written from the Years 1856 to 1860*, ed. Julia Dallas (London, 1870), p. 10.
71. Ibid., pp. 17, 51.
72. Ibid., p. 140.
73. Quoted in *Littell's Living Age*, 11 September 1869.
74. Frances Anne Kemble, *Further Records. 1848–1883*, 2 vols (London, 1890), vol. 2, p. 240.
75. Paul Langford, 'Manners and Character in Anglo-American Perceptions, 1750–1850', *Anglo-American Attitudes: From Revolution to Partnership*, eds Fred M. Leventhal and Roland Quinault (Aldershot, 2000), p. 81.
76. de Tocqueville, *Democracy in America*, p. 543.
77. A copy of this essay can be found at www.4literature.net/James_Russell_Lowell.
78. Bagehot, *The English Constitution*, p. 38.
79. Ibid., p. 41.
80. 'The American Executive', *Christian Examiner*, March 1866.
81. 'The American Constitution at the Present Crisis', *The Collected Works of Walter Bagehot*, ed. Norman St John-Stevas, 15 vols (London, 1974–1986), vol. 4, p. 283.
82. Bagehot, *The English Constitution*, p. 41.
83. The *Independent*, 22 March 1860.
84. Sewell, 'Queen of Our Hearts', p. 222.

Chapter 4

1. For a recent study of the tour see Ian Radforth, *Royal Spectacle: The 1860 Visit of the Prince of Wales to Canada and the United States* (Toronto, 2004). For a brief account see also Dana Bentley-Cranch, *Edward VII: Image of an Era 1841–1910* (London, 1992), pp. 20–34.
2. Kinahan Cornwallis, *Royalty in the New World; or, the Prince of Wales in America* (London, 1860), p. v.
3. *The Times*, 24 July 1860.
4. Cornwallis, *Royalty in the New World*, p. 249.

5. *Christian Observer*, 2 August 1860.
6. Daphne Bennett, *King without a Crown: Albert Prince Consort of England 1819–1861* (Philadelphia and New York, 1977), p. 328.
7. RA VIC/Z 466/23.
8. See Peter J. Parish, 'Confidence and Anxiety in Victorian America', *Victorianism in the United States: Its era and its legacy* (Amsterdam, 1992), pp. 1–18.
9. Frances Trollope, *Domestic Manners of the Americans* (New York, 1949), pp. 408–9.
10. Charles Dickens, *American Notes* (Gloucester, Mass., 1968), pp. 277–86.
11. Anthony Trollope, *North America*, 2 vols (Philadelphia, 1862), vol. 2, pp. 310, 322.
12. *San Francisco Bulletin*, 20 November 1860.
13. John Plunkett, *Queen Victoria: First Media Monarch* (Oxford, 2003), p. 200.
14. *New York Times*, 11 October 1860.
15. *Vanity Fair*, 21 July 1860.
16. RA VIC/Z 466/18.
17. *Littell's Living Age*, 1 December 1860.
18. *New York Times*, 22 September 1860.
19. *Deseret News*, 14 November 1860.
20. Cornwallis, *Royalty in the New World*, p. 163.
21. *New York Times*, 29 October 1860.
22. *Saturday Evening Post*, 3 November 1860.
23. *New York Times*, 29 October 1860.
24. John Gardner Engleheart, *Journal of the Progress of H.R.H. the Prince of Wales through British North America and his Visit to the United States* (London, 1860), p. 81.
25. Trollope, *North America*, vol. 2, p. 16.
26. Philip Shriver Klein, *President James Buchanan*, (Pennsylvania State University, 1962) p. 350; Elbert B. Smith, *The Presidency of James Buchanan* (Kansas, 1975), p. 72.
27. [Henry Adams], *Democracy* (New York, 1961), p. 57.
28. Cornwallis, *Royalty in the New World*, p. 186.
29. *New York Times*, 5 October 1860; Radforth, *Royal Spectacle*, p. 320.
30. Engleheart, *Journal of the Progress of H.R.H. the Prince of Wales through British North America and his Visit to the United States*, p. 82.
31. Anonymous, 'At the Grave of Washington', quoted in Cornwallis, *Royalty in the New World* p. 281.
32. *Littell's Living Age*, 3 November 1860.
33. *Saturday Review*, 13 October 1860.
34. *New York Herald*, 19 January 1861.
35. Philip Magnus, *King Edward the Seventh* (London, 1964), p. 39.
36. *Saturday Evening Post*, 20 October 1860.
37. *New York Herald*, 10 October 1860.
38. The Downs Collection of Manuscripts and Printed Ephemera at the Winterthur Library contains several dolls of the Queen and the Prince of Wales. Prince Albert tobacco, which is still for sale, appeared after the death of the Prince Consort, but it was not named for him but probably for Prince Albert Edward, later Edward VII.
39. *San Francisco Bulletin*, 21 November 1860.
40. *American Broadsides and Ephemera*, Series 1, no. 1621.
41. Quoted Radforth, *Royal Spectacle*, p. 347.
42. Ibid., p. 347.
43. *American Broadsides and Ephemera*, series 1, no. 261.
44. Radforth, *Royal Spectacle*, pp. 346–52.
45. *The Diary of George Templeton Strong: The Civil War 1860–1865*, eds Allan Nevins and Milton Halsey Thomas (New York, 1952), p. 45.
46. *Punch*, 14 July 1860.
47. Radforth, *Royal Spectacle*, p. 336.

48. Cornwallis, *Royalty in the New World*, p. 207.
49. *Harper's Weekly*, 27 October 1860.
50. Cornwallis, *Royalty in the New World*, p. 205.
51. *New York Times*, 18 October 1860.
52. Ibid., 13 October 1860.
53. *San Antonia Ledger and Texan*, 27 October 1860.
54. *New York Times*, 13 October, 1860.
55. Cornwallis, *Royalty in the New World*, p. 209.
56. *Saturday Evening Post*, 3 November 1860.
57. *Boston Daily Advertiser*, 16 November 1860.
58. *New York Times*, 13 October 1860.
59. Ibid.
60. *The Diary of George Templeton Strong: The Civil War 1860–1865*, p. 47.
61. Edmund C. Stedman, 'The Prince's Ball,' *Vanity Fair*, 20 October, 1860.
62. Lloyd R. Morris, *Incredible New York. High Life and Low Life of the Last Hundred Years* (New York, 1951), pp. 23–4.
63. Quoted in *Littell's Living Age*, 8 September 1860.
64. *Saturday Evening Post*, 20 October 1860.
65. *Harper's Weekly*, 1860, issue 8/18.
66. Engleheart, *Journal of the Progress of H.R.H. the Prince of Wales through British North America and his Visit to the United States*, pp. 96–7.
67. Ibid., pp. 98–9.
68. *New York Times*, 20 October 1860.
69. *Liberator*, 2 November 1860.
70. *Saturday Evening Post*, 29 September 1860.
71. Radforth, *Royal Spectacle*, p. 323; *Liberator*, 2 November, 1860.
72. Quoted in *Liberator*, 16 November 1860.
73. Ibid., 26 October 1860.
74. Radforth, *Royal Spectacle*, pp. 334–5.
75. Engleheart, *Journal of the Progress of H.R.H. the Prince of Wales through British North America and his Visit to the United States*, pp. 83–4.
76. *Liberator*, 31 December 1860.
77. Quoted in Bentley-Cranch, *Edward VII: Image of an Era*, p. 32.
78. *Lowell Daily Citizen and News*, 23 February 1861.
79. *Dallas Herald*, 7 November 1860.
80. *Bangor Daily Whig & Courier*, 31 October 1860.
81. *San Francisco Bulletin*, 21 November 1860. See also *Vermont Patriot*, 19 November 1860.
82. Magnus, *King Edward the Seventh*, p. 40.
83. The *Saturday Review*, 13 October, 1860.
84. See, for example, *New York Herald*, 20 October 1860.
85. *Vanity Fair*, 19 May 1860; *The Nassau Literary Magazine*, October 1860.
86. Bennett, *King without a Crown: Albert Prince Consort of England 1819–1861*, p. 328.
87. *New York Herald*, 9 December 1860.
88. For a discussion of the 1860 election see Richard J. Carwardine, *Lincoln* (Harlow, 2003), pp. 109–30.
89. See, for example, *Harper's Weekly*, 20 October 1860.
90. *New York Times*, 22 September 1860.
91. Quoted in Radforth, *Royal Spectacle*, p. 374.
92. Quoted in the *Farmer's Cabinet*, 25 January 1861.
93. *Diary of George Mifflin Dallas while United States Minister to Russia 1837 to 1839, and to England 1856 to 1861* (Philadelphia, 1892), pp. 415–18.
94. Quoted the *Farmers' Cabinet*, 4 January 1861.

95. *New York Herald*, 19 December 1860.
96. Stephen Fiske, *English Photographs* (London, 1869), p. 275.
97. Engleheart, *Journal of the Progress of H.R.H. the Prince of Wales through British North America; and his Visit to the United States*, pp. 100–1.
98. The *Independent*, 18 October 1860.
99. The *Monthly Religious Magazine and Independent Journal*, December 1860.
100. Radforth, *Royal Spectacle*, pp. 330–5.
101. Fiske, *English Photographs*, p. 276.
102. *Saturday Evening Post*, 3 November 1860.
103. *The Diary of George Templeton Strong: The Civil War 1860–1865*, p. 52.
104. Trollope, *North America*, vol. 2, pp. 310–11.
105. *New York Times*, 20 October 1901.

Chapter 5

1. *The Times*, 6 February, 1861, quoted in the *Farmers' Cabinet*, 1 March, 1861.
2. H. C. Allen, *Great Britain and the United States: A History of Anglo-American Relations (1783–1952)*, (New York, 1955), pp. 452–3.
3. *The Times*, 30 May 1861, quoted in Ephraim Douglass Adams, *Great Britain and the American Civil War*, 2 vols (New York, 1925), vol. 1, p. 97.
4. *Richmond Daily Dispatch*, 17 January 1861.
5. Ibid., 3 May 1861. See also 18 April 1861.
6. From the *Richmond Whig*, quoted in *The Independent . . . Devoted to the Consideration of Politics, Social and Economic*, 27 June 1861.
7. *Richmond Daily Dispatch*, 2 November 1861.
8. *Houston Telegraph*, 21 December 1864.
9. *The Journal of Benjamin Moran*, eds S. A. Wallace and F. E. Gillespie, 2 vols (Chicago, 1948), vol. 2, pp. 906–7.
10. Martin B. Duberman, *Charles Francis Adams 1807–1886* (Boston, 1961), p. 471.
11. Charles Francis Adams, *Dictionary of American Biography*.
12. RA VIC/Q 9/63.
13. On this issue see Charles Francis Adams, *Studies Military and Diplomatic 1775–1865* (New York, 1911), pp. 375–413.
14. See, for example, *Daily Evening Bulletin*, 20 November 1873; 23 July 1875; *Milwaukee Daily Sentinel*, 17 July 1875.
15. See, for example, *Christian Observer*, 30 January 1901; *Christian Advocate*, 31 January 1901; *The Independent . . . Devoted to the Consideration of Politics, Social and Economic*, 31 January 1901.
16. See, for example, *Boston Daily Advertiser*, 14 January 1862.
17. Adams, *Great Britain and the American Civil War*, vol. 1, p. 228.
18. *Godey's Lady's Book and Magazine*, May 1862.
19. *New York Times*, 25 December 1861.
20. 'Victorian Death Rituals', *Ancestry Magazine*, vol. 19, no. 5, September/October 1999.
21. *Richmond Daily Dispatch*, 13 February 1862.
22. Ibid., 28 December 1861.
23. RA VIC/M 65/63.
24. Queen Victoria to Mary Lincoln, 29 April 1865, RA VIC/Q 10/53.
25. Walter Bagehot, *The English Constitution* (Oxford, 2001), p. 41.
26. RA VIC/Q 10/70.
27. Quoted in Duberman, *Charles Francis Adams 1807–1886*, p. 471.
28. *Harper's Weekly*, (1868), issue 3/7; *The Eclectic Magazine of Foreign Literature*, January 1860.

29. Philip Magnus, *King Edward the Seventh* (London, 1964), p. 70.
30. Ibid..
31. Michael J. Sewell, 'Queen of Our Hearts', *Victorianism in the United States. Its era and its legacy*, eds Steven Ickingrill and Stephen Mills (Amsterdam, 1992), p. 224.
32. Henry Adams, *The Education of Henry Adams: An Autobiography* (Boston and New York, 1918), p. 195.
33. Stephen F. Mills, 'Introduction', *Victorianism in the United States: Its era and its legacy*, eds Steven Ickingrill and Stephen Mills, p. xiv.
34. Stephen Fiske, *English Photographs* (London 1869), p. 276.
35. See, for example, *The Sun* (Baltimore), 27 March 1875.
36. Louis J. Jennings, *Eighty Years of Republican Government in the United States* (New York, 1868), p. 36.
37. *Pomeroy's Democrat*, 15 May 1875.
38. *North American Review*, vol. 118 (Boston, 1874), pp. 1–6.
39. J. M. Bailey, *England from a Back-Window; with Views of Scotland and Ireland* (Boston, 1879), p. 81.
40. Fiske, *English Photographs*, p. 275.
41. *Old and New*, May 1873.
42. See Frank Prochaska, *The Republic of Britain, 1760–2000* (London, 2000), passim.
43. Anthony Trollope, *North America*, 2 vols (Philadelphia, 1862), vol. 2, p. 194.
44. *The Diary of George Templeton Strong: Post-War Years 1865–1875*, eds Allan Nevins and Milton Halsey Thomas (New York, 1952), p. 387.
45. See, for example, *Daily Evening Bulletin*, 19 January 1872; 20 November 1873.
46. Quoted in Elizabeth Longford, *Victoria R. I.* (London, 1964), p. 576.
47. *The Eclectic Magazine of Foreign Literature*, January 1860.
48. *American Broadsides and Ephemera*, Series 1, no. 11194.
49. *Old and New*, May 1873.
50. *The Galaxy. A Magazine of Entertaining Reading*, February 1874.
51. See, for example, *Daily Cleveland Herald*, 7 March 1870.
52. See the cartoon 'Fight between Gen. Tom Thumb and the Queen's Poodle' in the collection of the Center for Disability and Public History.
53. Andrew Ward, *Dark Midnight When I Rise: The Story of the Jubilee Singers Who Introduced the World to the Music of Black America* (New York, 2000), pp. 207–8.
54. RA, Queen Victoria's Journal, 7 May 1873.
55. See Noble Frankland, *Witness of a Century: The Life and Times of Prince Arthur Duke of Connaught 1850–1942* (London, 1993), p. 37.
56. *The Times*, 27 April 1872, quoted in *Harper's Weekly*, 1 June 1872. The correspondence between Queen Victoria and Miss Grant is cited in the *Daily Evening Bulletin*, 11 June 1872.
57. See Allen, *Great Britain and the United States. A History of Anglo-American Relations (1783–1952)*, chapter 14.
58. Frankland, *Witness of a Century*, p. 38.
59. *Darling Child: Correspondence of Queen Victoria and the Crown Princess of Prussia 1871–1878*, ed. Roger Fulford (London, 1976), pp. 257–8.
60. *Daily Arkansas Gazette*, 26 June 1875; *North American and United States Gazette*, 26 June 1875.
61. Walter Arnstein, 'Queen Victoria and the United States', *Anglo-American Attitudes: From Revolution to Partnership*, eds Fred M. Leventhal and Roland Quinault (Aldershot, 2000), p. 100.
62. Quoted in Sewell, 'Queen of Our Hearts', p. 211.
63. Ibid., pp. 211–12.
64. Frederick William Chapman, 'The Changed Significance of "Anglo-Saxon"', *Education*, vol. 20 (February, 1900), pp. 367–9.

65. *Darling Child: Correspondence of Queen Victoria and the Crown Princess of Prussia 1871–1878*, ed. Fulford, pp. 243–4.
66. *St Louis Globe-Democrat*, 10 November 1877.
67. John Russell Young, *Around the World with General Grant*, 2 vols (New York, 1879), vol. 2, chapter 2. See also www.pbs.org/wgbb,amex/grant.
68. *Bangor Daily Whig & Courier*, 25 November 1880. David H. Stam and Deirdre C. Stam, *Books on Ice: British and American Literature of Polar Exploration* (New York, 2003), p. 38.
69. The message to Mrs Garfield still resonated at the time of Queen Victoria's death. See the *Washington Post*, 23 January 1901.
70. RA VIC/Q 13/63–7.
71. RA VIC/Q 13/78, 81.
72. Arnstein, 'Queen Victoria and the United States', p. 100.
73. RA VIC/Q 13/118 and VIC/Q 13/131.
74. Edward Sandford Martin, *The Life of Joseph Hodges Choate as gathered chiefly from his Letters* (New York, 1927), p. 296.
75. Arnstein, 'Queen Victoria and the United States', p. 100.
76. Lowell Papers, MS Am 1659 (370). By permission of the Houghton Library, Harvard University.
77. *New York Times*, 22 June 1887.
78. Ibid.
79. Ibid., 22 August 1887.
80. *Dallas Morning News*, 23 June 1887.
81. Ibid., 16 June 1887.
82. *New York Times*, 22 June 1887.
83. Ibid. On Hewitt and Queen Victoria's views on the Civil War see Adams, *Studies Military and Diplomatic 1775–1865*, pp. 375–83.
84. *Wheeling Register*, 16 July 1887; *Dallas Morning News*, 21 June 1887.
85. *Albuquerque Morning Democrat*, 22 June 1887.
86. *Daily Tombstone Epitaph*, 25 March 1887.
87. See, for example, *Dallas Morning News*, 19 May 1887.
88. *Wheeling Register*, 13 May 1887.
89. *Chicago Daily Tribune*, 21, 23, 24 August 1887.
90. *Atlanta Constitution*, 21 June 1887.
91. *Dallas Morning News*, 19 June 1887.
92. Ibid., 20 June 1887.
93. Quoted in H. L. Mencken, *The American Language: An Inquiry into the Development of English in the United States* (New York, 1946), pp. 20–1.
94. See Reginald Horsman, *Race and Manifest Destiny: The Origins of American Racial Anglo-Saxonism* (Cambridge, Mass. and London, 1981).
95. Stuart Anderson, *Race and Rapprochement: Anglo-Saxonism and Anglo-American Relations, 1895–1904* (London and Toronto, 1981), p. 12.
96. Peter Mandler, *The English National Character: The History of an Idea from Edmund Burke to Tony Blair* (New Haven and London, 2006), p. 134.
97. Paul Kramer, 'Empires, Exceptions, and Anglo-Saxons: Race and Rule between the British and United States Empires, 1880–1910', *Journal of American History*, vol. 88, (March, 2002), pp. 1315–53. I would like to thank Eden Hammond for this reference.
98. Charles S. Campbell, *The Transformation of American Foreign Relations 1865–1900* (New York, 1976), pp. 335–6.
99. Anne Orde, *The Eclipse of Great Britain: The United States and British Imperial Decline, 1895–1956* (New York, 1996), p. 26.
100. Lodge to Roosevelt, 2 February 1900. *Selections from the Correspondence of Theodore Roosevelt and Henry Cabot Lodge, 1884–1918*, 2 vols (New York, 1925), vol. 1, p. 446.

101. Quoted in Anderson, *Race and Rapprochement: Anglo-Saxonism and Anglo-American Relations, 1895–1904*, p. 178.
102. Charles Wentworth Dilke, *Greater Britain. A Record of Travel in English-Speaking Countries during 1866–7* (Philadelphia and London, 1869), pp. v, 268.
103. Beckles Willson, *America's Ambassadors to England (1785–1928)* (New York, 1928), pp. 412–13.
104. Ibid., p. 413.
105. President McKinley to Queen Victoria, 28 May 1897. RA VIC/R 45/145.
106. Quoted in Sewell, 'Queen of Our Hearts', p. 217.
107. *New York Tribune*, 26 May 1898.
108. *New York Times*, 4 July 1897.
109. This essay has been republished in *The Complete Essays of Mark Twain*, ed. Charles Neider (Cambridge, Mass., 2000), pp. 189–99.
110. *Chicago Tribune*, 23 June 1897.
111. Karl Marx, *The Eighteenth Brumaire of Louis Napoleon* (New York, 1963), p. 1.
112. Twain, 'Queen Victoria's Jubilee', *The Complete Essays of Mark Twain*, pp. 189–90.
113. See *The Hawaiian Gazette*, 19 February 1897.
114. *Boston Daily Globe*, 13 February, 24 May 1897.
115. Ibid., 24 May 1897.
116. *Atlanta Constitution*, 16 May, 22 June 1897.
117. Ibid., 16 April, 23 June 1897.
118. *Chicago Tribune*, 13 June 1897.
119. Ibid., 22 June 1897.
120. Ibid., 23 June 1897.
121. *New York Times*, 21 June 1897.
122. Ibid., 27 June 1897.
123. Ibid., 16 June 1897.
124. Ibid., 23 June 1897.
125. *Chicago Daily Tribune*, 6 June 1897.
126. Ibid., 11 June 1897.
127. *New York Times*, 11 and 13 June 1897.
128. Ibid., 4 July 1897.
129. David Cannadine, *The Decline and Fall of the British Aristocracy* (New Haven, 1990), p. 398.
130. Constance Mary Harrison, *The Anglomaniacs* (New York, 1890), pp. 24–5, 76.
131. *New York Times*, 2 November 1897.
132. *Irish World and American Industrial Liberator*, 8 April 1899.
133. *Chicago Daily Tribune*, 26 June 1897.
134. *New York Times*, 24 June 1897.
135. *The Letters of Sidney and Beatrice Webb*, ed. Norman MacKenzie, 3 vols (London, 1978), vol. 2, p. 134.
136. *New York Times*, 23 January 1901.
137. *Christian Advocate*, 31 January 1901.
138. *Atlanta Constitution*, 23 January 1901.
139. William McKinley to Edward VII, 6 April, 1901. RA VIC/Add mss J/1507/20.
140. *Washington Post*, 25 January 1901.
141. Martin, *The Life of Joseph Hodges Choate as gathered chiefly from his Letters*, pp. 187–8.
142. *Atlanta Constitution*, 4 February 1901.
143. *Los Angeles Times*, 22 January 1901.
144. *Atlanta Constitution*, 4 February 1901.
145. Arnstein, 'Queen Victoria and the United States', p. 102.
146. *Boston Globe*, 3 February 2001.
147. *Atlanta Constitution*, 13 February 1901.

148. *Washington Post*, 3 February 1901.
149. *Boston Globe*, 23, 31 January 1901.
150. *New York Evangelist*, 31 January 1901.
151. *Atlanta Constitution*, 18 February 1901.
152. *Boston Globe*, 23 January 1901.
153. Prochaska, *The Republic of Britain, 1760–2000*, p. 75.
154. *Atlanta Constitution*, 18 February, 1901.
155. Quoted Bradford Perkins, *The Great Rapprochement: England and the United States, 1895–1914* (New York, 1968), p. 300.
156. Elinor Glyn, *Romantic Adventure* (New York, 1937), p. 97.
157. *The Best Loved Poems of the American People*, ed. Hazel Felleman (Garden City, NY, 1936), pp. 557–8. Quoted Arnstein, 'Queen Victoria and the United States', p. 103.
158. 'The American Constitution at the Present Crisis', *The Collected Works of Walter Bagehot*, ed. Norman St John-Stevas, 15 vols (London, 1974–1986), vol. 4, p. 283.
159. *Los Angeles Times*, 24 January 1901.
160. James Bryce, *The American Commonwealth* (New York, 1922), p. 14.

Chapter 6

1. *The Daily Inter Ocean*, 14 March 1889.
2. *New York Times*, 10, 12 February 1901.
3. Philip Magnus, *King Edward the Seventh* (London, 1964), p. 276.
4. J. I. Clark Hare, *American Constitutional Law*, 2 vols (Boston, 1889), vol. 1, p. 173.
5. *Knoxville Journal*, 9 February 1896.
6. *Dallas Morning News*, 30 July 1898.
7. Henry Jones Ford, *The Rise and Growth of American Politics: A Sketch of Constitutional Development* (New York, 1898), p. 293.
8. Garry Wills, *Inventing America: Jefferson's Declaration of Independence* (New York, 1978), p. 356.
9. *New York Times*, 27 January 1901.
10. George Burton Adams, *Why Americans Dislike England* (Philadelphia, 1896), pp. 26–7.
11. See F. K. Prochaska, *Philanthropy and the Hospitals of London: The King's Fund, 1897–1990* (Oxford, 1992), chapters 1–3; Frank Prochaska, *Royal Bounty: The Making of a Welfare Monarchy* (London and New Haven, 1995), chapter 5.
12. *Washington Post*, 19 May 1931.
13. David Cannadine, *The Decline and Fall of the British Aristocracy* (New Haven and London, 1990), p. 346.
14. *Boston Globe*, 14 April 1907.
15. *New York Times*, 2 June 1901.
16. Ibid., 27 June 1901.
17. *Hartford Courant*, 20 January 1903.
18. *Boston Globe*, 2 July 1902.
19. *New York Times*, 11 January 1906.
20. See Frank Prochaska, *The Republic of Britain, 1760–2000* (London, 2000), chapter 5.
21. *New York Times*, 22 September 1903; 19 September 1905; 17 December 1905; 21 July 1906; 7 October 1907; 17 May 1908.
22. National Archives, HO/144 contains the files of about 2,500 applicants for royal patronage between 1879 and 1920.
23. *Washington Post*, 31 March 1901.
24. *The Collected Works of Walter Bagehot*, ed. St John-Stevas, 15 vols (London, 1974–1986), vol. 5, p. 432.
25. *New York Times*, 8 May 1910.

26. www.spartacus.schoolnet.co.uk/USAEdecades.
27. Walter Bagehot, *The English Constitution* (Oxford, 2001), p. 34.
28. Sidney Lee, *King Edward VII. A Biography*, 2 vols (London, 1927), vol. 2, p. 427.
29. *New York Times*, 10 August 1902.
30. Vernon Bogdanor, *The Monarchy and the Constitution* (Oxford, 1995), p. 301.
31. Peter J. Parish, 'Confidence and Anxiety in Victorian America', *Victorianism in the United States: Its era and its legacy* (Amsterdam, 1992), p. 18.
32. *New York Times*, 24 August 1902.
33. *Current Literature*, August 1902.
34. See Marlene A. Eilers, *Queen Victoria's Descendants* (New York, 1997).
35. Theodore Roosevelt, *Letters*, 8 vols, ed. Elting E. Morison (Cambridge, Mass., 1951–1954), vol. 4, p. 1042.
36. *New York Times*, 5 April 1904.
37. Ibid., 24 May 1903.
38. *Boston Globe*, 24 December 1905; *Washington Post*, 8 October 1905.
39. *Roosevelt, Letters*, vol. 4, p. 1045.
40. Edmund Morris, *Theodore Rex* (New York, 2001). Stephen Graubard, *The Presidents: The Transformation of the American Presidency from Theodore Roosevelt to George W. Bush* (London, 2004) titles his chapter on Roosevelt 'To Be a King'.
41. Quoted in Lee, *King Edward VII*, vol. 2, pp. 427–8.
42. RA VIC/W 45/116, quoted in Lee, *King Edward VII*, pp. 430–1.
43. Lee, *King Edward VII*, vol. 2, p. 431.
44. RA VIC/W 45/126a.
45. RA VIC/W 45/359.
46. Reginald Horsman, *Race and Manifest Destiny: The Origins of American Anglo-Saxonism* (Cambridge, Mass., 1981), p. 302.
47. Quoted in *Washington Post*, 1 December 1901.
48. RA VIC/W 52/112.
49. RA VIC/W 53/19.
50. *Boston Globe*, 12 May 1910.
51. *Julius Caesar*, ed. T. S. Dorsch (London, 1958), p. 52.
52. Barbara Tuchman, *The Guns of August* (New York, 1963), p. 15.
53. *Hartford Courant*, 9 May 1910.
54. Ibid., 28 May 1910.
55. Quoted in Bradford Perkins, *The Great Rapprochement: England and the United States, 1895–1914* (New York, 1968), p. 266.
56. *New York Times*, 22 June 1910. For a good biography of the King see Kenneth Rose, *King George V* (London, 1983).
57. *New York Times*, 23 June 1911.
58. Ibid., 6 August 1911.
59. Noble Frankland, *Witness to a Century: The Life and Times of Prince Arthur Duke of Connaught 1850–1942* (London, 1993), pp. 280–3.
60. Henry Adams, *Democracy* (New York, 1961), p. 146.
61. *The Graphic*, 7 March 1914.
62. *New York Times*, 7, 8 May 1910.
63. *Los Angeles Times*, 13 December 1914.
64. Ibid., 19 July 1914.
65. Ibid., 9 October 1915.
66. Quoted in Philip Ziegler, *King Edward VIII: The Official Biography* (London, 1990), p. 85.
67. Admiral Halsey to Lord Grey, 22 September 1919, RA EVIIIPWH/VIS/OV/1919/US.
68. H. G. Chilton to Alan 'Tommy' Lascelles, 26 August 1919, RA EVIIIPWH/VIS/OV/1919/US.
69. See the Woodrow Wilson Papers in the Library of Congress, WP.DLC.

70. Prochaska, *The Republic of Britain, 1760–2000*, p. 171; Prochaska, *Royal Bounty: The Making of a Welfare Monarchy*, pp. 182–3.
71. *Thatched with Gold: The Memoirs of Mabell, Countess of Airlie*, ed. Jennifer Ellis (London, 1962), pp. 141–2.
72. Ziegler, *King Edward VIII*, pp. 115–16.
73. In recent years, political scientists have begun to write of Wilson as an absolutist 'quasi-monarch'. See Scot J. Zentner, 'Liberalism & Executive Power: Woodrow Wilson & the Founding Fathers', *Polity*, vol. 26, no. 4, 1994, pp. 579–99.
74. Graham Wallas, *Our Social Heritage* (New Haven, 1921), p. 223.
75. *A King's Story: The Memoirs of the Duke of Windsor* (New York, 1947), p. 147.
76. *The Washington Post*, 12 November 1919.
77. RA PS/GV/O 1548/182, quoted in Zeigler, *King Edward VIII*, pp. 120–1.
78. *A King's Story: The Memoirs of the Duke of Windsor*, pp. 147–9.
79. Ibid., p. 151.
80. *New York Tribune*, 19 November 1919.
81. Quoted in Ziegler, *King Edward VIII*, p. 121.
82. Quoted in ibid.
83. *Washington Post*, 7 November 1936. From Washington, the play moved to the Henry Miller's Theatre in New York, where it had 88 performances.
84. *Daily News* (London), 25 November 1919.
85. *Sunday Express*, 23 November 1919.
86. *Daily Telegraph*, 24 November 1919.
87. *Evening Standard*, 24 November 1919.
88. *A King's Story: The Memoirs of the Duke of Windsor*, p. 217.
89. Ibid., p. 200.
90. *Atlanta Constitution*, 27 August 1924.
91. Ziegler, *King Edward VIII*, p. 150.
92. *A King's Story: The Memoirs of the Duke of Windsor*, p. 203.
93. Frazier Hunt, *The Bachelor Prince* (New York, 1935), pp. 136–7.
94. RA PS/GV/0 1965/23.
95. See, for example, *New York Daily News*, 23 September 1924.
96. Howard to Stamfordham, 17 October 1924, RA PS/GV/0 1965/47.
97. *A King's Story: The Memoirs of the Duke of Windsor*, p. 203.
98. See Chris Rojek, *Celebrity* (London, 2001), chapter 1.
99. Elinor Glyn, *It* (New York, 1927), pp. 5–6. See also Joseph Roach, *It* (Ann Arbor, 2007), p. 4.
100. There is some dispute over the date of their first meeting. In her memoir, *The Heart Has Its Reasons*, Mrs Simpson put it at the end of 1930. In *The King's Story*, the Duke of Windsor put their first meeting in the autumn of 1931. Based on the letters of Wallis Simpson, Philip Ziegler puts their first meeting on 10 January 1931.

Chapter 7

1. *Wallis & Edward. Letters 1931–1937*, ed. Michael Bloch (London, 1986), p. 1.
2. Michael Bloch, *The Duchess of Windsor* (London, 1996), p. 50.
3. See Ziegler, *King Edward VIII: The Official Biography* (London, 1990), p. 224
4. *The Heart Has Its Reasons: The Memoirs of The Duchess of Windsor* (New York, 1956), p. 9.
5. Bloch, *The Duchess of Windsor*, p. 229.
6. Ibid., p. 50.
7. Harold Nicolson, *Diaries and Letters 1930–1939*, ed. Nigel Nicolson (London, 1966), p. 226.

8. *The Flower and the Nettle: Diaries and Letters of Anne Morrow Lindbergh, 1936–1939* (New York, 1976), p. 63.
9. *Chips: The Diaries of Sir Henry Channon*, ed. Robert Rhodes James (London, 1967), p. 50.
10. *Wallis & Edward*, p. 292.
11. *Chicago Daily Tribune*, 1 November 1936.
12. *Chips: The Diaries of Sir Henry Channon*, p. 30.
13. Ibid., p. 75.
14. Nicolson, *Diaries and Letters, 1930–1939*, p. 271.
15. *Washington Post*, 21 April 1935.
16. Ibid., 12 March 1936.
17. Ibid., 22 January 1936.
18. *Chicago Daily Tribune*, 22 January 1936.
19. *A King's Story: The Memoirs of the Duke of Windsor* (New York, 1947), p. 309.
20. *Washington Post*, 17 October 1936.
21. Ibid., 24 October 1936.
22. Quoted in *Chips: The Diaries of Sir Henry Channon*, p. 79.
23. Susan Williams, *The People's King: The True Story of the Abdication* (London, 2003), p.85.
24. *Washington Post*, 19 October 1936.
25. Ibid., 28 October 1936.
26. Ibid.
27. *Chicago Daily Tribune*, 29 October 1936.
28. *Washington Post*, 28 October 1936.
29. *New York Times*, 6 December 1936.
30. Ibid., 8 December 1936.
31. Ibid., 4 December, 1936.
32. *Washington Post*, 8 December 1936.
33. Ibid., 22 November 1936.
34. Ibid.
35. *Chicago Daily Tribune*, 9 December 1936.
36. *Washington Post*, 11 December 1936.
37. On British attitudes towards the King beyond the establishment see Williams, *The People's King: The True Story of the Abdication*.
38. Quoted in Ziegler, *King Edward VIII*, p. 321.
39. James Pope-Hennessy, *Queen Mary 1876–1953* (London, 1959), p. 577.
40. J. Bryan III and Charles J. V. Murphy, *The Windsor Story* (London, 1979), p. 312.
41. Quoted in Williams, *The People's King: The True Story of the Abdication*, p. 242.
42. *Chicago Daily Tribune*, 12 December 1936.
43. *Washington Post*, 11 December 1936.
44. Quoted in ibid., 1 January 1937.
45. Williams, *The People's King: The True Story of the Abdication*, p. 279.
46. *Washington Post*, 13 December 1936.
47. *Chicago Daily Tribune*, 9, 11 December 1936.
48. *Chips: The Diaries of Sir Henry Channon*, p. 85.
49. *Washington Post*, 13 December 1936.
50. *Los Angeles Times*, 11 December 1936.
51. Quoted in Jonathan Dimbleby, *The Prince of Wales: A Biography* (London, 1994), pp. 178–9.
52. Brian Harrison, *The Transformation of British Politics, 1860–1995* (Oxford, 1996), p. 343.
53. *New York Times*, 11 December 1936.
54. Quoted in ibid., 13 December 1936.

55. *Yale Daily News*, 13 May 1937.
56. *Los Angeles Times*, 18 April 1937.
57. Ibid., 11 May 1937.
58. Elliott Roosevelt and James Brough, *A Rendezvous with Destiny: The Roosevelts of the White House* (New York, 1975), p. 178.
59. *Los Angeles Times*, 26 April 1937.
60. Ibid., 12 May 1937.
61. Ibid., 22 April 1937.
62. *New York Times*, 13 May 1937.
63. *The Times*, 28 December 1937.
64. Roosevelt and Brough, *A Rendezvous with Destiny: The Roosevelts of the White House*, p. 149.
65. *New York Times*, 18 March 1905. See also Will Swift, *The Roosevelts and the Royals: Franklin and Eleanor, the King and Queen of England, and the Friendship that Changed History* (New York, 2004), p. 9.
66. *Yale Daily News*, 10, 12 March 1937.
67. David Reynolds, *From World War to Cold War: Churchill, Roosevelt, and the International History of the 1940s* (Oxford, 2006), p. 137.
68. Roosevelt to George VI, 17 September 1938, RA PS/GVI/PS 03400/003/01/001.
69. Roosevelt to George VI, 2 November 1938, RA PS/GVI/PS 03400/003/01/015.
70. Roosevelt and Brough, *A Rendezvous with Destiny: The Roosevelts of the White House* p. 230.
71. Eleanor Roosevelt, *This I Remember* (New York, 1949), pp. 183–4.
72. RA PS/GVI/PS 03400/003/01/004.
73. RA PS/GVI/PS 03400/003/01/005.
74. RA PS/GVI/PS 03400/003/01/018.
75. Quoted in *New York Times*, 9 November 1938.
76. *Los Angeles Times*, 21 October 1938.
77. On the visit, see Fred Leventhal, 'Essential Democracy: The 1939 Royal Visit to the United States', *Singular Continuities: Tradition, Nostalgia, and Identity in Modern British Culture*, eds George K. Behlmer and Fred M. Leventhal (Stanford, 2000), pp. 163–77; Reynolds, *From World War to Cold War* (Oxford, 2006), chapter 7.
78. *Scribner's Magazine*, vol. 195, February 1939.
79. RA PS/GVI/PS 03400/003/45/4.
80. Leventhal, 'Essential Democracy: The 1939 Royal Visit to the United States', pp. 171–2.
81. *Los Angeles Times*, 9 June 1939.
82. Roosevelt and Brough, *A Rendezvous with Destiny: The Roosevelts and the White House*, p. 235.
83. *New York Times*, 11 June 1939.
84. Swift, *The Roosevelts and the Royals*, pp. 122–3.
85. *Los Angeles Times*, 18 May 1939.
86. *New York Times*, 11 June 1939.
87. Rose Fitzgerald Kennedy, *Times to Remember* (New York, 1995), p. 215.
88. RA PS/GVI/PS 03400/003/18/23.
89. Quoted in Robert Rhodes James, *A Spirit Undaunted: The Political Role of George VI* (London, 1998), p. 163.
90. RA PS/GVI/PS 03400/003/45/2.
91. Reynolds, *From World War to Cold War*, p. 143.
92. Quoted in Sarah Bradford, *George VI* (London, 1989), p. 396.
93. RA PS/GVI/PS 03400/003/01/054.
94. John W. Wheeler-Bennett, *King George VI: His Life and Reign* (New York, 1958), p. 390.
95. Roosevelt and Brough, *A Rendezvous with Destiny: The Roosevelts and the White House*, p. 235.

96. Eleanor Roosevelt, *This I Remember* (New York, 1949), pp. 184, 198. There is a further description of the departure of the King and Queen in Eleanor Roosevelt, *On My Own* (New York, 1958), pp. 30–1.

97. Wheeler-Bennett, *King George VI: His Life and Reign*, pp. 502–3.

98. Reynolds, *From World War to Cold War*, p. 147.

99. Swift, *The Roosevelts and the Royals*, chapter 9.

100. Leventhal, 'Essential Democracy: The 1939 Royal Visit to the United States', p. 174.

101. RA PS/GVI/PS 03400/003/45/2.

102. Swift, *The Roosevelts and the Royals*, p. 82.

103. David E. Koskoff, *Joseph P. Kennedy: A Life and Times* (Englewood Cliffs, New Jersey, 1974), p. 200.

104. RA GVI/PRIV/03/K/3. This letter is quoted in full in Wheeler-Bennett, *King George VI: His Life and Reign*, pp. 419–20.

105. Laurence Leamer, *The Kennedy Men, 1901–1963: The Laws of the Father* (New York, 2001), p. 147.

106. Quoted in Stephen Graubard, *The Presidents: The Transformation of the American Presidency from Theodore Roosevelt to George W. Bush* (London, 2004), p. 403.

107. Kennedy, *Times to Remember*, p. 192.

108. Ibid., p. 194.

109. Ibid., p. 198.

110. Robert Dallek, *John Kennedy: An Unfinished Life* (London, 2003), p. 56.

111. Edward R. Murrow, *This Is London* (New York, 1941), pp. 152, 174–5.

112. On this issue see Fiona MacCarthy, *Last Curtsey: The End of the Debutantes* (London, 2006).

113. Quoted in Bradford, *George VI*, p. 610.

114. Quoted in *In Search of Light: The Broadcasts of Edward R. Murrow 1938–1961*, ed. Edward Bliss, Jr. (New York, 1967), p. 207.

115. *Washington Post*, 8 February 1952.

116. Bradford, *George VI*, p. 611.

117. Dorothy Laird, *Queen Elizabeth the Queen Mother* (London, 1966), pp. 277–8.

118. *New York Times*, 7 February 1952

119. *The Papers of Dwight David Eisenhower*, 21 vols (Baltimore, 1970–2001), vol. 13, part 4, chapter 7, pp. 947–8.

120. The letter has disappeared. See Swift, *The Roosevelts and the Royals*, p. 292.

121. *In Search of Light: The Broadcasts of Edward R. Murrow 1938–1961*, p. 209.

122. *Washington Post*, 7 February 1952.

Chapter 8

1. *In Search of Light: The Broadcasts of Edward R. Murrow 1938–1961*, p. 209.

2. *Chicago Daily Tribune*, 29 March 1953.

3. Ben Pimlott, *The Queen: A Biography of Elizabeth II* (London, 1996), p. 217.

4. *Los Angeles Times*, 2 June 1953.

5. See '50 facts about The Queen's Coronation', www.royal.gov.uk. Robert Lacey, *Royal: Her Majesty Queen Elizabeth II* (London, 2002), pp. 175–82.

6. *Chicago Daily Tribune*, 2 June 1953.

7. *New York Times*, 2 June 1953.

8. *Christian Science Monitor*, 1 June 1953.

9. '50 facts about the Queen's Coronation'.

10. *Washington Post*, 3 June 1953.

11. Margaret Lane, 'The Queen is Crowned', *New Statesman*, Coronation Issue, June 1953; Sir Charles Petrie, *The Modern British Monarchy* (London, 1961), p. 198.

12. *Washington Post*, 3 June 1953.

13. *Chicago Daily Tribune*, 9 June 1953.

14. Willie Hamilton, *My Queen and I* (London, 1975), p. 14.
15. Lacey, *Royal: Her Majesty Queen Elizabeth II*, p.181.
16. *New York Times*, 3 June 1953.
17. David Cannadine, 'The Context, Performance and Meaning of Ritual: The British Monarchy and "The Invention of Tradition", c. 1820–1977', *The Invention of Tradition*, eds Eric Hobsbawm and Terence Ranger (Cambridge, 1984), p. 158.
18. On this issue see Tom Nairn, *The Enchanted Glass: Britain and its Monarchy* (London, 1988).
19. '50 facts about The Queen's Coronation'.
20. *Wall Street Journal*, 20 February 1953.
21. Lacey, *Royal: Her Majesty Queen Elizabeth II*, pp. 181–2.
22. *Los Angeles Times*, 9 June 1953.
23. *Chicago Daily Tribune*, 2 June 1953.
24. *Richard Dimbleby: Broadcaster*, ed. L. Miall (London, 1966), p. 83.
25. Gerald Dorfman, 'Coronation Memories', *Hoover Digest: Research and Opinion on Public Policy*, no. 4, 2002.
26. *Chicago Daily Tribune*, 1, 2 June 1953.
27. Sarah Bradford, *America's Queen: The Life of Jacqueline Kennedy Onassis* (London, 2000), pp. 88–9.
28. *Los Angeles Times*, 1 April 1953.
29. Ibid., 26 April 1953.
30. *New York Times*, 13 May 1953.
31. Ibid., 30 May 1953.
32. *Christian Science Monitor*, 26 May 1953.
33. *New York Times*, 2 May 1953.
34. Ibid., 4 January 1953.
35. *Los Angeles Times*, 2 June 1953.
36. *Chicago Daily Tribune*, 30 May 1953.
37. Ibid., 9 June 1953.
38. *Christian Science Monitor*, 17 June 1953.
39. *Chicago Daily Tribune*, 26 April 1953.
40. Ibid., 23 May 1953; *Washington Post*, 3 June 1953.
41. Quoted in Cannadine, 'The Context, Performance and Meaning of Ritual: The British Monarchy and the "The Invention of Tradition", c. 1820–1977', p. 157.
42. *The Papers of Dwight David Eisenhower*, 21 vols (Baltimore, 1970–2001), vol. 18, part 2, chapter 3, pp. 243–4.
43. Dwight D. Eisenhower, *The White House Years. Waging Peace 1956–1961* (New York, 1965), p. 214.
44. Quoted in Pimlott, *The Queen*, pp. 283–4.
45. *Washington Post and Times Herald*, 13 October 1957.
46. *New York Times*, 16 October 1957.
47. Merriman Smith, *A President's Odyssey* (New York, 1961), p. 4; *The Papers of Dwight David Eisenhower*, vol. 18, part 3, chapter 6, pp. 502–3.
48. *Washington Post and Times Herald*, 12 August 1957.
49. *New York Times*, 17 October 1957.
50. Eleanor Roosevelt, *On My Own* (New York, 1958), p. 36.
51. Pimlott, *The Queen*, p. 284.
52. *New York Times*, 17 October 1957.
53. Pimlott, *The Queen*, p. 284.
54. *Washington Post and Times Herald*, 13 October 1957.
55. *New York Times*, 23 October 1957.
56. *Daily Herald*, 23 October 1957.
57. *The Papers of Dwight David Eisenhower*, vol. 20, part 8, chapter 20, p. 1816. For Eisenhower's description of his visit to Balmoral see *The White House Years. Waging Peace 1956–1961*, p. 420.

58. Dermot Morrah, *The Work of the Queen* (London, 1958), pp. 37–44. See also Pimlott, *The Queen*, pp. 294–5.
59. Gore Vidal, *Palimpsest: A Memoir* (New York, 1995), pp. 372.
60. The cartoon appeared in the *Evening Standard; New York Times*, 6 June 1961.
61. *Washington Post and Times Herald*, 27 December 1961.
62. *Chicago Daily Tribune*, 29 January 1963.
63. Nixon's speech drew on a speech prepared by his staff. See Memorandum, Stephen Bull to Richard Nixon, 16 July, folder 'Beginning July 12, 1969,' box 81, President's Office Files, White House Special Files, National Archives at College Park, MD.
64. *Washington Post and Times Herald*, 19 July 1970.
65. *New York Times*, 17 July 1970.
66. Memorandum, Henry A. Kissinger to Richard Nixon, 18 July, folder 'Beginning July 12, 1969', box 81, President's Office Files, White House Special Files, National Archives at College Park, MD.
67. Jonathan Dimbleby, *The Prince of Wales: A Biography* (London, 1994), p. 149.
68. Anthony Holden, *Charles Prince of Wales* (London, 1979), p. 226.
69. *Chicago Tribune*, 16 July 1976
70. *Christian Science Monitor*, 9 July 1976.
71. *New York Times*, 7 July 1976.
72. *Chicago Daily Tribune*, 27 February 1977.
73. *Washington Post*, 2 June 1977
74. *New York Times*, 7 June 1977.
75. Geoffrey Kabaservice, *The Guardians: Kingman Brewster, His Circle, and the Rise of the Liberal Establishment* (New York, 2004), p. 447.
76. *New York Times*, 6 June 1977.

Chapter 9

1. On this issue see John Plunkett, *Queen Victoria: First Media Monarch* (Oxford, 2003).
2. See Tom Nairn, *The Enchanted Glass: Britain and its Monarchy* (London, 1988), chapters 1, 3.
3. Walter Bagehot, *The English Constitution* (Oxford, 2001), p. 41.
4. *New York Times*, 12 July 1981.
5. Quoted in Jonathan Dimbleby, *The Prince of Wales: A Biography* (London, 1994), p. 290.
6. Ibid., p. 292.
7. *Evening Standard*, 7 January 1975.
8. Quoted in *The New Republic*, 22 September 1997.
9. Dimbleby, *The Prince of Wales: A Biography*, p. 290; *New York Times*, 31 July 1981.
10. *Los Angeles Times*, 29 July 1981.
11. Ibid., 28 July 1981.
12. *Chicago Tribune*, 9 July 1981.
13. *New York Times*, 17 April 1981; *Chicago Tribune*, 7 June 1981; *Los Angeles Times*, 2 June 1981.
14. *Chicago Tribune*, 21 June 1981.
15. *Los Angeles Times*, 21 May 1981.
16. Ibid., 30 July 1981.
17. Ibid., 29 July 1981.
18. Toasts of the President and Queen Elizabeth II at a Dinner Honoring the President at Windsor Castle in England, 8 June 1982, *Public Papers of Ronald Reagan*.
19. Ben Pimlott, *The Queen* (London, 1996), p. 487.
20. Ibid.

21. Toasts of the President and Queen Elizabeth II at a Dinner Honoring the President at Windsor Castle in England, 8 June 1982.
22. Ronald Reagan, *An American Life* (New York, 1990), p. 387.
23. *The Diaries of Ronald Reagan*, ed. Douglas Brinkley (New York, 2007), p. 244.
24. Reagan, *An American Life*, p. 373.
25. Bill Clinton, *My Life* (New York, 2004), p. 439.
26. For details, see David Hackett Fischer, *Albion's Seed: Four British Folkways in America* (New York and Oxford, 1989), pp. 834–9. See also http://burkes-peerage.net/Lib.
27. Thomas P. O'Neill, *Man of the House: The Life and Political Memoirs of Speaker Tip O'Neill*, with William Novak (New York, 1987), p. 314.
28. Stephen Graubard, *The Presidents: The Transformation of the American Presidency from Theodore Roosevelt to George W. Bush* (London, 2004), p. 586.
29. *Time*, 16 November 1985.
30. *New York Times*, 10 November 1985.
31. Quoted in Dimbleby, *The Prince of Wales: A Biography*, p. 382.
32. *Washington Post*, 3 November 1985.
33. *New York Times*, 5 November 1985.
34. *Los Angeles Times*, 9 November 1985.
35. Andrew Neil, *Full Disclosure* (London, 1996), p. 207. See also Sally Bedell Smith, *Diana in Search of Herself* (New York, 1999), p. 151.
36. Tina Brown, *The Diana Chronicles* (New York, 2007), pp. 245–7.
37. *Washington Post*, 10 November 1985.
38. *Christian Science Monitor*, 8 November 1985.
39. H. J. Roberts, *Princess Diana, The House of Windsor and Palm Beach: America's Fascination with 'The Touch of Royalty'* (West Palm Beach, 1998), p. 10.
40. Dimbleby, *The Prince of Wales: A Biography*, p. 385.
41. Percy Black, *The Mystique of Modern Monarchy* (London, 1953), p. 59.
42. *Washington Post*, 10 November 1985.
43. *New York Times*, 5 November 1985.
44. *Chicago Tribune*, 9 November 1985.
45. *Wall Street Journal*, 27 November 1985.
46. *New York Times*, 5 November 1985.
47. *Time*, 11 November 1985. Dimbleby, *The Prince of Wales: A Biography*, pp. 388–9; Sarah Bradford, *Diana* (New York, 2006), pp. 136–41.
48. P. D. Jephson, *Shadows of a Princess* (New York, 2000), p. 132.
49. *New York Times*, 1 February 1989.
50. Ibid., 3, 4 February 1989.
51. *Sunday Times*, 21 June 1987.
52. Ben Pimlott, 'Monarchy and the Message', *Politics and the Media: Harlots and Prerogatives at the Turn of the Millennium*, ed. Jean Seaton (Oxford, 1998), p. 91.
53. *Chicago Tribune*, 12 November 1985.
54. Ibid.
55. *New York Times*, 28 November 1988.
56. Antony Jay, *Elizabeth R: The Role of the Monarchy Today* (London, 1992), pp. 87, 90.
57. *New York Times*, 16, 17 May 1991.
58. Ibid.; Pimlott, *The Queen*, p. 538.
59. *New York Times*, 21 May 1991.
60. Ibid., 21, 22 May 1991.
61. Ibid., 21 June 1992.
62. Jephson, *Shadows of a Princess*, p. 409.
63. Brown, *The Diana Chronicles*, pp. 420–1
64. Joseph Roach, *It* (Ann Arbor, 2007), p. 171.
65. *Newsweek*, 22 December 1997.

66. *The New Republic,* 22 September 1997.
67. www.state.gov/secretary/former/powell/remarks/2002/13459htm.
68. *People's Weekly,* 17 June 1996.
69. Brown, *The Diana Chronicles,* p. 18.
70. *Daily Mail,* 4 September 1997, quoted in Roach, *It,* p. 146.
71. *The New Republic,* 22 September 1997.
72. Ibid., 29 September 1997.
73. *Time,* 15 September 1997.
74. *New York Times,* 3 September 1997.
75. *Newsweek,* 15 September 1997.
76. *U.S. News & World Report,* 3 August 1998.
77. *American Journalism Review,* November 1997.
78. See Frank Prochaska, *Royal Bounty: The Making of a Welfare Monarchy* (London, 1995), p. 97.
79. *Newsweek,* 15 September 1997.
80. Quoted ibid.
81. *American Journalism Review,* November 1997.
82. *Journal of the Market Research Society,* October 1997.
83. *American Journalism Review,* November 1997.
84. *Time,* 15 September 1997.

Chapter 10

1. The Harris Poll #14, 11 March 1998. The poll was taken between 11 and 15 December 1997.
2. Harriet Beecher Stowe, *Sunny Memories of Foreign Lands,* 2 vols (Boston, 1854), vol. 1, p. 18.
3. Louis B. Wright, *Culture on the Moving Frontier* (Bloomington, 1955), p. 15.
4. David Hackett Fischer, *Albion's Seed: Four British Folkways in America* (New York and Oxford, 1989), p. 6.
5. Campbell Gibson, 'The Contribution of Immigration to the Growth and Ethnic Diversity of the American Population', *Proceedings of the American Philosophical Society,* vol. 136 (June, 1992), p. 166.
6. Russell Kirk, *America's British Culture* (New Brunswick, New Jersey, 1993), p. 1.
7. Samuel P. Huntington, *Who Are We? The Challenges to America's National Identity* (New York, 2004), pp. 45, 59.
8. *The Writings of Thomas Jefferson,* 20 vols, ed. Albert Ellery Bergh (Washington, D.C., 1904), vol. 7, p. 312.
9. *New York Times,* 5 November 1985.
10. Henry Jones Ford, *The Rise and Growth of American Politics: A Sketch of Constitutional Development* (New York, 1898), p. 369.
11. *The Letters of Thomas Babington Macaulay,* ed. Thomas Pinney, 6 vols (London, 1974–1981), vol. 6, p. 96.
12. *The New York Times Magazine,* 17 June, 2007, p.14.
13. *Littell's Living Age,* 27 October 1860.
14. See, for example, Jeremy Paxman, *On Royalty* (London, 2006), pp. 279–80.
15. James Bryce, *The American Commonwealth* (New York, 1922), p. 14.
16. *Christian Science Monitor,* 9 May 1953.
17. Walter Bagehot, *The English Constitution* (Oxford, 2001), p. 41.
18. William Blackstone, *Commentaries on the Laws of England,* 4 vols (Oxford, 1765–1769), vol. 1, p. 242.

INDEX

References to illustrations are in bold